Legacy:

History of Nursing Education
at the University of British Columbia,
1919-1994

Glennis Zilm and Ethel Warbinek

Legacy:

History of Nursing Education at the University of British Columbia, 1919-1994

UNIVERSITY OF BRITISH COLUMBIA
SCHOOL OF NURSING

ISBN 0-88865-234-8

Canadian Cataloguing in Publication Data

Zilm, Glennis.
  Legacy

  Includes bibliographical references and index.
  ISBN 0-88865-234-8

  1. University of British Columbia. School of Nursing. 2.
Nursing—Study and teaching (Higher)—British Columbia—
Vancouver. I. Warbinek, Ethel. II. University of British
Columbia, School of Nursing. III. Title.

RT81.C22V395   1994   610.73'071'133   C94-910411-6

University of British Columbia School of Nursing
2211 Wesbrook Mall
Vancouver, BC V6T 2B5
(604) 822-7417

Distributed by UBC Press
University of British Columbia
6344 Memorial Rd
Vancouver, BC V6T 1Z2
(604) 822-3259
Fax: (604) 822-6083

Design and typesetting by Brenda and Neil, Typographics West
Index by Annette Lorek
Printed and bound in Canada by D.W. Friesen & Sons Ltd.

Contents

Illustrations

Photographs were obtained from several sources and acknowledgment is given below. Where no indication of the source is given, the photograph is from the University of British Columbia School of Nursing Archival Collection.

CHAPTER 3

CHAPTER 4

CHAPTER 6

CHAPTER 7

Foreword

What began in 1918 as the first university Nursing program in Canada has now become a centre for nursing education that offers undergraduate, graduate, and doctoral degrees. What was a course offered, at its inception in 1919-1920, to four special students has become, in 1993-1994, a program for more than 500 students with more than 167 men and women registered in first year alone. What was a response, at the opening of this century, to health care needs such as influenza epidemics and high infant mortality is a program that searches for responses, as the century closes, to AIDS epidemics and the special needs of the rapidly growing population of dependent elderly. Although the full story of the last 75 years cannot be covered in detail, this book offers a peek into the evolution of the School of Nursing at the University of British Columbia.

As I read about the struggles during the genesis of the Nursing program at UBC, I am struck by similarities to the present. Financial support was sparse then, as now, and slim budgets have been one of the chronic, unrelenting problems that the School has faced. No doubt, budgets in the future will continue to be anorexic, so it is interesting to see the innovative ways that leaders in the School have worked creatively within and around constraints imposed by lack of funds.

Support from other disciplines, although improved in recent years, was nonexistent in the early years. In fact, as I reflect on a letter written by the College of Physicians and Surgeons in 1918, I cannot help but laugh. Asked to comment on the proposal for a Nursing department at the University, the College stated that "overtraining nurses is not desirable and results largely in the losing of their usefulness." Those of us in the present can quickly find the irony in this statement and marvel at how one discipline can try to decide upon the fate and requirements of another. Another comment in the letter, that "theoretical branches of nursing are of very little use in the sick room," is equally humorous for its ignorance and for the presumptuousness of the writers. So, some things have changed, but recognition by some University disciplines of "faculty status" for Nursing remains elusive.

As I mentally transport myself back in time, I cannot help but feel the sense of abandonment, frustration, and humiliation that those nurses interested in developing the program must have felt. I also became aware of the tenacity of the creators of the School and I quietly thank them. They obviously held a strong vision of the future, but realized that convincing others would be the most painstaking task. We have come a long way since those days, but we still may have a long way to go.

We are fortunate finally to have the story of the growth of the School contained in words and pictures in a book. As I grow older, understanding my roots, both personal and professional, has become a priority. Just as I want to know where I came from, I want to know where my profession came from – and this book offers some insights. One of the authors spoke at a lunch I attended, and I left sizzling with excitement of the stories from the past. To know what Nursing at UBC has gone through, and to understand a smidgen of what our nursing predecessors must have felt, provides us with a connection between past and future that we could never otherwise attain.

This book also provides a broad context against which to view the position of women, nursing as a profession, and society's beliefs about health during the past 75 years. And, oh, what changes have occurred. Without this written record, the stories of many significant people and events were hidden from general knowledge. As we struggle to piece together the larger picture of nursing history in B.C. and Canada, this book provides a small but illuminating segment. We do not have to agree with all that has gone on in the past, but it certainly gives us a context against which to plan for the present.

We must also be cognizant of what the past can offer us for the future. Exploring history can help us to prepare for the challenges of the future. We can and must learn from those who have come before us. This book shares not only the successes and the beautiful anecdotes that warm our hearts, but also delves into some of the challenges faced by previous generations of UBC nurses during the past 75 years. We can benefit from their trials and errors.

When I was pursuing my own graduate studies, one of my professors said something that has always stayed with me. She said that, although it is important to analyze and form our own opinions of the accuracy and strength of any written record, including historical research, we must always thank those individuals who took the time and the risks inherent in being the first to put their theories and thoughts on paper. Once something is in print, it invites close scrutiny, which may include not only compliments but also criticisms and challenges to the content. The task that began many years ago with Beth McCann collecting pictures, clippings, and stories about the School and its graduates has evolved into a long project involving numerous people. To those who did the work and risked the criticism, especially Glennis Zilm and Ethel Warbinek, I honour and respect your dedication to the daunting task of preparing our first published history.

The story of the first 75 years is now on record. Here's to the next 75.

Linda Gomez, President
Nursing Division, UBC Alumni
Spring 1994

Preface

This book provides an overview of the history of the Nursing program at the University of British Columbia over its first 75 years. It started as a labour of love by Elizabeth (Beth) Kenny McCann, who began planning for a book to celebrate the history of the UBC School of Nursing in the early 1980s. She spent a year on sabbatical just before her retirement in 1982 working on the project, and did a number of interviews, sent questionnaires to many graduates, and amassed an enormous but unorganized volume of files, letters, papers, notes, tapes, photographs, and memorabilia. When she died unexpectedly, her friend and colleague Elizabeth (Betty) Cawston and her sister Anna McCann collected these and gave them to the School of Nursing. This collection has formed the basis of an archives for the School of Nursing and was a major source of information for this book.

A major force in the history of the program has been the individuals who foresaw the effects of changing trends, who anticipated and envisioned the future, and who responded to the challenges. This book identifies the leaders and focuses on their achievements. As well, it provides an overview of the faculty and students of the various eras, using anecdotes to illustrate events characteristic of specific eras. Interviews reveal that, in the memories of graduates, it is people who are recalled, not course materials! Unfortunately, we could not include everything and everyone; there are still many gaps and many stories to be told.

In 1991, when we took on the work of completing Beth's task for the 75th anniversary of the School's founding, we never anticipated how exciting and how challenging this project would be. Beth had left a rough outline, which suggested the idea of organizing the book by the terms of the various directors, an idea that we adopted and expanded from her few pages of notes. The excitement has been in the growing realization that the contributions of the UBC School to nursing and health care have been enormous but that few people realize how many and how important these actually are. The contributions have not been recorded and therefore are essentially unknown to the present generation of nurses. We saw an opportunity to rectify this deficit.

It was also exciting to collect stories from individuals and receive their cherished memorabilia. We uncovered previously unknown materials that gave life and lustre to the big picture that was slowly developing. As the pieces came together, they also provided insights and led to a greater understanding of how past events continue to influence the present. We could see that, without a recorded history, actions often were – and are – ineffective.

The challenges came because we had not considered how little of the nursing history of Canada, British Columbia, and UBC has been collected or documented. Our nursing history is rich, exciting, and surprisingly colourful – but, with a few important exceptions, it has not been recorded. In the 75 years of the School, only one previous attempt at writing the story was made; this was by Evelyn Mallory in the late 1960s, and a small typewritten manuscript survives. A beacon in the darkness was the excellent biography of Ethel Johns by Margaret Street, but this covered only a brief period in the history of the School. An examination of the history of public health nursing in B.C. by Monica Green was extraordinarily helpful, as were master's theses and unpublished reports that touched on historical nursing events in B.C, particularly those of Margaret Kerr, Irene Goldstone, Nora Whyte, Cheryl Entwistle, and Cristina Pepe. Two histories of the School of Nursing at the Vancouver General Hospital, by Anne Cavers and Nora Kelly, and hard-to-find histories of other B.C. hospitals and schools of nursing also provided relevant background data.

But 75 years is a long time. Retrieval of information from primary sources was a daunting task. The mass of "unrefined data" from which to draw was enormous. The information on individuals who made contributions was too extensive for one book. We sometimes spent days verifying details to complete a single sentence.

Given the paucity of recorded histories of nursing in general and of the UBC Nursing program in particular and the immense volume of uncollected, uncatalogued, and rapidly disappearing primary sources on which to draw, we wish only to state that this book should be viewed as a *beginning* attempt – a proem – to a definitive history of Nursing education at the University of British Columbia. We have amassed a collection of materials as large as that of Beth McCann's that now must be added to the Archival Collection in a way that will make this more useful for historical researchers of the future. The book is only part of a larger history project that will eventually see the development of a permanent School of Nursing Archival Collection, which we hope will, one day, be part of the Special Collections Division of the UBC Library.

In this book, we have tried to create what Norman Cantor and Richard Schneider describe as "an historical picture out of a mass of disorganized and insignificant data."[1] In examining this data, we have been obliged to make judgments – for example, in the selection of the material we presented, and in the examination of the relationships between various bits of data. We have tried not only to present *what* happened but also to discover *how* and *why* things happened. Any view of history is a snapshot caught at a particular time. It may be true that history does not change, but the point from which history is viewed is constantly changing and the lens of each viewer is different as well – and that creates a different vision.

Many people assisted in various ways with this book and we would like to acknowledge the contributions of a few of the most helpful. The Nursing Division of the UBC Alumni provided the impetus for the project to be completed for the 75th anniversary celebrations and provided start-up funding. The School of Nursing then provided strong support for the project and funded the publication of the book. Funds were also obtained from the President's Office for assistance in obtaining and copying photographs.

Marilyn Willman, the director of the School, was a valuable source of information and made the archival documents of her office available to us. She also provided cogent and incisive comments on the preliminary drafts and assisted with editing and proofreading. The support staff of the UBC School of Nursing, especially Tere Rostworowski and Lydia Kwan, also provided practical help. Nursing students Natalie Bland, Tamara Stafford (later MacLeod), and Anne Keski-Salmi, who were hired to transcribe interviews and catalogue Beth McCann's files, also did more than was expected in their jobs and contributed to the overall project.

We also need to acknowledge the assistance in finding materials, verifying details, and answering general queries that we received from many libraries and their staffs: Woodward Biomedical Library (especially Lee Perry and Anna Leith); UBC Library Special Collections (especially Chris Hives and Frances Woodward); Canadian Nurses Association Helen K. Mussallem Library (especially Elizabeth Hawkins Brady and Martha Impersol); Registered Nurses Association of B.C. Helen Randal Library (especially Joan Andrews, Carol MacFarlane, and Randy Tywoniuk); B.C. Court House Library; Vancouver Public Library; New Westminster Public Library; Surrey Public Library; B.C. Cancer Agency Library (especially David Noble); Ken Kaye Memorial Library, Forensic Psychiatric Services (especially Heidi Dysarsz); University of Alberta Archives and Records Office (especially Faye Hutchinson and Mary Jean MacKenzie); University of Saskatchewan Library and Archives (especially Cheryl Avery); Saskatchewan Registered Nurses Association Library (especially Alice Lalonde), and the Library of the Canadian Red Cross Society in Toronto.

We also had help with photographs from UBC Biomedical Communications and UBC Media Services and from the Learning Resource Centre of the UBC School of Nursing. The UBC Alumni Association (especially Deborah Apps, Mary Scott Molson, and Fyfe Brown) encouraged us throughout the project. The staff of UBC Press, especially Jean Wilson, who reviewed and edited the manuscript, and George Maddison, who guided it through production, were extraordinarily generous and helpful.

We also acknowledge the debt that we owe to the many, many alumni, who shared memories, answered questions, and provided documents. Only a few of these could be mentioned in the chapters, but others also provided background and verification. Six nursing friends who gave support and encouragement over the years we worked on the book deserve particular mention: Esther Paulson, Monica Green, Betty Cawston, Margaret Street, Anne Wyness, and Helen Shore. We also wish to thank our families – especially Rudi and Anita Warbinek and Valerie Chapman – who provided constant support and a touching faith that we really would complete the book.

Any first attempt to record history will undoubtedly have errors and omissions. The responsibility for these is ours alone.

History allows for self-discovery based on the inheritance from those who have gone before. We hope that those who read this history will have a better understanding of how nursing education at UBC came into being and of how the complex forces throughout the past 75 years have converged to create today's UBC School of Nursing.

Legacy:

History of Nursing Education at the University of British Columbia, 1919-1994

CHAPTER ONE

A Climate for Change

When Marion Fisher, Margaret Healy, and Beatrice Johnson accepted their degrees of Bachelor of Applied Science (in Nursing) at the University of British Columbia convocation on Thursday, May 10, 1923, they made history. They were the first to acquire university degrees in nursing in Canada – or indeed anywhere in the entire British Empire. Several universities in the United States offered nursing programs, which led to a combined university degree in nursing plus a hospital diploma. The program offered through the University of British Columbia and the Vancouver General Hospital, which began in 1919, was the first in Canada, however, and marked a recognition of the need for stronger and better educational preparation for nurses. As Ethel Johns, the director of the program, said of this movement into university settings: "We are building here for the future [... and] we earnestly hope that the foundation will be well and truly laid."[1]

The foundations were "well and truly laid," but the future has been a long time coming. When the UBC program began, some far-sighted leaders saw this as a first step to get nursing education out of hospitals, where student nurses often were exploited for service needs at the expense of their educational goals. Nursing leaders wanted nursing in the educational system – which, at that time, meant in universities. In the 1960s and 1970s, some nursing education moved into the newly formed community colleges, although the programs were shortened to two years. Since then, the move toward the baccalaureate degree as the educational foundation for nursing has continued, and is now the stated goal of most nurses' organizations in Canada. With the development in 1989 of a collaborative program between the University of B.C. and the Vancouver General Hospital, all hospital-based programs in B.C. finally closed. As well, by 1994 all diploma nursing programs had established links with degree-granting institutions, which is a move to the philosophy of higher education for nursing.

Development of university programs for nursing at the end of the 1910s appears, when looked at with hindsight, inevitable; pressures of the times were moving in this direction. The world-wide economy of the period was generally good, especially in Canada, which was going through an enormous period of population growth through massive immigration from Europe. Many of these immigrants helped open the West, and in 1905 this led to creation of the Prairie provinces from the undeveloped North-Western Territory.

British Columbia, which had joined Confederation in 1871, received its promised railway link with eastern Canada in 1887. Towns and cities sprang up like mushrooms throughout the province at the turn of the century, in some part related to the Klondike Gold Rush (1897-1899) and to the railway-driven prosperity for the interior of the province. The "golden years" of 1900 to 1914 saw Vancouver's population increase from 27,000 to more than 113,000.[2] The lumber, mineral, and fishing resources spurred an economic boom leading to land speculation and major construction, especially in the centres of Victoria and Vancouver. Despite some economic fluctuations, this period of prosperity for most British Columbians generated growth of an affluent middle class, and led to major changes in educational and health status.

After Canada entered World War I on August 4, 1914, British Columbians, including many nurses, volunteered for overseas duty. The area continued to prosper through war contracts for munitions and ship building. Women, who had struggled to enter the work force during the preceding era, suddenly found the demands for their services increased and their economic status improved as well.

Between 1900 and 1918, the party system emerged in British Columbia, mainly under the leadership of Richard McBride, who led the Conservative Party as premier for a relatively stable period from 1903 to 1915. He was fortunate to take office just as the new fishing and lumbering industries in the province achieved stability and at a time when labour strife in other areas also came to a halt.[3] A major political problem of the period concerned immigration to the West Coast from Asia. British Columbia had a long history of Chinese immigration. The first Chinese came as part of the province's Gold Rush of the 1850s and, because they proved themselves hard workers, were welcomed as domestic servants and labourers, for example for the building of the Canadian Pacific Railway, although racism was prominent. A large Chinatown had sprung up in Vancouver. In February 1900, however, the large number of immigrants from Britain influenced the Legislative Assembly to adopt the slogan "British Columbia is British" as the politicians moved their support for Canada's entry into the Boer War.

During the early 1900s, B.C. politicians continued to lobby the federal government for a "head tax" on Chinese residents; this idea had first been broached in 1878 to control Chinese immigration. Although all men had obtained the vote for a brief period when B.C. entered Confederation in 1871, "Native Indians" and Chinese were disenfranchised in 1874 and the Japanese lost their vote in 1895. Despite repeated attempts to change these discriminatory laws, the Chinese did not again receive the vote until 1947, and Japanese and aboriginal peoples were not able to vote until 1949.[4,5,6]

Throughout the early 1900s, Asian immigration was a burning issue. In 1907, a significant rise in numbers was reported, with more than 8,000 Japanese, more than 2,000 Sikhs, and, despite the head tax, nearly 1,500 Chinese entering that year.[7] The Asiatic Exclusion League was formed in 1907 and, following one of its meetings, a mob attacked the Chinatown properties in a riot that shocked the city.[8] One related outcome was the disenfranchisement of East Indians in 1907; their right to vote was returned in 1947.[9]

The reaction of the white majority was not directed only at the Chinese. Because Japanese immigrants tended to establish their own communities, for example in Steveston and in "Little Tokyo" in Vancouver, the local white population frequently referred to them as "the Japanese menace."[10] In 1914, another incident illustrated the racial tensions; more than 350 East Indian immigrants, who had arrived aboard the *Komagatu Maru*, were prevented from landing by immigration officials. For two months the ship lay anchored in the harbour and was finally forced to depart without any of the passengers or crew being able to enter the province.[11,12]

The combination of these 19th century social pressures of what has been summed up as "immigration, industrialization, urbanization, and capitalism"[13] profoundly changed the way education and health care, both previously carried out in the home, were offered. Both education and health care increasingly came into the public domain. Along with these came the rise of new professions, which can be viewed as a consequence partly of industrialization and partly of advances in scientific and technological knowledge.

EMPHASIS ON EDUCATION

The turn of the century saw an increased interest in education. B.C.'s public school system had been co-educational since its inception, but with increased prosperity in the province, students were remaining in classrooms longer and high school education was becoming the norm. Interest was also being expressed in establishing university education in the province.

Training schools for nurses were among the first higher-level educational institutions in B.C. The first Canadian nursing program to be based on the educational model developed by Florence Nightingale was the Mack Training School for Nurses, which opened in St. Catharines, Ontario, in 1874. British Columbia's first Nightingale-based nursing program opened at Victoria's Royal Jubilee Hospital in 1891.[14] Florence Nightingale's far-reaching influence on nursing education had caused many changes in nursing, one of which was that it had become largely a female occupation by the end of the 1800s. Because of this, nursing at that time was considered a temporary career, lasting only until marriage. However, changes in health care and scientific advances were also affecting nursing.

Until the turn of the century, hospitals were for the homeless and for those who could not afford private nursing care in their homes. Surgery was done either in the patient's home or in the doctor's office. All care in hospitals usually was given by students working under the direction of one or two trained matrons or supervisors; almost all graduates left the hospital to work as private duty nurses in patients' homes. These graduate nurses filled roles which in the 1990s are termed "independent practice"; they were paid by their patients for bedside care in the home or by the community if they did teaching and health promotion. Payment for health care in the 1910s and 1920s was the responsibility of the individual patient or family; medical and nursing care insurance was non-existent. Private plans, such as Metropolitan Health Insurance, were just beginning to be set up. Early nursing leaders talked of government-sponsored plans; by the 1930s, nurses such as Florence Emory and Ruby Simpson were recommending government insurance programs.[15]

Moreover, advances in medical and surgical technology were changing the roles of hospitals. Introduction of anesthesia and development of more extensive and sophisticated surgical procedures meant sicker patients. This created a demand for nurses who had more education and better scientific understanding. Health care was benefitting from increased scientific knowledge. For example, the "germ theory" had been accepted, and rapid advances in medical and surgical treatment were evident. Ether had been introduced and care in hospitals was gradually replacing the time-honoured tradition of care in the home. An interest in better public health measures, including clean water supplies, improved sanitation, and control of infectious diseases, was also apparent.

Vancouver's first hospital was a tent facility used by the Canadian Pacific Railway (CPR) for its workers in 1886, only months after a devastating fire had all but destroyed the city. The CPR soon moved into a wooden building, in which the city had an interest. Then, in September 1888, the Vancouver City Hospital, run as a department of the city, opened in a two-storey wooden building at the corner of Beatty and Pender streets; it contained two large public wards of 16 beds each.[16,17] By 1899, there were demands for a Vancouver training school for nurses, which opened that same year.[18] By 1902, a board of directors had completed plans for a private, non-profit medical institution, to be re-named the Vancouver General Hospital. A 5½-acre site on the southern slope across False Creek, far from downtown in the area called Fairview, was purchased for $5,500 by the city from the Canadian Pacific Railway.[19] In January 1906, the move was accomplished, with 47 patients being transported across the Cambie Street plank bridge to three new wards in a modern brick building. In 1907, three isolation cottages – for people with diphtheria, scarlet fever, and other infectious diseases – were opened as well as tents for those with tuberculosis. These contagious

Figure 1.1 City Hospital located between Pender, Beatty, and
Cambie Streets, 1888.

Figure 1.2 Vancouver City Hospital grounds, 1902.
The hospital was vacated in 1906 when the move to Fairview occurred.
The white square on the left is an outside cloth blind to diminish glare in the
operating room. A.M. Robertson, medical superintendent, is reclining on
the lawn. Note the style of the cap worn by the nursing students.

Figure 1.3   Vancouver General Hospital students class of 1908 with
Lady Superintendent Albertine Macfarlane in centre, without a cap.

Figure 1.4   VGH Ambulance donated by the Women's Auxiliary in 1902.
Its handsome carriage lights were said to be the envy of every local coachman.

Figure 1.5   Isolation cottages. Three wooden cottages were erected
in 1907 on 12th Avenue between Willow and Heather streets. They housed
patients with infectious diseases and were destroyed in 1927.

diseases were major health problems of the time and the new public health
measures required isolation for public protection. Student nurses assigned to
these wards lived with the patients in the cottages. The 180-bed hospital of
1906 more than tripled in size over the next eight years.[20] The population of
Vancouver was expanding rapidly during this period and frequently there
were long waiting lists for surgery. Student nurses lived in one wing of the
hospital until 1907, when a separate nurses' residence was opened. A second
residence also opened at the Fairview site in 1915.

The Provincial Normal School, for education of teachers, opened in
Vancouver in 1899 with 50 students.[21] Although the Normal School had no
building until 1908, classes were held in various city schools under the
direction of William Burns, one of the provincial inspectors of schools.

Two theological colleges to train ministers for the growing numbers of
churches in B.C. were also among the first post-high school institutions.[22] In
1881, the Methodist Church opened a college in New Westminster, eventually to become known as Columbian College. The Presbyterian Church
founded Westminster Hall, a theological college in Vancouver, in 1907.

The original notion of a university in B.C. came in 1877 from John Jessop,
the provincial superintendent of education,[23,24] and was strongly supported
by the local politicians. The first legislation for a B.C. university was passed
in 1891, but a dispute over location between Victoria and Vancouver led
to the failure of this attempt. As a temporary measure, affiliation of B.C.
high schools with eastern Canadian universities was made possible through

Figure 1.6   Vancouver General Hospital building 1916.

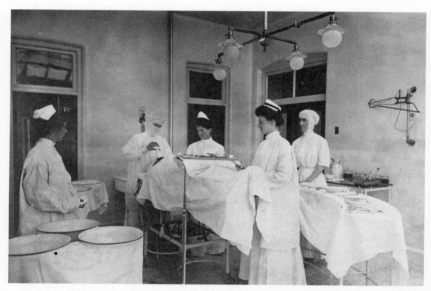

Figure 1.7   Operating room at Vancouver General Hospital in 1906. Note the administration of ether by drops. Nurses are gowned but no masks are worn.

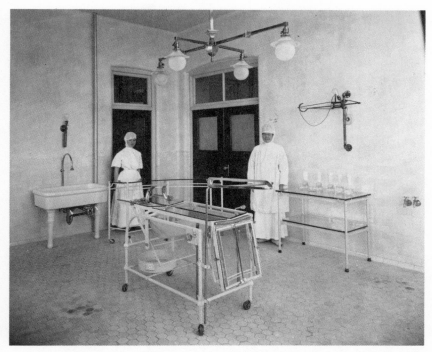

Figure 1.8   Caseroom, Vancouver General Hospital, 1908, with nurses Miss
Hastie (later Montgomery) and Miss Stone (later Wilson).

Figure 1.9   East and West wings of the nurses' residence on 10th Avenue and
Heather Street, built 1907-1908 (Old Home).

legislative acts passed in 1894 and 1896; Vancouver High School affiliated with McGill University in 1899 to offer first year arts courses.[25] In 1906, students were first able to complete degrees in the province through acts that established the McGill University College of B.C. However, public demands for a provincial university continued.

In 1908, Henry Esson Young, a physician, was provincial secretary and minister of education in the Richard McBride's government. He was influential in gaining the passage of an act to establish the University of British Columbia. In 1910, the government endowed 175 acres at the tip of Point Grey as a permanent home for the new university.[26] A competition was announced for a master plan for what was envisioned even then as a world-class facility. The provincial legislature provided $500,000 in funds to begin clearing the site and starting the buildings, with another $1 million, an enormous sum for the time, promised in 1914.

Frank F. Wesbrook, a physician, was named the first president in 1913 after a notable administrative career at the University of Minnesota.[27] President Wesbrook, along with the enthusiastic Board of Governors and Senate, originally scheduled the opening for the fall of 1913, but delays prompted a request to McGill University College for the continuation of its program for

Figure 1.10   New nurses' home erected in 1914 on the northwest corner of 12th Avenue and Heather Street. It later became the interns' residence, still standing in 1994. Note the wooden isolation cottages in left background.

Figure 1.11   Room in the new nurses' residence 1915.

two more years. Canada's entry into World War I, in August 1914, turned attention and funds away from grand university plans to the war effort. Enthusiasm continued for the university, however, and the decision was made to use old, vacant, wooden buildings on the Fairview property of the Vancouver General Hospital as temporary quarters. On September 1915, the new University of British Columbia quietly opened its doors to 379 registrants in what was known as the "Fairview Shacks." These included a small, three-floor former hospital building that was used for classrooms.

Figure 1.12   Army tents on the University's Fairview site.

Figure 1.13   "Fairview Shacks" with
Vancouver General Hospital in the distance.

Despite the diversion of provincial moneys away from the university and
into the war effort, the student population continued to grow in the three
faculties of the time: Arts, Agriculture, and Applied Science. By 1918,
enrolment had grown to 273 women and 265 men.[28] This predominance of
females was regarded as "temporary" because of the numbers of young men
who were serving overseas in the armed forces. The numbers of women,
however, was evidence of another trend of the time.

A GROWING FEMINISM

One of the most important social happenings of the period was the emergence of the Women's Movement in the late 1800s and early 1900s. This
early feminism was an important social pressure in British Columbia, where
women had joined in the agitation for suffrage. Women obtained the vote in

1917 in B.C., the fourth province to gain the franchise, and the Canada Election Act of 1918 gave them voting rights in federal elections. Their participation in the War helped spur their efforts to achieve a measure of equality, although at the end of the War women were strongly encouraged to leave the work force, and married women employed by the federal government were legislated out of their jobs.[29]

This period also saw the development of women's organizations, or women's clubs, so women could support one another and make their collective voices heard in the demands for better educational, employment, and political opportunities. The Local Council of Women was formed in 1895, with one of its goals the improvement of the health of women during the childbearing period. Because of this, local councils of women were particularly interested in the development of schools of nursing and improvements in public health nursing care in the home. While Countess Ishbel Aberdeen, wife of Canada's Governor-General, was in Vancouver helping to organize its local council, the idea of a visiting nursing service was suggested to her by two Vancouver women.[30,31] Lady Aberdeen, with the help of the National Council of Women (the Canada-wide association of the local councils), was to bring this idea to fruition. In 1897, she succeeded in organizing the Victorian Order of Nurses for Canada, which was based in Ottawa, but soon had established several branches, including one in Vancouver.[32] By 1914, the Vancouver Local Council of Women had 5,000 members[33] and was a strong, effective voice for women.

The University Women's Club, made up of women graduates of out-of-province universities, was formed in 1907 and proved vigilant in its support for women's education – especially for the equality of opportunity for women at UBC.[34] Largely because of its activities, two women were included in the 15 elected members of the first UBC Senate. One of these, Evlyn Kierstead Farris, was also the first woman named, in 1917, to the Board of Governors.

Despite these advances, opportunities for women students at the university were limited mainly to the Faculty of Arts, with few opportunities for women to enter professional fields. This undoubtedly was a factor in the introduction of a department of nursing when the idea was finally broached.

A GROWING PROFESSIONALISM IN NURSING

Well before the turn of the century, nurses in Canada were critical of the hospital-controlled nursing education programs. Mary Agnes Snively, one of the most prominent leaders, was a Canadian-born graduate of New York's Bellevue Hospital training program and "lady superintendent" of the school at the Toronto General Hospital. She was instrumental in the formation, in 1892, of the American Society of Superintendents of Training Schools for

Nurses. The American and Canadian leaders who established this group were concerned about the quality of nursing education and the fact that students were exploited to provide care at the expense of their studies. Isabel Hampton (later Robb), a Bellevue-trained Canadian who was head of the highly regarded nursing school of the Johns Hopkins Hospital, had set new educational standards there. Placed in charge of a nursing section for the Chicago World's Fair in 1893, she was instrumental in arranging for Ethel Bedford Fenwick to be invited to speak.

Ethel Gordon Manson (later Bedford Fenwick) had been a matron of St. Bartholomew's Hospital in London and the first to promote the idea of professional autonomy for nurses. In the 1880s, Ethel Bedford Fenwick was actively organizing nurses in Britain and leading a call for state examinations and registration of nurses to protect the public. Lavinia Dock and Isabel Maitland Stewart described this revolutionary idea as "probably equal in its daring to Miss Nightingale's"[35] because it led to emergence of national associations and to recognition of nursing as a profession unique and separate from medicine.

Ethel Bedford Fenwick's efforts led to development of the British Nurses Association in 1887 and the International Council of Nurses in 1899. When she spoke at the Chicago World's Fair, she stimulated Canadian and American nursing leaders to form national associations out of the burgeoning alumnae groups being formed by each hospital school. At first, Americans and Canadians formed one association, the Nurses' Associated Alumnae of the United States and Canada, with Isabel Hampton as its first president. Because legal requirements made it essential for organizations to be on national lines, the Canadian nurses withdrew. In 1907, the Canadian Society of Superintendents of Training Schools for Nurses was formed, with Mary Agnes Snively as president. Mary Agnes Snively had also represented Canada at the first meeting of the International Council of Nurses in 1899 and was elected its treasurer. However, Canada itself did not have an organized professional group and could not become an ICN member. Under Mary Agnes Snively's leadership, nurses from alumnae associations, other groups such as school nurses, and the developing province-wide associations formed the Canadian National Association of Trained Nurses (CNATN). Through this latter organization, which could represent all nurses in the country, Canada was admitted into the International Council of Nurses in 1909. CNATN changed its name in 1924 to the Canadian Nurses' Association.[36] (The apostrophe was later dropped from the official title.)

Nurses in B.C. formed a province-wide association in 1912.[37,38] The inaugural meeting of the Graduate Nurses Association of B.C. (GNABC) was held in New Westminster in the fall and Scharley Wright (later Bryce Brown), a school nurse in New Westminster, was elected first president. Helen Randal, the new superintendent of nurses at the Vancouver General

Figure 1.14

Helen Randal, Superintendent of Nurses, Vancouver General Hospital, 1912-1916. First registrar and inspector of training schools for Graduate Nurses Association of B.C., a position she held from 1918 to 1941. Editor of The Canadian Nurse, 1916-1924. The RNABC library is named in her honour.

Hospital, was appointed to head a committee to secure legislation for registration. By December she and her committee had met with Premier Richard McBride. Despite an extensive postcard campaign by nurses to all members of the legislature, the bill was delayed, first because the cabinet decided it should be presented as a private member's bill and then because of the outbreak of World War I. In 1916, the bill was again to be presented, but was withdrawn when the nurses discovered that the government intended to have nursing controlled under the College of Physicians and Surgeons, which had been established in 1886 to govern medical standards in the province.

A new, revised bill was finally passed and in April 1918 the Registered Nurses Act became law.[39] Helen Randal was appointed Registrar. Under the new act, nurses who graduated from approved programs and passed standard tests could have their names listed on a register maintained by the association, call themselves "Registered Nurses," and use the initials "R.N." after their names. The act also established some minimum standards for training schools.[40]

The B.C. association had, in 1914, affiliated with the Canadian National Association of Trained Nurses and B.C. nurses began to take an active role in national affairs. When the national association decided, in 1916, to purchase The Canadian Nurse from the Toronto General Hospital Alumnae, which had founded the journal in 1905, the B.C. association supported the move. Helen Randal became the journal's editor (part-time), as well as B.C.'s Registrar, and the editorial offices were moved to Vancouver.[41,42]

The new association was also anxious to improve educational standards for nurses in the province. The first survey of B.C. training schools for nurses was made in 1919 by the Registrar, with a recommendation for annual inspections. The association was concerned about the growing numbers of training schools attached to small hospitals; any hospital that had at least 15 beds could establish a training program, even if these were only maternity beds. The association, under the new act, began to take action to force these small schools to join with larger programs so that students would have a more balanced nursing education. These and other less successful endeavours to improve nursing educational standards in the province led to many controversies until the association's authority was upheld in a legal opinion in 1926.[43]

B.C. nurses were also active on national committees, especially on committees related to nursing education. The Society of Superintendents, which in 1917 changed its name to the Canadian Association of Nursing Education (CANE), especially was concerned about standards for nursing education. Leaders in the organization, such as Mary Agnes Snively, Helen Randal, Ethel Johns of the Winnipeg General, and Mary Ardcronie MacKenzie of the Victorian Order of Nurses, strongly believed that nursing education should be controlled by educational institutions rather than hospitals or employing agencies. They, as well as several of their American colleagues, were beginning to believe that all nursing education belonged in universities.

THE MOVE TO UNIVERSITY EDUCATION

Ethel Johns summarized this viewpoint in her first address to a mass meeting when she became director of nursing at the Vancouver General Hospital in 1919.[44] She explained that when she was serving on Manitoba's Royal Commission on Public Welfare she found that the commissioners and the politicians were looking to nurses for leadership in health questions, for teaching, and for a vitalizing force in community life. Unfortunately, she found that the quality of nursing education was not good enough to prepare such leaders. She stressed that educational institutions would have to open their doors so that nurses could take up the challenges of health care. "Do you think any preparation too broad and deep for such a task as this?" she asked. "Do you think we can rest satisfied with what we have? It is good, but not good enough."[45]

This move to university preparation had begun in Scotland in 1893, when students at the Glasgow Infirmary received short courses in theoretical instruction at St. Mungo's College before they began their practical work at the hospital.[46,47] In the United States, in 1897, the University of Texas in Galveston was the first to establish links with a hospital, and the school of nursing there had come under the medical department, although student nurses were not required to meet university level standards.[48] The first university course for graduate nurses was opened at Teachers College, Columbia University, New York, in 1899; students could take courses in "hospital economics" to suit their needs as teachers and administrators. In 1907, M. Adelaide Nutting, who had followed Isabel Hampton at Johns Hopkins Hospital School of Nursing, moved to Columbia to receive an appointment as professor in a new "department of household administration" (the name was later changed to reflect a nursing emphasis), under which the division of hospital economics was placed.[49] Then, in 1909, came the first full university nursing program, at the University of Minnesota, followed in quick succession by nursing programs at several other universities in the United States.

Canada was not far behind. The Graduate Nurses Association of Ontario in 1905-1906 had approached the University of Toronto requesting it offer a course for nurses.[50] The proposal, "although kindly received, was never acted upon."[51] Helen MacMurchy, a physician who until 1911 had been the first editor of *The Canadian Nurse*, carried out a survey of Canadian universities in 1918 to find out to what extent they were involved in education of nurses.[52] McGill had given the most promising reply, indicating that steps were being taken toward university preparation for nurses.

Frank Wesbrook, president of the three-year-old University of B.C., had replied that lectures by the head of the Department of Bacteriology, R.H. Mullin, were given to nurses at the nearby Vancouver General Hospital. Frank Wesbrook had helped to inaugurate the department of nursing at the University of Minnesota, and had been in touch with Adelaide Nutting about university education for nurses. He could foresee a department or school of nursing at UBC "may be possible, in the future, [but] ... at the present time ... we have made no arrangements."[53]

Strong support for the move in B.C. to university preparation for nurses came from doctors associated with the public health movement. Organization of public health services in B.C. began in 1893 with the establishment of the Provincial Board of Health.[54] C.J. Fagan, secretary of the Board, recommended as early as 1908 that nurses should visit schools and homes to help educate the public about better infant and child care and to assist in reducing the incidence of tuberculosis and other communicable diseases.[55] The first "school nurse" in Vancouver was appointed in 1910 by the city to help supervise the health of 9,800 children in Vancouver's 16 schools.[56] In 1911, a provincial act to provide for medical inspection in schools was passed, but a lack of physicians to carry out this work led to use of "school nurses" throughout the province. The need for such care is indicated by the 1914 statistics that showed the death rate in children under age two was a startling 25 per cent.[57] The Provincial Board of Health recommended use of more and better prepared nurses. Henry Esson Young, minister of education and responsible for the provincial board of health, wanted better educated nurses who could provide more comprehensive public health care and family health teaching.

Nursing leaders of the time recognized that the nursing education programs prepared graduates only for curative work in hospital settings. Information on prevention, family education, and community leadership was not taught, despite the fact that once nursing students graduated they went out to work in the community. Any preparation for public health work was usually done through short courses in public health for graduates. For example, the University of Alberta offered such a short course early in 1919 when eight nurses completed a special course before joining the Alberta public health nursing staff.[58]

A major concern of the Canadian Nurses' Association's Special Committee on Nurse Education in 1914 was that hospital-based schools did not offer a broad-based liberal education and well-qualified young women were not entering nursing but were going into university courses in other fields.[59]

DEVELOPMENT OF UBC'S NURSING PROGRAM

All these factors contributed to the demands in B.C. for a university-based nursing education program. As well, the activities of nurses in World War I and in the care of the Spanish flu victims in the world-wide epidemic of 1918-1919 imparted a glorification of nurses; this was among influences that led to the opening of the Department of Nursing at UBC. Nurses had served magnificently in field hospitals, often near the front lines, and had become icons to be emulated by women. Even women's fashions were influenced by the shorter, more practical length of the skirts of nurses' uniforms. The influenza epidemic killed more than 50 million people world-wide and 50,000 in Canada and brought home to the public the need for better health care generally. During the height of the epidemic in B.C., the university was closed for five weeks and the auditorium and classrooms turned into wards for flu patients.[60] President Wesbrook and several students died from this virulent flu. Victims generally progressed rapidly to a toxic pneumonia with severe nosebleeds that required packing. Treatment was symptomatic and good nursing care was essential: tepid sponges for high fevers, mustard plasters for chest congestion, and fluids for dehydration. The dedication of the nurses from the nearby Vancouver General Hospital was duly noted and authorities also awakened to the need for better health education generally, which could be done by public health nurses.

Although organized medical groups questioned development of a nursing program at UBC (at the time, a faculty of medicine at UBC was not even a dream), UBC's Department of Nursing owes its early start to four highly influential physicians: Malcolm T. MacEachern, Henry Esson Young, Robert E. McKechnie, and R.H. Mullin.

Figure 1.15

Malcolm T. MacEachern, first General Superintendent of Vancouver General Hospital, 1913-1923.

Malcolm T. MacEachern, later to be recognized as one of Canada's and North America's most able hospital administrators,[61] had been medical superintendent of the Vancouver General Hospital since 1913. He had been a leader in the Hospital Standardization Movement, which was gaining momentum across Canada and the United States, and he was interested in quality education for nurses, both for his own highly regarded institution and generally. As medical and administrative head of Vancouver General Hospital, he worked closely with Helen Randal. He attended many national meetings of the Canadian Hospitals Association and would have known of and perhaps met Ethel Johns, Mary Agnes Snively, and Mary Ard. MacKenzie. He was supportive of the idea of a department of nursing education within a university. In fact, he wanted to see a University of British Columbia Department of Nursing as the central institution for education of all nurses in the province, with various approved (and only approved) hospitals used for practical portions of the program.[62]

The influential Henry Esson Young, who was provincial secretary and minister of education for British Columbia from 1908 until 1915, had become secretary of the Provincial Board of Health and Provincial Medical Officer in 1916. He, too, definitely favoured more education for nurses, and especially favoured advanced education in public health. As the minister responsible for school health, he had promoted the School Medical Inspection Act of 1911. This legislation called for every school child in the province to have a physical examination every year. He and C.J. Fagan had appointed the first provincial school nurse in 1913 and soon most centres also had school nurses (either under the provincial department or through the local school board). As well, he was concerned about shortages of trained public health inspectors and believed well qualified public health nurses would fill these roles – and maintained they would fill them better than non-nursing inspectors.[63]

Robert E. McKechnie was, at this crucial time, chancellor of UBC and presided over the Senate. He was also a strong member of the education committee for the School of Nursing at Vancouver General Hospital and a close working colleague of Robert MacEachern and Helen Randal. R.H. Mullin, another supporter of university education for nurses, was director of laboratories at VGH and head of the Department of Bacteriology at UBC, with each institution paying half his salary. He gave lectures to student nurses at Vancouver General Hospital and strongly supported the idea of nurses working in the community when they graduated.

In February 1919, the Senate considered a letter from Robert MacEachern asking the University to take over instruction of nursing students through a Department or Chair of Nursing. Robert McKechnie, as chairman of the Senate meeting, explained in detail the proposal and a committee was struck to meet with the Education Committee of VGH and report back to Senate.[64] On March 5, the committee reported the plan was "practical and offers the University a desirable and legitimate field of activity."[65] Shirley P. Clement, the first UBC graduate to become a member of the Senate, voiced opposition to the recommendation that a department be established, arguing that if the University were to give degrees in nursing it should demand some general education, such as a year in Arts, as was required of other students in Applied Science disciplines. Because of this objection, the report was accepted in principle, but referred to an enlarged committee for further study and recommendations.

In May 1919, the Senate received the report of the enlarged committee and proposed to the Board of Governors that a Department of Nursing be established in connection with the Faculty of Science, leading to a degree of B.Sc. (the degree designation was later changed). The Board of Governors approved this at its May 26th meeting,[66] and the stage was set for the first baccalaureate nursing degree program in Canada, to open in the fall of 1919. The approved program called for two years of university courses, two years in an *approved* hospital program, and a final year at UBC. The Board of Governors had been advised that Vancouver General Hospital would pay the salary of the head of the nursing department, and approval was thus given on the grounds that the University would have no financial responsibility (a move that turned out to be hampering for the new director).

At the time the proposal passed, the lady superintendent of VGH, Maude MacLeod, was leaving to be married and a search was on for a person who would be both director of nursing at the hospital and head of the new Nursing department at the University. Largely because of the efforts of

Malcolm MacEachern and, no doubt, Helen Randal, Registrar for B.C. nurses and a previous superintendent at VGH, Ethel Johns was approached, first informally and then formally, to take the position. Her name had also been recommended to the search committee by Teachers College, despite the fact that she had not completed academic qualifications for a degree.[67] Her application was accepted in August by VGH and announced to the UBC Board of Governors at its September meeting. She arrived in Vancouver and began her new role on October 1, 1919. The Nursing program had officially started.

CHAPTER TWO

The Ethel Johns Years
1919 to 1925

Figure 2.1

Ethel Johns, Superintendent of
Nurses at Vancouver General Hospital,
1919-1922. First head of the Department
of Nursing at UBC, a position she held
from 1919 to 1925.

Ethel Johns' role in the development of the UBC Nursing program has been
described as that of "midwife."[1] The metaphor is highly suitable for,
although she was not there at its conception, it was indeed her hand that
guided the new program into being. She became the first director of the UBC
Nursing program, appointed in August of 1919 to be both superintendent of
nurses at Vancouver General Hospital and head of the newly approved
Department of Nursing at the University of British Columbia. She remained
for only six years, a turbulent time during which she set a secure foundation.
She left to become field director of nursing programs in Europe for the
Rockefeller Foundation and to fill a variety of influential positions in the
United States before returning to Canada in 1933 to become editor of *The
Canadian Nurse*. A life-long writer and influential speaker, she was author of
three books, a series of 16 delightful pamphlets (later compiled into another

book), several major reports, more than 100 articles and editorials, and numerous speeches and presentations. Among the awards that she received was an Honorary Doctor of Laws from Mount Allison University and the Mary Agnes Snively Memorial Medal from the Canadian Nurses Association. She died in Vancouver in 1968.[2]

Her tenure with the UBC Nursing department, from 1919 to 1925, reflected the social, economic, educational, cultural, political, scientific, and technological climates of the period. However, she and the young women who entered the first Canadian degree program during this period also helped shape the events for the following decades. When she arrived, Ethel Johns was a strong, dynamic leader, one who already had been instrumental in shaping the forces that led to the early introduction of university-level approaches to nursing education. She had the foresight to see that a strong, science-based, liberal education for nurses belonged in the university system, paid for from educational budgets. She accepted the challenges of trying to bring such a program into being, using the forces, described in Chapter 1, that prompted acceptance of higher education for women. Despite these forces, however, she faced daily roadblocks placed in her path by some academics and some medical men. This proved an interesting and demanding period.

The fact that the UBC program succeeded is a tribute both to her skills and to the enthusiasm and support she received from nurses and from a small handful of medical and public leaders who supported these goals. It is also a tribute to the dedication of the young graduates of the program who went out into the community and brought about changes in the way health care was delivered. Their contributions have not been adequately reported or acknowledged in histories over the years, but change health care they did.

ETHEL JOHNS' EARLY LIFE

Ethel Johns' early life and nursing experiences helped colour her visions of what a university program should be. Ethel Mary Johns was born in England May 13, 1879. When she was 11 years old, first her father, then her mother emigrated to Canada, to northern Ontario. Ethel and her brother Owen, two years younger than she, remained behind in boarding schools near her maternal grandmother's home in northern Wales. Two years later, when Ethel was 13, the two children journeyed alone, by ship and railway, to join their parents in Canada. They were eventually "set down" by the train crew in northwestern Ontario to meet their mother at the local Hudson's Bay Post. From there, they went by canoe to the Wabigoon Reserve, near the Manitoba border, where her father had an appointment as teacher.

During her years on the Reserve, the young Ethel lived a secluded life, but became interested and involved in learning the Ojibway language and culture. Despite the lack of a formal high school education, Ethel Johns was exposed to a wide range of classics under the tutelage of her teacher parents and received an education far beyond the quality found in the public school systems of the time. In particular, she showed a talent for writing that was to prove a vital part of her career. Following the death of her father in 1895, the family remained on the Reserve, with Mrs. Johns taking over her husband's teaching appointment.

When Ethel was just 17, a chance meeting with E. Cora Hind had profound and lasting effects. Cora Hind was an independent, free-spirited woman who had moved to Manitoba in 1881 with hopes of becoming a reporter for the *Free Press*.[3] Although she was unable to secure a reporter's job, she mastered the new technology of the typewriter, which was just being introduced, and eventually set up her own typist's office. She did some freelance writing on the side and when she met the Johns family she was on a trip to write about life in the lumber camps of northern Ontario.[4] The 35-year-old woman, who soon became internationally known for her articles on prairie grain and livestock shipments, and the young Ethel Johns struck up the beginnings of a life-long friendship, at most times carried out by mail. Under what today might be called the "mentorship" of her friend Miss Hind, in 1899 the 20-year-old Ethel Johns, who writes that she "had always wanted to be a nurse,"[5] entered the Training School for Nurses at the Winnipeg General Hospital.

The School for Nurses, when she entered, was only 12 years old, and had gone through the growing pains common to hospital schools before the turn of the century.[6] Ethel Johns was one of 19 students in her class, which happened to include a young woman named Isabel Maitland Stewart. Isabel Stewart was destined to become, along with Ethel Johns, an international nursing leader and is well-recognized today in American nursing as a vital influence on nursing education in the United States. The students were fortunate to have a new Lady Superintendent, Adah Patterson, and her hand-picked assistant, Cassie Thompson. Both were graduates of the already-famous Johns Hopkins Hospital School of Nursing; Adah Patterson was a Canadian who had enrolled at the Baltimore school and who remained on staff after graduation and thus worked with Isabel Hampton (later Robb) and Adelaide Nutting.[7]

EARLY PROFESSIONAL CAREER

Ethel Johns had limited opportunities as a nurse graduating in 1902. The main employment was in patients' homes and, during the next 10 years, she did various stints of private duty, broken with experiences such as relief night supervisor, head of the operating room, and head surgical nurse at large hospitals in both Winnipeg and nearby American centres. Those early experiences in private homes made a lasting impact on Ethel Johns and coloured her caring and concern about the plight of those who needed round-the-clock care but could not afford to pay for it.[8] In 1907, she finally achieved a permanent position in the "high-tech" area of her time – in charge of the brand new X-ray department of the Winnipeg General.

During this early part of her career, she was also involved with the launching of two important nursing organizations: the Alumnae Association of the Winnipeg General Hospital and the Manitoba Association of Graduate Nurses. She was present at the inaugural meeting of her alumnae association and, although rather bored with the early meetings,[9] she began to recognize the importance of nursing associations and networks. This was the beginning of 50 years involvement with nursing groups at local, provincial, national, and international levels.[10] As well, with Isabel Stewart as business manager, she started a nursing magazine – the *Nurses' Alumnae Journal* – and became its first editor. In addition, she began to write for the relatively new national quarterly magazine called *The Canadian Nurse*, which had been launched in Toronto in 1905.

In her writings, and then in an outstanding public address in Winnipeg in 1910, Ethel Johns stressed the need for standardization of nursing educational programs and for standardized provincial nursing examinations. As well, she began to champion a move, already under way in eastern Canada, for registration for nurses. As a result of the efforts of Ethel Johns and her like-minded friends, Manitoba was, in 1913, the second province in Canada to achieve a Nurse Registration Act.

Around this time she visited selected hospitals in the Chicago area and had opportunities to observe an affiliation between one hospital and the medical school at the university. She came away convinced that the goal for nursing education should be affiliation with a university. Before she could see this newest idea bear fruit in Canada, however, she made several major career moves, including a position as lady superintendent at McKellar General Hospital in Fort William, Ontario, and as head surgical nurse at the Good Samaritan Hospital in Los Angeles, California.

By 1914, she had saved up enough money to enter the course at Teachers College, Columbia University, where Isabel Stewart had gone earlier to continue her education and was now a junior instructor. A family crisis soon after her arrival in New York meant she had to divert most of her savings back to her family in California, but thanks to Clara Noyes, the outstanding lady superintendent at Bellevue, she obtained a part-time job (in the central linen room) that enabled her to remain at Columbia for a year.[11] There she studied under some U.S. nursing legends: Mary Adelaide Nutting, Annie Goodrich, and Lavinia Dock. Unfortunately, her finances did not allow her to complete her degree and, after what she described as "my wonderful year,"[12] she left to become superintendent of the Children's Hospital of

Winnipeg. Her position there was also as head of the school of nursing and she did a great deal of the teaching.[13]

When she returned to Winnipeg in the summer of 1915, she renewed her activities in Canadian nursing associations. She was elected corresponding secretary of the Manitoba Association of Graduate Nurses, and prepared, for its annual meeting, a paper on the importance of nursing journals. She was asked to become head of a committee on standardization of training schools for the Canadian Society of Superintendents of Training Schools (whose first president had been Mary Agnes Snively); through this committee she established ties with other important national leaders, including Jean Gunn, superintendent of nurses at the Toronto General Hospital and then secretary-treasurer of the Canadian National Association for Trained Nurses. Through the Society for Superintendents, Ethel Johns became well acquainted with its president, Helen Randal, who was superintendent of nurses at the Vancouver General Hospital (1912-1916), which, with its 600 beds and seven operating rooms, was the second largest hospital in Canada (after the Toronto General).[14]

Helen Randal, about this time, was also "editor, business manager, secretary, stenographer and everything else"[15] of *The Canadian Nurse* (1916-1924) when it was purchased by the national nurses' association. She also was the driving force behind and then president (1917-1919) of the Graduate Nurses Association of British Columbia, which was lobbying hard with the government for registration. Helen Randal and Ethel Johns were active too in the Canadian National Association for Trained Nurses. In 1917, when the two organizations held a joint meeting in Montreal, Ethel Johns made an impassioned speech on the deficiencies of many Canadian training schools and on the woes of the apprenticeship system of nursing education. She contended that a training school needed to be financially independent of the hospital and that students needed a broad-based, liberal education. At that meeting, she was elected secretary of the national nurses' association, a position she was to hold for three years, and elected second vice-president of the Society of Superintendents, which voted at the meeting to change its name to the Canadian Association of Nursing Education (CANE).

In 1918, the two rapidly strengthening national nursing organizations again held a joint meeting, this time at the University of Toronto, with Adelaide Nutting and Isabel Stewart as the chief guest speakers. Ethel Johns once again presented a paper, this time commenting on the need for nurse teachers to be educated to teach. At this same meeting, Helen MacMurchy's report on her survey of universities across Canada, to discover if any were involved with education of nurses, was read.[16]

During this 1917-1919 period, possibly thanks to her candour about health care needs in her local speeches and to her friendship with the respected journalist Cora Hind, Ethel Johns was appointed by the Manitoba Government to the Public Welfare Commission of Manitoba. As part of her responsibilities on the commission, she visited hospitals throughout Manitoba. As a result, the "Nursing" section in the commission's Interim Report sharply criticized the hospital training system for nurses and, as one of its recommendations, suggested that the University of Manitoba should be involved in the education of nurses.[17]

Although this two-year stint as commissioner was an exceedingly busy one for Ethel Johns in addition to her position at the Children's Hospital, she continued with her work with the provincial and national organizations. She also was involved in a political issue in Manitoba in February 1919 when proposed amendments to the province's Minimum Wage Act would include provisions for student nurses. The Manitoba nurses' association vigorously opposed the provisions. Mabel Gray, then superintendent of nurses at the Winnipeg General Hospital and corresponding secretary for the provincial nurses' association, was asked to present a resolution to the legislative committee proposing the amendments. Ethel Johns, as secretary of the national nurses' association, was asked to organize a national delegation to speak to the legislative committee. The nurses' organizations opposed the move on the basis that, although the pupil nurses' hours were overly long and their stipends inadequate, they should not come under the Minimum Wage Act because they should not be considered employees of the hospital but students who were in the hospital for educational purposes and not as a working force.[18]

An appreciation of just how "advanced" were the positions of the early nursing leaders comes from a review of Ethel Johns' presentations to various groups during 1916 to 1919. Frequently and eloquently she promoted the idea of university education for nurses. Although her workload in Winnipeg was heavy, she was often on the speakers' circuit. The year 1919 was a momentous one for her in many ways; the report of the Manitoba Public Welfare Commission had been well in advance of its time in social policy areas and had involved her in public controversy; for example, the commission had touched on compulsory health insurance. Then, in May and June of 1919, Winnipeg's post-World War I labour unrest exploded into one of the hot-bed centres of a General Strike that affected cities from Vancouver to Halifax with workers all across Canada taking part. In Vancouver, more than 10,000 workers went out[19] and the strike lasted 25 days.[20] In Winnipeg, the strike lasted longer, involved almost 30,000 workers, and created deep divisions on political grounds. Those opposed to the strikers linked them with the Communist Revolution. Finally the federal government passed the Riot Act, leading to a clash involving police and troops against the workers on "bloody Saturday."[21]

The strike extended to the city's hospitals and as superintendent of the Winnipeg Children's Hospital Ethel Johns was in the front trenches; she was management, although her sympathies were with the workers.[22] The strike committee generally exempted deliveries to the hospital. The nurses were not on strike and children of many of the workers were in hospital. "The diseases they were suffering from were chiefly due to starvation,"[23] Ethel Johns wrote in later years to the author of a book about the Strike.[24] Because of one heart-tearing incident over repairs to a wind-damaged roof where hospital officials forced her to reject offers of free help from the striking workers, she made the decision that she would have to leave the Hospital. As soon as the Strike was ended, she handed in her resignation.[25]

She then found another door had opened. She was offered the opportunity to become superintendent of nursing at the Vancouver General Hospital and head of the Department of Nursing at the four-year-old University of British Columbia.

ORGANIZING THE DEGREE PROGRAM AT UBC

Ethel Johns arrived in Vancouver to take up her duties on October 1, 1919. Her appointment was heralded by the Vancouver General Hospital, which had agreed to pay her full salary so that the University need not bear the costs of the new Nursing department; the choice was less enthusiastically received by the University Senate, because she did not have an academic degree.[26] Malcolm MacEachern's letter to President Leonard S. Klinck, the first dean of agriculture who had been appointed president on the death of Frank Wesbrook, praised Ethel Johns highly,[27] however, and subsequent events proved she was well-suited for the onerous tasks of organization of the program.

Senate minutes reveal her excellent capacity for organizing and presenting the course outline that eventually was accepted. Much more detail is con-tained in the proposals for the Nursing department than in those from other departments, such as Home Economics and Theology, which also were seeking approval at about the same time. Perhaps because of the wealth of detail, however, the Senate members queried small points and recommended minor changes.

Nursing became one of 21 departments under the only three faculties (Arts, Agriculture, Applied Science) at UBC in 1919-1920. The plan for the nursing degree program approved by the Senate in October 1919 was for a five-year program calling for two years of university study (at least one of which must be at UBC), two years in a program at an *approved* hospital affiliated with UBC, and a final year of study at UBC.[28] This became the prototypical pattern for most university nursing programs in Canada; it was referred to as the 2+2+1 or non-integrated program, and was typical of most Canadian programs until the University of Toronto established an integrated program in 1942.[29]

The UBC model approved by the Senate contained certain criteria that were not included in early programs in other parts of Canada and the United States. For example, in the UBC program, the Vancouver General portion of the course was much more closely allied with UBC because of the shared campus and the common director. As well, the hospital school's program had to be declared "approved" by the University Senate. The Vancouver General, which had passed the brand-new survey carried out by the Standardization Committee of the American College of Surgeons, was considered a model institution of its time.[30]

The Senate quibbled over some initial wording proposed by Ethel Johns, especially that the first two years in the program would be "equivalent of two years of Arts" and removed this phrase.

Still, when the program is examined closely, the first two years are seen to be more rigorous than required for most Arts degrees. The requirements for those in the first two years of the Nursing Department were:

First Year: English 1 and 2, History 1, Mathematics 1 or Latin 1 or French 1, Physics 1, Chemistry 1, Biology 1

Second Year: English 3 and 4, Chemistry 2, Philosophy 1, Economics 1, Bacteriology 1 and 2.[31]

Description of the fifth-year courses, which would be mainly Nursing courses and limited to those enrolled in the department, was referred to committee to be brought back to the Senate at a later date.

When it approved the basic program, the Senate also made provision for graduate nurses who had matriculation standing and were from approved programs to take the three university years if they applied to the University within two years of graduation. This "privilege" for post-registration training was withdrawn in 1925.[32]

Although organization of the fifth year of the degree course was not final, one of Ethel Johns' first acts was to meet with and interview young women who were interested in the nursing degree program. She looked for those whose educational backgrounds made it possible for them to be enrolled in *second* year.

One of these young women was Beatrice Fordham Johnson (later Wood), who had entered the Vancouver General Hospital nursing course in September 1919. This 20-year-old woman was from a prominent Vancouver family, whose father later was one of B.C.'s Lieutenant Governors. She had graduated from Crofton House private school at age 16 and had taken some courses at the University. However, she became ill while at UBC. She described this in an interview years later: "I was one of these bronchial people and had been warned about TB and taken out before I finished the year."[33] She then went to New York to stay with her godmother and took two years at Finch Junior

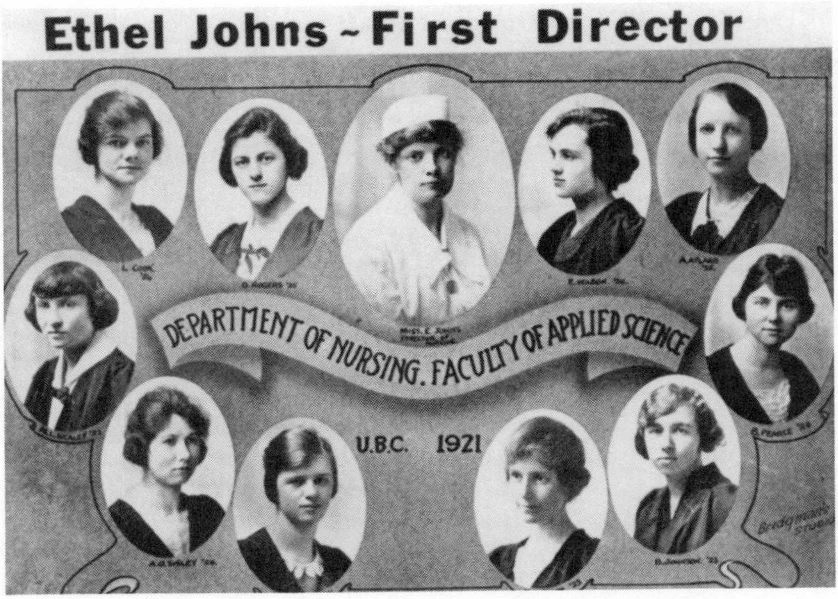

Figure 2.2   Ethel Johns with students enrolled in the UBC
nursing program in 1921. Top L-R: Louise Cook, Dorothy Rogers,
Ethel Johns *Director*, Everilda Wilson, A. Aylard.
Centre L-R: Margaret Healy, Beatrice Pearse. Lower L-R: A.O. Sisley,
Esther Naden, Marion Fisher, Beatrice Johnson.

College where she majored in drama. On her return to Vancouver, she found that the family was leaving for Florida for a year and had rented their home. As she had no place to stay she decided to enter the nursing school where she could stay in residence. She had just started at VGH when she heard about the proposed UBC Nursing program. Her father called his friend Malcolm MacEachern to inquire about the course. She was then interviewed by Ethel Johns and taken out of the VGH program and, along with Marion Fisher, was granted permission by Senate to enter second year.[34]

Marion Fisher (later Faris) had also entered the VGH program. She had taken one year in the UBC-McGill program in 1913, but then went to Normal School and taught for three years before she decided she wanted to become a nurse. She was a probationer in the fall of 1919 when she was called to see Ethel Johns. "She called me down and I was kind of scared and I expected something. Instead she smiled very awkwardly and told me to sit down. She outlined what they were thinking of – I can't remember the details – about having this school and she was looking for certain people who had a year at university."[35]

Two other young women – Margaret Healy and Esther Naden – were also enrolled at the University and applied to enter the first class of the Nursing program. In an interview in 1987, Esther Naden (later Gardom) recalled that she had always wanted to be a nurse but her mother had strenuously objected and so she had entered UBC instead. "To my great delight, I learned of the degree course in Nursing just [as I was] starting the second year. Without telling my parents, I registered for second year in Nursing."[36] Because of her mother's death soon after she entered the hospital portion, however, Esther Naden had to leave for a period and did not graduate until the second class in 1924.

Bea Johnson noted that the 1919-1920 university year was heavy on the sciences and "was a very strenuous year."[37] As female students in this era usually enrolled in humanities courses, these nursing students no doubt had a number of science courses to make up so that they would achieve the Senate's goals. During this year, the students also were asked to decide whether they wished to graduate in public health or administration. Bea Johnson recalled, "Well, you looked at all the administrators and you didn't want that."[38] All of the first students chose public health.

At the Senate meeting of February 18, 1920, the curriculum for the fifth year was presented and approved. The program included general subjects to be taken by all nursing students, but they then had to choose one of two options – Pedagogy or Public Health – for the rest of their subjects (see Box 1).

THE PUBLIC HEALTH CERTIFICATE COURSE

Perhaps it was not surprising that the early students in the UBC program selected the public health option; as noted earlier, organization of public health departments throughout the province and the nation was a major trend. Public health nursing could be considered a glamour and growth industry for women at the time. The International Red Cross Society during the 1914-1918 World War recognized that the young men called up for military duty could have benefitted from better health education during their early years. The League of Red Cross Societies thus turned to preventing disease (especially tuberculosis, venereal diseases, and malaria) and promoting health as its post-War goal. The Canadian Red Cross Society called for courses for public health nurses to achieve these ends and in 1920 offered special subsidies to five universities to establish postgraduate instruction in public health nursing.[39]

The UBC Senate was offered one of these subsidies by the provincial Red Cross branch. The Red Cross proposed to pay up to $5,000 a year for three years for the salary of a professor appointed to a Red Cross Chair of Public Health, starting in April 1920.[40] The Senate accepted and expressed its "appreciation of this generous offer" and referred the matter to faculty.

Box 1 Curriculum for Fifth Year Academic Work, Department of Nursing

In her [sic] fifth year, the student will attend the session of the University. Two major subjects are offered, of which the student, with the consent of her [sic] advisors, may elect (1) Teaching and Administration of Schools for Nurses (2) Public Health Nursing. Students selecting Pedagogy will take Courses A and B. Those selecting Public Health will take Courses A and C.

A. General.

Psychology
Sanitary Science
Practical Application of Sociology
Statistics
Nutrition
Physical Education

B. Pedagogy

Students selecting the Pedagogy option will in addition take the following subjects:

Principles of Teaching
History of Education
Teaching of Nursing Principles and Contemporary Problems
Teaching Practice
Supervision in Hospital Training Schools

C. Public Health

Students selecting Public Health Option will in addition take the following subjects:

Principles of Public Health Nursing and Contemporary Problems
Principles of Public Health Teaching
Medical Inspection and School Nursing
Control of Communicable Diseases
Principles of Modern Social Work
Administration of Institutes.

Source: Senate Minutes, Wednesday, February 18, 1920, p. 140.

R.H. Mullin, who was head of the Department of Bacteriology, head of the Provincial Laboratories, and on the medical staff of Vancouver General, was considered the logical choice, but he elected to share his salary with a nurse to ensure the course was truly a nursing course. A Department of Public Health, separate from the Department of Nursing, was set up under the Faculty of Arts, with R.H. Mullin as its head. The nurse chosen to design and teach the first special 14-week public health nursing course was Mary Ardcronie MacKenzie, who had been Chief Superintendent of the Victorian Order of Nurses (VON) from 1908 to 1917.

Mary Ard. MacKenzie (she signed herself this way and was generally referred to by friends and colleagues as Mary Ard., possibly to distinguish her from Mary Agnes Snively) was well suited to take this position. She was born in Toronto in 1869 and took her Bachelor of Arts degree at the University of Toronto in 1892, then took a "Higher School" Teacher Certificate with specialist standing in modern languages in 1893. She had taught in high schools and had been principal of a high school in Sherbrooke, Quebec, before taking her nursing training at Massachusetts General Hospital in Boston in 1901 and additional training from the Sloan Maternity Hospital in New York. She was the second president of the Canadian National Association for Trained Nurses (1912-1914), following Mary Agnes Snively. As Chief Superintendent of the VON, she would have visited the developing VON branches in B.C. and would have known all the small Canadian network of nursing leaders, including Ethel Johns and Helen Randal. She had long recognized the need to expand training programs in district nursing initiated by the VON around the turn of the century. She now believed university programs could and should augment, even take over, these VON programs. When she left the VON, she accepted three short appointments in the United States, first as Superintendent of Nurses, University of California in San Francisco, State Supervisor, Tuberculosis Nurses, Oklahoma, and Superintendent of Visiting Nurse Association, Denver, Colorado.[41] In today's terms, the first of these might be called postgraduate education and the others might be best described as "consultancies." She apparently was pleased to return to Canada to join the newly established Department of Public Health at UBC as Red Cross Instructor. She presented the first short course for graduate nurses.

Twenty-six nurses graduated with a Certificate in Public Health Nursing from this first course, which began November 15, 1920. Students took six weeks of academic work followed by eight weeks of field work.[42] The UBC Calendar of 1921-1922 stated that "the aim of the course is to afford such instruction to graduate nurses entering the public health field as will assist them in dealing with problems of sanitation, economics, and education that will be met in a public health service and to give them a broader understanding of present-day nursing problems."[43] The course content is described in Box 2.

Box 2

Outline of the Short Course in Public Health Nursing, November 1920–
March 1921.

1. *Academic Work:*

(1) Twelve lectures on each of the following:
 (a) Public Health Nursing,
 (b) School Hygiene,
 (c) Communicable Diseases,
 (d) Modern Social Problems.

(2) Six lectures on each of the following:
 (e) Teaching Principles,
 (f) History of Nursing Education,
 (g) Social Service Problems,
 (h) Personal Hygiene,
 (i) Medical Aspects of Infant and Maternal Welfare,
 (j) Tuberculosis,
 (k) Mental Hygiene,
 (l) Sanitation.

(3) Occasional lectures on Provincial Legislation,
 Municipal Health Departments, Voluntary
 Organizations, Delinquent and Deserted
 Children, etc.

(4) Excursions to special health features in and around
 Vancouver.

2. *Field Work:* For field work the class was divided into sections of
appropriate size, each of which received from one to two weeks'
instruction and experience under trained workers in the actual
operation of each of the following branches:

1. Urban School Nursing,
2. Tuberculosis Problems,
3. District Nursing,
4. Health Centres and Rural School Nursing,
5. Child Welfare,
6. Medical, Social Service, and Relief Organizations.

Source: UBC Calendar, 7th session, 1921-1922, p. 186.

During their courses, the students received classes from some 20 well-known and prestigious specialists, including Henry Esson Young, former minister of education and now provincial officer of health, and Frank T. Underhill, Vancouver medical health officer. One important lecturer was Judge Helen Gregory MacGill of the B.C. Juvenile Court, the first woman who had been appointed a judge in B.C. Leonard S. Klinck, president of UBC, and M.F. Angus of the Department of Economics, UBC, also gave lectures to the nurses as well as Malcolm MacEachern and Ethel Johns and a host of other nurses, social workers, and economists. The field work was given at local branches of the VON at Vancouver, Saanich, and Colwood, and at the Rotary Institute for Chest Diseases in Vancouver, the Vancouver School Board and City Health Department, and the Social Service Department run by the Women's Auxiliary of the Vancouver General Hospital.

Saanich was selected for field work experience because it was the first provincially-run health centre to be established in B.C. The Saanich public health centre opened in 1919, with financing from local taxes and grants from the Provincial Board of Health; in 1920, the Cowichan Health Centre at Duncan and the Rural Esquimalt Nursing District at Langford (near Victoria) were established.[44] As well, Vancouver, Victoria, and several other cities such as New Westminster had established boards or departments of health and had hired nurses, usually designated as school nurses, to work in them.

This emphasis on health reflected the prosperous and expanding times as the province's population reached a half million people and industrial growth expanded. B.C.'s salmon, herring, and halibut fishing markets were developed and added to the economic strength from lumber and steel exports. Other industrial development included foundries, sugar refining, shipbuilding, pulp and paper, printing, flour milling, food products, and glass and rubber making.[45] Grain exports were increasing and the B.C. government of Premier John Oliver was lobbying Ottawa for reduction in rail freight rates so that the western port could expand even more. In 1920, he successfully ran for majority re-election of his Liberal party on a platform of road-building throughout the province.[46] Technology was advancing and even mail was taking to the air; the first Canada-U.S. airmail flight occurred from Vancouver to Seattle on March 3, 1919.[47]

These prosperous times led Henry Esson Young, who became the Provincial Health Officer from 1916 (and held the position until his death in 1939), to exploit the awakening public conscience with what was to become a province-wide Public Health Service. He had two main objectives for the early 1920s: an educational program that would equip nurses for public health district work and a network of health centres in local districts throughout the province through which these nurses would work. The district would set up a community board to administer the service. In some districts, part of the funds came from the Provincial Department of Education, which had agreed to pay

Figure 2.3   The Cowichan Health Centre in Duncan opened in 1920 and
provided office, clinic space, and living quarters for public health nurses.

the same grant for a public health nurse as for a teacher.[48] The individual public
health nurse would be a generalist working especially to improve the health of
children and families. A major portion of the work included infectious disease
control, especially identification and control of tuberculosis. As well, the nurse
would introduce well-baby clinics and school health programs that would
promote better education for the public.

THE FIRST CERTIFICATE GRADUATES

The early certificate courses reflected these needs of the time and their first
graduates were instrumental in making these objectives work throughout the
province. A look at the early careers of some graduates of the first certificate
class reflects how these young women managed to take health care to the
people of B.C.

Four of the nurses to enrol in the first short course in Public Health
Nursing were recent graduates of the Royal Jubilee Hospital School of
Nursing in Victoria and brief notes on their nursing careers follow: Louise
Elizabeth Buckley (later Jones) (1918), Winnifred Ehlers (later Keighley)
(1919), Margaret Miriam Griffin (later Dowell) (1920), and Muriel Caroline
Harman (1920).[49] Louise Buckley graduated from the course with first-class
honours and joined the School Health Department in Saanich. The small
community of Saanich, later a part of the Greater Victoria area, had been the
first of the provincially-run health centres and was a model for the rest of the

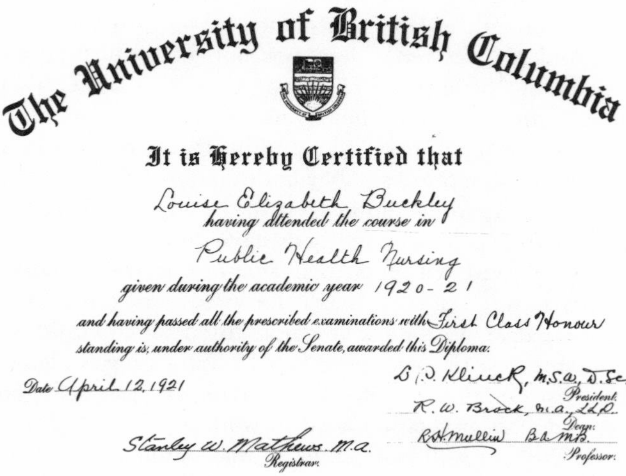

The University of British Columbia

It is Hereby Certified that

Louise Elizabeth Buckley
having attended the course in

Public Health Nursing

given during the academic year 1920-21

and having passed all the prescribed examinations with First Class Honour
standing is, under authority of the Senate, awarded this Diploma:

Date April 12, 1921

L. D. Klinck, M.S.a, D.Sc.
President
R. W. Brock, m.a, Ll.D.
Dean

Stanley W. Mathews, m.a.
Registrar

R.A. Mullin, B.a. m.b.
Professor

Figure 2.4   The first Diploma in Public Health Nursing was awarded to Louise Buckley, April 12, 1921. There were 26 graduates in this first class.

Figure 2.5   Saanich War Memorial Centre opened in 1919, the first health centre to be established in the province. It had hospital beds, living space for the nurses, and office and clinic space.

province. In an interview in the early 1980s, Louise Buckley recalled that she had introduced hot lunches for the Saanich school program, a "first" in ensuring that students received at least one hot, healthful meal a day. She recalled the necessity of learning to change tires on the VON's model-T Ford, which was rather a high technology item for the nursing staff as horses-and-buggies were still much more common on the roads than cars.

Margaret Griffin also went as a public health nurse to Saanich and recalled that she received $43 a month and her board; the wage came partly through money from the municipality and partly through donations and fees. Saanich public health nurses lived in a comfortable home built by the municipality as a war memorial health centre; a married couple were hired to cook and maintain the grounds.[50] With these amenities, the Saanich Health Unit soon became a desirable area for field work for UBC's nursing students.

Muriel Harman won the $100 Red Cross Prize given for the highest marks in the course and after graduation went to work for the VON in Burnaby. She established the first well-baby clinic in that municipality. These VON nurses, as well as the public health nurses in some districts, frequently offered nursing care in the home, including a 24-hour service which was especially common for maternity care and home deliveries. Many people at that time carried a Metropolitan Life Insurance Policy, which covered the cost of some health care, including these home visits.[51] For the others, the VON made a small charge, if the family could afford it, or provided as much service as was possible without charge. Muriel Harman later went to a Bible College in Toronto and then as a nurse-missionary to the Belgian Congo (later Zaire); after 37 years as a nurse and teacher she was captured by forces opposed to independence and was machine-gunned to death in 1964.[52]

Winnifred Ehlers, whose grandmother had been a Red Cross nurse during the American Revolution,[53] went to Eagle Bay as one of two Red Cross nurses in the Shuswap area northeast of Kamloops. The Red Cross, which was funding the UBC course, had decided to set up eight nursing stations in isolated districts of the province and wanted to employ graduates of the course.[54] When the other nurse married, Winnifred Ehlers took over both parts of the district. Although the Red Cross provided cars for nurses in some of the districts, she used horse and buggy in the summer and horse and cutter in winter, even crossing the lake on the ice when it was frozen over. In articles describing the work of the early nurses in the Shuswap area, one author recalls receiving care typical of the time:

As a small child in Blind Bay, I remember Nurse Winnie Ehlers making her regular visits to the school. Knowing that some of the children were unable to buy toothbrushes and paste, she told us how to clean our teeth with a clean cloth and salt. She lectured the pupils on personal hygiene – how to wash our hands and keep our fingernails clean. She also showed, using a doll, the correct way to care for and hold a baby. This was useful information for older children with newborn siblings. She showed parents how to deal with headlice [sic] and how to control ringworm with a solution made by soaking coppers (pennies) in vinegar. It left a nasty brown stain, I recall. I remember when goitres were a common problem, and for nine days each month for a period of three months, we were given a glass of water and an iodine capsule first thing in the school day.[55]

This same author notes that the nurse made a monthly visit to the school, checking for head lice, goitres, bad teeth, infectious rashes, ringworm, and enlarged tonsils. One month Winnifred Ehlers examined this young girl's throat and made a note to ask the doctor, on his annual visit, to check the tonsils, which the doctor then said must be removed. The youngster, whose mother had died, was accompanied on "the biggest adventure of my life" by Nurse Ehlers; the two had to travel to the rail line on the mail truck when the mail carrier made his weekly visit, then by train (of which the youngster had seen only pictures) to Kamloops where she was fascinated by sidewalks, street lamps, and a "box on the wall" into which the nurse talked. Following the operation and return journey, the youngster was a celebrity as "the first in the family to see the wonders of 'outside'."[56]

Another member of the first public health certificate class, Christina West Thom, was hired following graduation by the Red Cross in Kamloops. The Kamloops Junior Red Cross Auxiliary had been formed during the War and, after a short hiatus, re-formed to assist in health education; it welcomed the idea of a Red Cross nurse and paid half the initial annual salary of $166.72, while the city agreed to pay the other half.[57] By May of 1921, Christina Thom had opened a weekly well-baby clinic. This was a new idea and mothers at first had to be convinced of the concept of a clinic for well babies, not sick ones. She also began classes in home nursing and hygiene, offered in the high school to teenage girls and through evening classes to adults. Christina Thom also visited the schools giving classes and weighing and measuring more than 6,800 students in 1922; underweight children received home visits and had their diets supplemented with cod-liver oil at school.[58]

Ida May Snelgrove recalled her field work experience in the new health centre in Duncan.[59] She was one of the few, however, who did not make direct use of her public health certificate, but instead continued to do private duty nursing until her marriage in the 1930s.

Josephine (Jo) Peters was another of the graduates of the first certificate class to go into the provincial public health service. After receiving her certificate, she went to work for the Rotary Clinic in Vancouver, a position sponsored by the Rotary Clubs to help provide care for tuberculosis patients. Tuberculosis continued as a leading cause of death, with one in 10 deaths attributed to this "white plague," as it was frequently called. By the 1920s, however, medical science had advanced to the point where it was possible to control its spread through good public health measures. The Provincial Board of Health had responsibility for control of tuberculosis and had appointed a Travelling Medical Officer. Clinics were held at intervals throughout the province to identify patients and their contacts, and a central province-wide registry was established. Seriously ill patients were admitted to special TB wards or to the Tranquille Sanatorium, near Kamloops, which was on property that had been purchased by the Anti-Tuberculosis Society in 1907[60] ; the "San" became a provincial institution in 1921. The local public health nurses followed up patient care for those at home and for all contacts, teaching them about infection control, rest, nutrition, and personal care.[61] In 1924, thanks to funding assistance from the Anti-Tuberculosis Societies (and later through the Christmas Seal campaigns), Josephine Peters was appointed first as Travelling Nurse then as Tuberculosis Nursing Supervisor for the Provincial Health Services, a position she held with distinction until her retirement in 1948. During her career, she saw many changes as tuberculosis care improved. Use of X-rays to assist in diagnosis had begun during the 1910s and, during the early 1920s, the main treatment was to go "on the cure." The latter meant absolute rest lying in a reclining position, preferably in a dry climate, good nutrition, and good personal hygiene, which was especially important to control the spread of the infection.[62] Pneumothorax as treatment for TB had been introduced for the seriously infected, but such surgical treatment, radical for the era, was limited in the early days to those who had one sound lung. Management of hemorrhage during a violent coughing spell was essential nursing knowledge and early textbooks recommended a "hemorrhage basket," with morphine sulphate, atropine, and nitroglycerine (the 1920s equivalent of a "crash cart").[63]

Tuberculosis was an everyday menace in the 1920s, and overworked nurses frequently contracted it. A generally accepted maxim in schools of nursing in the early part of the century was that one nurse from every class likely would die from TB. Marion Fisher (later Faris), who was one of the first three nurses in the UBC degree program, went to the TB San at Tranquille as a patient immediately following her graduation in 1923. She recalls that she had been diagnosed early and was not an advanced case; after about a year she went to Gabriola Island to complete her recovery. "Miss Johns was so thoughtful; she sent over books to read and so on," she recalled in an interview.[64] Esther Naden (later Gardom) recalled that she had five close friends – two nurses and three non-nurses – die of TB in the early 1920s, "It was very prevalent at the time. Bone and joint TB was common because of the unpasteurized milk; unpasteurized milk does not cause pulmonary TB – at least it didn't seem to. Tremendous numbers of children had scars on their necks from tuberculous glands."[65]

Margaret Allan Thatcher, a certificate graduate in 1922, had a more rewarding personal experience with the family tragedies that could result from TB contacts. In 1924, a young mother had to be admitted to Tranquille, leaving two small twin babies behind. A child welfare worker asked Meg Thatcher, who was at home caring for her ill father at the time, to take in the twin boys as foster children because they were TB contacts, malnourished, and needing special care. The boys remained throughout their young childhood with Meg Thatcher and, although this was unusual for a single woman to do in this era, she eventually adopted them about six years later and raised them as her own.[66]

CHANGES IN THE PUBLIC HEALTH COURSE

Almost immediately following graduation of the first 26 students from the certificate course, a decision was made to lengthen it. The certificate course was given by the Department of Public Health, which was part of the Faculty of Arts and Science and entirely separate from the Department of Nursing, although no doubt there was communication and collaboration. Under R.H. Mullin and Mary Ard. MacKenzie, the certificate course was lengthened to three months of academic work at the university followed by four months of field work in the various branches of public health.

The enrolment of 14 in the second certificate course in 1921-1922 included some nurses who had already been working in public health, but who recognized the importance of a sound theoretical basis. For example, Helen E. Kelly had already some experience opening the Esquimalt unit, but recalled that social service and child welfare were essential in the daily life of a public health nurse.[67] During the course, emphasis was placed on these subjects, which would not have been covered in the hospital training programs of the time. As well, field work was offered in six specific services: general visiting nursing, child welfare, urban school nursing, rural nursing, tuberculosis, and settlement and social service.[68]

The following year, 1922-1923, the public health certificate course was extended once again. R.H. Mullin believed that four months was "much too short a time for the course" and it was extended to a full academic year.[69] This extension also was necessary because the three fifth-year students from the nursing degree program were taking this public health nursing option along with the certificate students. The academic work was given in the first term and the field work was given in the second. Twelve nurses enrolled in the certificate course, which brought the total to 52 for the certificates issued under the initial Red Cross funding.

In June of 1923, Mary Ard. MacKenzie's contract, which had been covered under the Red Cross funding, was up, and she did not wish to renew it. She left the University, and her departure suddenly placed a great deal of responsibility for the teaching of courses in both the Department of Public Health and the Department of Nursing on the shoulders of Ethel Johns.

In recognition of her increased duties, the UBC Board of Governors approved the appointment of Ethel Johns as an Assistant Professor, and for the 1924-1925 year increased her salary by $300 to $2,800 annually.

The public health nursing certificate courses were to continue under the Department of Public Health, but in August 1924, R.H. Mullin suddenly died. He had been a strong supporter of the nursing courses and Ethel Johns considered him a "staunch friend and wise counsellor."[70] She now had to take over additional teaching responsibilities in the Public Health course. Hibbert Winslow Hill took over R.H. Mullin's responsibilities as head of the two departments, Bacteriology and Public Health, both under the Faculty of Arts; this led to some administrative problems and reorganization of the departments soon began. Amalgamation was achieved through a new Department of Nursing and Health, under the Faculty of Applied Science, with Hibbert Hill as head.[71] Reginald W. Brock, who was dean of the Faculty of Applied Science, said that the work of the two previous departments was closely interwoven and that it would make for better cooperation and more effective administration. The end of Red Cross funding was no doubt a factor in the amalgamation. The decision to name Hibbert Hill as head related to Ethel Johns' lack of academic credentials, but the nursing community was not pleased with this apparent loss of autonomy.

THE GROWING DEGREE PROGRAM

In addition to her duties with the public health certificate course, Ethel Johns' top priority was development of the nursing degree program or, as she described it, "the new experiment in nursing education."[72] She had to balance her commitments as director of nursing at the Vancouver General (and thereby also head of its nursing school) with her role as head of the Department of Nursing. The fact that the two institutions still were occupying the same site made the job somewhat easier. Students in the first degree courses said how helpful Ethel Johns was in ensuring that those taking University courses were able to be freed from ward duties to attend campus lectures and events. Such preferential treatment inevitably led, however, to some resentment on the part of VGH students, who frequently had to "cover" for the UBC students when they went off wards for campus courses.

Ethel Johns had addressed these concerns in her first speech to staff and pupils soon after she arrived. She stressed that the Hospital's excellent reputation was a major factor in the University giving recognition to nursing and in its selection as the affiliated hospital.

This hospital is to be one of the laboratories, as it were, in this province where the new experiment [of degree programs] is to be tested ... This is where you come in. You have got to demonstrate to the University and to the public that work done in the wards of this hospital by the rank and file of the staff and pupils is so good that it is worthy of University recognition. No other department in the University has to submit to such a searching test as this. The Department of Nursing will be under judgment as to results from the moment of its inception, before a single student shall have received her degree. If the work done here in the wards is only mediocre, then we shall have failed. The University and other bodies – we must live up to them, or we shall be thrust aside.[73]

She emphasized the honour as well as the responsibility that every nurse in the Hospital should feel in taking part in opening these new doors for nurses and women to achieve university-level entry for their education.

Maude McLeod, a former superintendent at VGH, in an article published in *The Canadian Nurse* about the same time, also discussed the benefits to nursing that the new degree program would ensure. She wrote that it was "not only a great boon to the nursing profession, but allows the University to extend its service in another direction and enter an extremely useful field, and no doubt this arrangement will have a stimulating effect on all training schools throughout our Province and make them adopt higher standards."[74] (See also Box 3.)

Box 3
Advantages of University Education for Nurses, 1919.

The following summary of advantages for the University of B.C. and the Vancouver General Hospital was made by Maude McLeod, former superintendent of nursing, in an article in *The Canadian Nurse* in November 1919.

　　　First – The connection of our training school with the University will bring it to a much higher plane and attract the best type of young women.

　　　Second – The teaching will be more thorough, systematic and efficient – casting no reflection whatsoever on the past, where the teaching was done under many handicaps, and, considering everything, excellently well done.

　　　Third – The great advantage [is] to the patient in not being subjected to the untrained nurse, inasmuch as this system will bring into the wards nurses who are now fairly well qualified to take care of a patient.

　　　Fourth – The connection of the training school with higher education and ... modern advancements ... will be more stimulus for ... nurses and attract the best class of young women to take the course.

Source: McLeod, Maude. (1919). The university and the training school for nurses, Vancouver General Hospital. *The Canadian Nurse*, 15 (11), p. 2101.

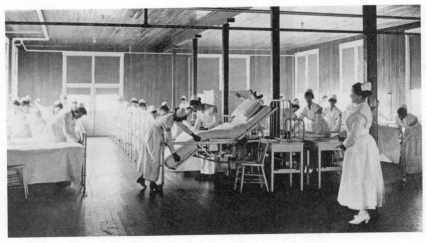

Figure 2.6   Nursing instruction in Heather Annex
after the influenza epidemic, circa 1919.

By fall of 1920, students were enrolling in the Department of Nursing at
the beginning of the academic year. Ethel Johns continued to accept young
women who had already taken their first university year into second year. As
well, she accepted some who had a second university year and could,
therefore, enter the 28-month clinical portion of the course given at the
hospital (in other words, enter at the third year). Students who were missing
some required science courses were allowed to take these while they were
taking the clinical portion of the course.

The degree program also had opened nursing's doors to some young
women who had graduated from high school but who could not enter
nursing programs because they were not the required 20 years of age. These
young women frequently had more university courses than were required,
which eventually led the Department of Nursing to propose a so-called
"double degree" program. These students took a six-year program, where a
student could take three years of Arts and Nursing courses, then the clinical
portion, and a final year that included both nursing and arts courses. Starting
in 1930, these students began receiving both a BA (Bachelor of Arts) and a
BASc (Nsg) (Bachelor of Applied Science in Nursing).

CLINICAL PORTION OF THE COURSE

Ethel Johns drew up a curriculum outline for the clinical portion of the
degree course; this covered the third and fourth years in hospital. She then
took it to the UBC Senate for approval. It appeared in the *University
Calendar 1922-1923* and reflected the improvements that she and the VGH

Figure 2.7   Vancouver General Hospital nurses or students in nursing station, circa early 1900s. Note the style of the cap.

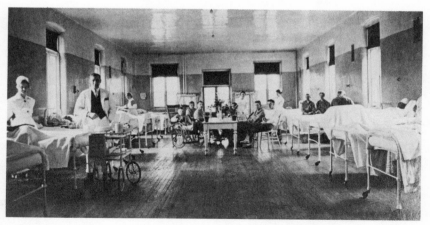

Figure 2.8   Men's surgical ward in Heather Pavilion 1918. These open wards remained in use until 1993 when the last two were closed.

staff had achieved in the Hospital's teaching program. She was proving an excellent and able administrator for the 1,200-bed Hospital, which was fast gaining a nation-wide reputation as an outstanding teaching institution. In addition to herself and her Assistant Director, Maud Buttle, the nursing staff included R.W. Tassie, instructor of nurses, M. McArthur, demonstrator to nurses, and B. (Bertha) Marsden, supervisor at Infants' Hospital.[75] The remaining graduate staff included: three night supervisors; nine supervisors of departments (such as the Operating Room, TB and Infectious Diseases Unit, and Men's Surgical); five graduates in charge of wards; and 33 other graduates, including 22 in the Military Annex (which was for returned soldiers and which was staffed mainly by graduate nurses and by 32 ward assistants and not by student nurses). A booklet published to attract students into the program in 1919 indicated a nursing staff of 47 graduates and 190 pupil nurses for the 1,200 patients.[76] This ratio of graduate nurses to pupil nurses was exceptionally high for hospitals of this era, although this number of nursing staff must have been hard pressed to provide the hands-on quality of physical care demanded by patients of the time.

The students in the Hospital program when Ethel Johns arrived included six from the previous graduating class who were completing their course because of time lost to illness, 51 seniors (third year), 44 intermediates (second year), 71 juniors and probationers, and five postgraduate students.[77] This was a total of 177 compared to the usual complement of 190.

Although these students at VGH still gave a large portion of patient care, they had achieved a major breakthrough in their hours of duty; the school was one of the first in Canada to achieve the eight-hour day that was being recommended by labour unions. VGH students generally worked a day shift that could be 7 a.m. to 3 p.m. or a 7 a.m. to 7 p.m. "split shift" with four hours off in the afternoon. The other two shifts were 3 p.m. to 11 p.m. and 11 p.m. to 7 a.m. Classroom hours were in addition to these shifts. The day shift usually made allowance for students to work the split shift so they could attend classes; those on afternoon or night duty had to get up to attend classes when these were offered. Students also received one half-day off during the week and a half-day off on Sundays. After the six-month probationary period, students received $6 a month for the remainder of the first year, $8 a month for the second year, and $10 a month for the third year; this was a relatively high amount when the starting salary for most graduates was $60 a month. All students were required to pay for breakages, however, and Bea Johnson (later Wood) recalled dropping a tray of glass thermometers that meant that she did not receive any stipend for two months.

The fact that university students were taken off wards to attend university classes sometimes led to some animosity from VGH students. Esther Naden (later Gardom) recalled that "the university girls were not welcome on the wards as they had to be away so much."[78] This meant that other nurses would

Figure 2.9   Class of nursing students at Fairview. Those in the forefront are
probationers (without caps). Public health nursing students are wearing dark hats.
Nursing classes were held at Fairview until the Department of Nursing was
located on the top floor of the Science building in 1925.

have to cover the workload while the student was at class. She recalled a
typical day on a ward where she was a "treatment nurse" for two months.
"Many of the patients ... were having hot fomentations. For eight or nine
hours a day I did nothing but put on hot fomentations. Some doctors ordered
them hourly, some every two hours, some three. By the end of two months I
was an expert. Quite a trick to do a good fomentation!"[79]

Writing years later, Ethel Johns remarked on the difficulty that the first
university students often faced from their colleagues:

> In the hospital, they were marked women and the slightest infringement of
> regulations was punished as though it had been a violation of the decalogue.
> Worst of all, they were held aloof by the hospital student nurses and were
> regarded as giving themselves insufferable airs. In the university, they were
> singled out for scorn and rebuke unless they displayed superior intelligence on
> all and every occasion. But there was a stubborn loyalty among these harried
> little groups. They carried the weight of the young enterprise on their young
> shoulders and they saved the day.[80]

Some of the workloads for students were exceptionally heavy. Marion
Fisher (later Faris) recalled one of her experiences when she was in charge, all
alone, on a busy women's ward, including the typical large room for 30
patients plus four semi-private and five private patients, on the 11 p.m. to
7 a.m. shift. She noted that she "had the privilege" of calling the float nurse if

there were an emergency or if she could not finish all the night treatments before 7 a.m.

Beatrice Johnson (later Wood) reflected, however, that the university students found tremendous satisfaction in the challenge of being the first:

> Like all pioneers, we found a tremendous satisfaction in accomplishing our purpose. With the sympathetic understanding and forceful drive of our three mentors [Ethel Johns, Malcolm MacEachern, and R.H. Mullin] behind us, we couldn't help catching the spirit of the thing. It was exciting to be first in the new field. It was stimulating to find that a good many doctors and nurses (especially the Heads) heartily disapproved of the experiment. It made us more determined than ever to prove our point.[81]

The students considered Ethel Johns an excellent teacher and mentor. In addition to her administrative duties, she assisted the four instructors and demonstrators in the VGH nursing program by carrying a large portion of the classroom teaching. Florence Innes, who graduated in 1926, recalled her as "a very dynamic person, but demanding."[82] Bea Johnson (Wood) stated that Ethel Johns had impressed upon them the importance of their pioneering roles, and that they had to do well, and that they must not fail. "She terrified us all."[83] As Bea Johnson (Wood) recalled:

> Well do I remember studying in my room night after night until "Lights Out" bell rang; then sneaking quietly downstairs, through the darkened corridors, into the big lecture room, and there, with "Mr. Bones" the skeleton occupying one ghastly corner, I would pace back and forth, learning Chemical formulae by moonlight![84]

The classrooms at this time were mainly located in the Vancouver General Hospital itself and in the nearby buildings that had already become known as the "Fairview Shacks." Enrolment in the University had expanded greatly and the temporary buildings on the hospital site were overcrowded. The nursing students joined in the protests over the inadequate facilities and, on October 28, 1922, they marched with the other 1,200 students from downtown Vancouver out to the Point Grey campus on what is known as The Great Trek.[85] The three degree students proudly carried a banner proclaiming themselves as the first to be enrolled in a university nursing program in the British Empire. They and the certificate students also climbed onto the girders of the unfinished Science Building for one of the famous photographs of the event, with the Nursing banner proudly waving from the second storey. Florence Innes of the Class of 1926 recalled throwing stones into the clearing that later became the Cairn that still graces the Mall in front of the Chemistry Building.

Figure 2.10   UBC buildings at Fairview. The three-storey brick and stone Arts building is surrounded by wooden "shacks." When UBC moved to Point Grey in 1925, Vancouver General Hospital took over the buildings vacated by UBC. The Arts building became the provincial headquarters for the Division of TB Control and is still standing in 1994. Others were converted to residences and used as classrooms for nursing students.

Figure 2.11   UBC students assembled outside the Arts building at Fairview. After 10 years, UBC moved to Point Grey in 1925.

Figure 2.12   Great Trek parade from downtown Vancouver to Point Grey,
October 29, 1922. Students were protesting delays in the opening of the campus.

Figure 2.13   Nursing students in the Great Trek parade, October 22, 1922.
The first three students to graduate in 1923, Marion Fisher, Margaret Healy, and
Bea Johnson, carried the nursing banner.

Figure 2.14   UBC students assembled on girders of the unfinished Science building. Students had paraded from downtown Vancouver to Point Grey to spur the government to release funds to complete construction of the University. Nursing banner reads: First University in Brit Empire to grant degrees.

Figure 2.15

Cairn located on Main Mall in front of the Chemistry building constructed of stones placed there by students. Inscription reads: To the glory of our Alma Mater Student Campaign 1922-23.

Despite the heavy academic and clinical load for the nursing students, there was a great deal of camaraderie. Those in the certificate course wanted a kind of "alumnae group" that would meet at least once a year so that graduates could keep in touch. The first meeting of the "U.B.C. Nurses' Club," with 24 graduates and undergraduates attending, was held on April 21, 1923 at the Cosy Corner Tea Rooms on Hastings Street in downtown Vancouver. Total cost of the dinner for the 24 nurses was $18. The minutes record this as being "in honour of those graduating in Public Health at the University of B.C. in the 1923 Class." Both the degree and the certificate graduates were included, and the group elected Josephine Peters as president and Mary Ard. Mac-Kenzie as honorary president. Dues were set at 50 cents each.

A minute book of this early alumni association, which met once a year to honour the graduating classes, is in the UBC School of Nursing Archival Collection, showing the details of the annual meetings from 1923 to 1943, with much detail and notes on the activities and members.

The Science Girls' Club, for undergraduates in the degree program, also was started by students during this period. Florence Innes and Margaret Kerr, class of 1926, were instrumental in getting this going. Florence Innes recalled the club this way:

> Margaret Kerr was the driving force and it was called the Science Girls' Club because we were under the Faculty of Applied Science and our degree was Applied Science. I never particularly cared for the name, but anyway it went on for a long time. It was a very interesting group. You see the membership was all of the people registered in nursing from the first year to the final year so that as you registered and went through this group you knew all of the people who were ahead of you for four or five years.[86]

These early clubs were the forerunners of the UBC Nursing Alumni Division and the Nursing Undergraduate Society (NUS).

Marion Fisher (Faris) described Ethel Johns as a superb teacher and as inspirational about the ideas and ideals of nursing, which she considered the noblest of professions.[87]

Ethel Johns was a tall, slender woman with reddish-blonde hair when she was director of the Department of Nursing. She had a commanding presence, and one student described her as having "a fresh vitality about her ... [and as being] a woman of *great* courage."[88]

As Director of Nursing at VGH, Ethel Johns faced some major problems during 1920 and 1921, including a rapid increase in numbers of patients, overcrowding in the student nurses' residence (which meant she could not increase enrolments further), and major staffing shortages. She also remained active in provincial and national nursing associations and was taking an increased executive role in hospital associations.[89] A number of influential physicians opposed the degree program,[90] which put great pressure on her dual position. At the end of 1921, Ethel Johns became a full-time faculty member at UBC and Kathleen Ellis, who was also a supporter of the degree program, took over as Director of Nursing at VGH. However, Ethel Johns continued as Director of Nursing Education at VGH until mid-1922.

In 1921, the UBC Board of Governors took over more of the financial responsibility for the new Department of Nursing by doubling the $600 portion of the annual salary paid by the University for her part-time role; however, half of this $1,200 salary came through the Department of Public Health. The total budget from the University for the Department of Nursing for 1922-1923 was $800 and for the Department of Public Health was $7,010.[91]

In her new full-time role, although the salary did not immediately increase, Ethel Johns began working with the University administration to admit graduates from qualified nursing programs who could return to the University and take the three campus years required for the degree. During the summer of 1922, she also visited Saskatchewan and gave a short summer course for eight nurse superintendents at the University of Saskatchewan. At UBC, she also gave a short certificate course in Teaching and Supervision that could be taken by highly-qualified experienced nurses along with the degree candidates.

In the fall of 1923, her salary was increased to $2,500 a year, charged in full to the Department of Nursing, and she began teaching the fifth-year nursing courses to the three graduating students. At the beginning of the 1924-1925 academic year, the Red Cross funding stopped and the two departments were joined as the Department of Nursing and Health. The total budget for the new combined department in 1924 rose to $7,610.[92] (See Box 4.)

Box 4
Budget for Department of Nursing and Health, 1924-1925

Professor and Head, Dr. R.H. Mullin	$2,500
Assistant Professor, Ethel Johns	$2,800
Instructors	$1,000
Stenographer	$ 660
Equipment and Supplies	$ 650
	$7,610

Source: University of B.C. Board of Governors Minutes, 1924.

Ethel Johns remained extremely active in nursing and hospital associations, believing this a major part of her academic role. Among her additional
duties was membership on the new nation-wide Committee on the Training
and Education of Public Health Nurses and she was invited to speak at the
U.S. National League of Nursing Education (later the National League for
Nursing) convention, held in Seattle. She chaired one session of the convention, at which was presented the report of a study, funded by the Rockefeller
Foundation, on nursing and nursing education. The Rockefeller Foundation
had been set up with a $100 million endowment in 1913 by American
billionaire John D. Rockefeller, Jr., and was especially involved in worldwide
programs to fight hunger and improve public health; the Foundation was
especially supportive of health and public health education issues during the
1920s. Ethel Johns summed up the conclusions of the study and of the
convention by noting that nursing believed "that our schools have not been
what we want our schools of nursing to be, and ... we believe the importance
to the community of our work justifies the university school."[93] Despite these
conclusions, however, she continually had to battle for support for the
nursing degree program at home in B.C.

The UBC Senate had approved "short courses in post-graduate work for
nurses holding institutional and teaching positions" to be held at UBC in the
summer of 1923, which Ethel Johns was to direct. These summer courses,
which today might be classed as continuing education, were well received.
Seven nurses registered for a six-week course in teaching, four enrolled in the
two-week course in administration, and 33 private duty nurses attended a
four-day institute.[94]

The enrolments in the Department of Nursing were steadily increasing
during the Ethel Johns years, with the largest group – 16 students – entering
first year in 1924-1925. Some of these students either withdrew or deferred
because of illness, and the average size of the total enrolment in the five years
of the degree program was about 30. Ethel Johns arranged the university
course work for these students, supervised their work and their educational
program in the hospital, and generally mentored them throughout their
courses. The one-year certificate programs in public health and in teaching
and supervision, although reduced in size at the conclusion of the Red Cross
funding, also continued to attract nurses, with six graduating in 1923-1924
and three in 1924-1925.

While all these developments were occurring in the Nursing department,
the social and political climate in B.C. had remained fairly steady. After a
post World War I economic recession, British Columbia, like much of the
rest of the world, had responded to the Roaring Twenties with an economic
boom, rapid growth, and unbridled optimism. Prohibition had been introduced, but by the mid-1920s had been repealed in favour of government
controlled liquor sales. Automobiles were replacing horses and buggies and

B.C. had even made the switch, on January 1, 1922, to the North American pattern of driving on the right-hand side of the road.

A few new inroads had been made by the women of the period, who were consolidating advances achieved by the suffragists as a result of the War. Agnes Campbell Macphail of Ontario had been the first women elected to the House of Commons in Ottawa in 1921. The same year, Mary Ellen Smith of B.C. had made history by being the first woman appointed to a cabinet position in the B.C. Legislature – the first in the Commonwealth. Even the fashions reflected a new look, with shorter skirts and bobbed hair. The short skirts of the Flapper were partially attributed to the fashion changes that nursing sisters had introduced overseas to deal with the muddy conditions of the war zones.

The population of Vancouver reached 126,000 by 1925[95] and both St. Paul's and the Vancouver General were expanding to meet the growing demands for hospital and public health care. This growth was also reflected with the opening in 1921 of a new North Vancouver District General Hospital, needed to meet the growth of the North Shore population to about 13,000.[96] The bridge across the Second Narrows for access to the communities of North and West Vancouver, previously only reached by ferries, was completed in 1925.

Nursing power had come to the fore, as well. By 1922, all nine provincial nursing associations in Canada had achieved legislation that gave them power to register and set out improved standards for the education and training of nurses. The Graduate Nurses' Association in B.C. had offered its first examinations for registered nurses in 1921. All UBC nurses had to sit these exams. Standards for hospitals had also been approved and those hospitals that did not meet approved standards in B.C. were no longer able to have nursing schools. Helen Randal, as B.C. Registrar, had surveyed all schools of nursing in the province and drawn up standards for approval. The UBC Senate accepted this, in that only graduates from approved schools could enter the certificate programs, although the Nursing department did not achieve its earlier dream that all approved schools in the province could be used for the clinical portions of the program.

Because of the growth of university nursing programs, the Victorian Order of Nurses for Canada had closed its "training centres." The Order established a policy of offering scholarships, but was relying on the output from the certificate courses to meet the public health nursing needs.

Health care science and technology had also advanced during this period. For example, by 1923, hospitals in British Columbia had begun using the brand-new insulin treatment for those with diabetes.[97] Nursing science also was advancing and, in 1921, Bertha Harmer, director of the School for Graduate Nurses at McGill University, published the first Canadian nursing textbook, called *Principles of Nursing*.[98] All these events created a supportive environment for the new UBC Nursing department.

END OF THE ETHEL JOHNS ERA

By the end of the 1923-1924 academic year, the department had taken root. The first degree students had graduated, the diploma programs had proven strong enough to continue following the end of the Red Cross funding, and the graduates were being welcomed throughout the province. The UBC Senate and Board of Governors had sanctioned the Department of Nursing and undertaken its funding. But trouble was on the horizon.

R.H. Mullin had been a strong supporter of the Department of Nursing. He had become its titular head when the Senate had questioned Ethel Johns' lack of academic credentials, although in effect she ran the department. His untimely death in the summer of 1924 led to the appointment of Hibbert Winslow Hill as head of the Department of Nursing and Health and as head of the Department of Bacteriology. President R.E. McKechnie and Dean of Applied Science Reginald W. Brock continued to support Ethel Johns in her position, but she began to feel the need to turn over the reins to someone with the required academic qualifications. In notes, years later, for her autobiography, Ethel Johns made special reference to these difficulties where her lack of academic rank "was a serious handicap at every turn."[99] She also recognized that her lack of experience at university schools meant that she was not prepared for the opposition the degree course encountered:

> Medical men disapproved, except for a handful who stood by it through thick and thin. Graduate [nursing] staff were not particularly friendly. Few had any

Figure 2.16

Ethel Johns. After she resigned as Head of the Department of Nursing at UBC in 1925, she went to work for the Rockefeller Foundation. In 1933 she became editor of *The Canadian Nurse*, a position she held until 1944. This picture was taken in 1933.

academic experience, though quite a number had postgraduate courses in various special branches. Students in [the] three-year course were understandably hostile since the course for the University was six months shorter than theirs…. Attitude of university students was excellent. If it had not been for their loyalty and perseverance the course would have perished.[100]

Just at this time she was offered the opportunity to go to work for the Rockefeller Foundation as Special Member of the Field Staff in Nursing Education for central Europe. Her commitment had been recognized during the National League of Nursing Education convention and a Rockefeller representative had visited the UBC Department of Nursing. Rockefeller workers were welcomed around the world and this opening represented an irresistible challenge for Ethel Johns. Given the situation at UBC, she decided to accept the Rockefeller position. Her resignation was accepted by the Board of Governors in April 1925, to be effective at the beginning of the 1925-1926 academic year.[101]

At the time of her leaving, she was honoured at a reception by the Graduate Nurses Association of B.C. Her most treasured memories, however, were tied to the tribute from the students in the UBC program, who presented her with the gift of a grey leather correspondence case, which she kept all her life. The small silver plaque was engraved, simply: "Miss E. Johns, from your girls at U.B.C., July 1925."[102]

CHAPTER THREE

The Mabel Gray Years
1925-1941

Figure 3.1

Mabel Gray, Nursing head of the
UBC Department of Nursing and
Health, 1925-1941

When Mabel Gray accepted the position as nursing head of the UBC Department of Nursing in 1925, the University was in the midst of a generation of rapid economic growth and exciting developments. The Nursing program was well established and well supported by the administration and by the public. The graduates were welcomed throughout the province, and public health nurses were respected and admired for their contributions to education, health promotion, and prevention of disease. Then came the challenge of the greatest depression Canada has ever known and a struggle to maintain the fledgling professional department in a University racked by fiscal restraint. Mabel Gray proved a capable, determined, and dependable leader throughout this period. She managed to maintain the progress that had been made and, in her quiet way, stabilized and nurtured the program for 16 years.

Like Ethel Johns, Mabel Gray had moved to the Canadian West and was a graduate of the Winnipeg General Hospital school of nursing.[1] She was born July 26, 1880, in Brampton, Ontario, to Samuel Gray and his wife Francis (nee Sargent). The Gray family had come to the Brampton area from England about 1823 and Samuel was born there in 1843. Samuel and Francis had two children, Milton, born 1879, and Mabel. A few years later, the family moved to Ottawa, where Samuel was stationed as a member of the civil service. His duties moved him to Winnipeg and then Regina, where the young Mabel spent her school years. She was described by her high school principal as "one of the very best pupils we have ever had in our school."[2] She obtained her teaching certificate from a normal school in Regina, enabling her to teach in the North-West Territories of Canada (Saskatchewan did not become a province until 1905). She also obtained her certificate for Manitoba and taught school both in Plum Coulee, N.W.T, and in Carberry, Manitoba. She cherished dreams of entering medicine, but in 1904 decided to enter nursing, and graduated from Winnipeg General Hospital in 1907. After a brief stint there as a staff nurse, she was appointed instructor and then assistant superintendent of nurses.

In 1914, just a few months before the outbreak of World War I, she took over as superintendent of nurses and principal of the school of nursing at Winnipeg General. The hospital was going through a period of rapid growth, but when the war began many senior nursing staff enlisted for overseas service. This loss of staff placed a great strain on the educational program, and the 12-hour shifts and heavy workloads for students and staff were of great concern to Mabel Gray. She used her political acumen to ask the board of trustees to establish a Training School Committee. Through this committee she gained a measure of financial independence for the school and its students.[3]

In 1918, the worldwide influenza epidemic hit Winnipeg, with great waves of sufferers needing hospital care. As well, the flu affected some 20% of the student nurses and one-third of the graduate staff, and Mabel Gray was forced to close the teaching program for a period. Building on the wide support elicited for the heroic efforts of the nurses during the epidemic, she put through many other educational reforms, including adoption of the standard curriculum being recommended by the Canadian National Association for Trained Nurses. Like Ethel Johns, who was superintendent of the Children's Hospital in Winnipeg, Mabel Gray helped representatives of the schools lobby in favour of a private member's bill in the Manitoba legislature that called for an eight-hour day for students in schools of nursing. In her report before a committee of the whole legislature, Mabel Gray stressed that a nursing program

was a professional school – not a trade school or factory – and that a school and its students should have the same freedom to develop the course, and to carry out essential practice in the hospital wards, as any other group of professional students.[4]

In 1919, recognizing the growing importance of public health nursing, Mabel Gray left Winnipeg General to take the one-year program at Simmons College School of Public Health Nursing in Boston. She received her certificate in June 1920. She returned to Canada to set up a course for "nursing housekeepers," which was jointly sponsored by the University of Saskatchewan, the Saskatchewan Registered Nurses Association, and the Canadian Red Cross Society.[5] The three agencies had agreed to hire a supervisor for a one-year "nursing housekeeper" program, which was to be given in smaller hospitals throughout the province. The goal of the program, which also was supported by the national nursing association, was to provide a "secondary nurse," who would work in homes in the rural areas where the shortage of nurses was acute, especially so during the flu epidemics of the previous winters. Nine students completed the course in 1921 and 16 in 1922. But difficulties were developing.[6] Although there was no shortage of applicants, those who completed the course had difficulty finding employment at the suggested rate of $3 a day. New and improved hospitals were springing up, and the trend was toward admission to hospital rather than care in the home, even for maternity cases. Furthermore, many nurses had returned from war-time duty, the nursing shortage was over, and registered nurses were not supporting the plan.

Mabel Gray's appointment with the University of Saskatchewan course was her main position, for which she received about $2,400 a year; the money came mainly from the Red Cross, with the University and the Association also each paying a portion and covering her travel expenses to hospitals around the province. Her office was in Red Cross headquarters in Regina (although the University was located in Saskatoon). She also had the part-time position of Registrar and was the first, and for a time the only, paid staff of the Saskatchewan Registered Nurses Association. During this time, she was active in the Canadian National Association for Trained Nurses (which changed its name in 1924 to Canadian Nurses Association [CNA]). She served first as Saskatchewan representative to the CNA Board, then was elected to positions as honorary secretary and, later, first vice-president. When Flora Shaw, president of CNA, died in office in 1927, Mabel Gray took over the presidency for the remaining term (1927-1928) and was president when the CNA and the Canadian Medical Association commissioned the study of nursing education in Canada by George Weir.

Various correspondence in its archives indicates that the University of Saskatchewan was interested in starting a Department of Nursing, although this did not materialize until much later. However, in the summer of 1922, the University, with the assistance of Mabel Gray, arranged for Ethel Johns to come from the UBC Department of Nursing to give a "Short Course for Superintendents and Instructors in Schools of Nursing" at the summer school on the Saskatoon campus. This was "the first of its kind to be given in any University in Canada."[7] The two-week course was well received and 10 superintendents of the major hospitals in the province and from Winnipeg's St. Boniface Hospital wrote glowing evaluations, as did the Saskatchewan Registered Nurses Association.

During these years, Mabel Gray kept in touch with Ethel Johns, whom she had known in Winnipeg. As well, she would have met Helen Randal and other B.C. nursing leaders and would have known about the development of the nursing programs at UBC and other universities. Her advanced approach to nursing education has been described as "fearless and enlightened, ... eminently practical and sane."[8] During this time, according to some sources, she also took additional courses at Teachers College, Columbia University, although she did not obtain a degree.

In the summer of 1925, Mabel Gray went for an interview for the position being vacated by Ethel Johns at UBC. She did this with the full approval of W.C. Murray, president of the University of Saskatchewan, who felt it would give her the scope to be involved with a nursing program which was not yet possible in Saskatchewan.[9] The Red Cross had already decided to discontinue its support for the Nursing Housekeepers' Course and when Mabel Gray was appointed at UBC the University of Saskatchewan decided to discontinue its interesting experiment with that program.

DEPARTMENTAL CHANGES

When Mabel Gray accepted the UBC position as assistant professor in the Department of Nursing and Health, she was 45 years old, well-known as a national nursing leader, and at the peak of her career. However, as had been the case with Ethel Johns, and despite her practical qualifications, she did not have a degree. Hibbert Hill therefore continued as professor and head of the Department, although to the nursing community and to the students Mabel Gray was considered the "head." He remained in charge of the Department of Bacteriology as well, but taught in the nursing program. His 13-hour course titled "Public Speaking and Parliamentary Procedure" was addressed to diploma and final-year degree students and he also taught courses in epidemiology, preventable diseases, public health, and vital statistics. This increased cooperation suggests that Mabel Gray achieved a better working relationship with him than Ethel Johns had managed.

Mabel Gray's students remember her as warm, caring, "lady-like," dedicated, and quiet. She was well-liked by the students. When she arrived, she was the only full-time faculty member in the nursing department and so carried a formidable teaching load. The academic program for the degree

Figure 3.2   Science building, completed in 1925. Department of Nursing
was on the fourth floor and remained there until 1946.

students was still five years when she came. The first and second years were
wholly academic, with one nursing course in each year (Introduction to
Nursing in first year and History of Nursing in second year). In first year, the
students had one elective choice from mathematics, Latin, French, or history;
other required courses were English (both years), physics, chemistry, and
biology in first year and zoology, bacteriology, economics, and philosophy in
second year. As well, an anatomy and physiology course, adapted especially
for nurses, was given during the second year by Mabel Gray.

In the four-month summer period between first and second years, nursing
students entered a probationary program at the Vancouver General Hospital.
Immediately following the second-year exams, students began a 28-month
hospital program, merging with the VGH students already enrolled there.
During these years, the students had only the two-week holiday breaks
allowed VGH student nurses. During their clinical experience in hospital,
Mabel Gray also continued to oversee and supervise the UBC students. She
established good and close working relationships first with Kathleen Ellis,
who was Director of Nursing until 1929, and then with Grace Fairley.

For the final year, UBC students returned to campus and specialized in
either public health nursing or in teaching and supervision in schools of
nursing. Most courses in the fifth year also were offered in the one-year
diploma/certificate programs, although degree students took three additional
academic subjects. For those taking public health, the program did not allow
electives, although those who selected teaching and supervision were given
options either from the sciences or from the public health course. Field work
requirements in the final year involved half of each week and all of the last
four weeks of the second term. For field work, those taking public health

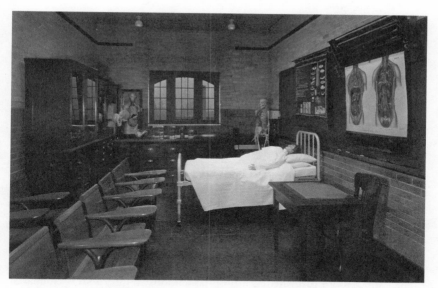

Figure 3.3 Nursing laboratory in the Science building, 1931, furnished as a hospital demonstration room with charts, skeleton, hospital bed, and doll called "Judy."

Figure 3.4 Reading room in the Science building, circa 1926, which had a limited collection of books and journals such as *The Canadian Nurse*. The room was shared with students majoring in bacteriology.

went to the Victorian Order of Nurses branches, the Vancouver Rotary Clinic for Diseases of the Chest, the Provincial Mental Hospital at Essondale, the Provincial Department of Health, the Medical Department of the Vancouver School Board, the Government Venereal Disease Clinic, and the Department of Child Hygiene for the City of Vancouver. Those taking teaching and supervision had field work experiences at the Vancouver General Hospital in addition to some public health field experiences. The list of guest lecturers through these years remained impressive, with well-known public figures such as Henry Esson Young and George Weir continuing to participate in the program.

The University had moved to the Point Grey campus and the Department of Nursing and Health was in the new Science building (later generally referred to as the Chemistry building). Nursing shared the building with the departments of Bacteriology, Chemistry, and Physics. Half of the fourth floor housed the Nursing and the Bacteriology departments, and three rooms, including a small office for Mabel Gray, were assigned to Nursing and Health. The nursing classes were given in a nursing laboratory typical of the time, a small room furnished as a hospital demonstration room with charts, skeleton, hospital bedstead, and Chase doll – called a "Judy." An adjoining reading room housed current nursing periodicals and reference materials and was shared with students majoring in bacteriology. Mabel Gray reported that fifth year students also used the bacteriology laboratories "for the more advanced research work in nursing technics."[10]

UNIVERSITY GROWTH

The early portion of Mabel Gray's stay at UBC, from 1925 to 1929, was the golden age of the "roaring twenties." By 1929, the population of Vancouver had grown to 229,000 (with 83 millionaires!) and an average weekly industrial wage of $29.20.[11] Vancouver itself was growing rapidly, with expansion south to the new suburb of Kerrisdale along the interurban tracks and west along Broadway toward the University gates.

UBC also continued to grow rapidly. In 1923, the Board of Governors approved a one-year teacher training course to prepare university graduates for teaching. At the time, most teachers, especially those who taught in elementary schools, were prepared at the provincial normal school, which was not part of the University. However, UBC also offered many of its arts and sciences courses during its summer sessions, which began in July 1922, and these were directed mainly to teachers. The summer sessions proved highly popular, reaching a 1920s peak enrolment in 1927 of 487.[12] In 1925, the University approved a separate Department of Education; before that the education programs had been under the Department of Philosophy. The new Education department also tried to meet needs of working teachers by ensuring that courses were scheduled in late afternoons or Saturday mornings.

In 1929, UBC began a two-year course leading to a diploma in "social service" (social work) and a four-year program leading to a Bachelor of Commerce. During the latter part of the decade, the students also contributed to the growing new campus at Point Grey by raising funds for a gymnasium and for playing fields; they did this through a bond, and despite the Depression they were able to pay this off by 1935. The Alumni Association also assisted, equipping the gym.[13]

Mary Bollert was appointed Advisor of Women in 1921 and became Dean of Women in 1922. This latter title had been eagerly sought by the Women's Undergraduate Society, which wanted recognition of women on campus as well as practical assistance for female students, such as counselling and financial aid. As was typical of the times, certain restrictions were placed on female students not living at home. There were no residences on campus, so living accommodations for women students had to come from a list of "approved boarding houses." Male and female students, unless of the same family, could not live in the same boarding house without Senate approval, and young women, under age 25, had to have an "older person" living in their residences. The cost of a room was about $8 to $12 a month, and with board was about $35.[14] During their hospital years, nursing students moved into the VGH student residence.

In 1925, the provincial government, on the recommendation of the provincial health officer, appointed Hibbert Hill, in addition to his other duties, as medical health officer for the Point Grey area, including the campus. In 1927, a public health nurse was added to this new unit, allowing for continuous operation of a local health office in the Auditorium. The nurse supervised student health and provided first aid. Equipment for the office had been provided as a gift of the graduating class of 1927.[15]

NURSING'S PROGRESS

The 1920s had been good for nursing. The provincial associations had achieved their goals of registration of nurses and most hospitals now only took qualified, or registered, staff. Some nurses now were asking for registration to be dominion-wide. Compulsory registration (later called mandatory registration) was being discussed as well, and a recommendation to this effect was introduced at the 1934 biennium of CNA.[16] Hospital standards had improved, and the larger teaching hospitals were undergoing accreditation, which had been a legacy of Malcolm MacEachern. At the beginning of the 1920s, CNA President Jean Gunn had recommended development of a national public health policy, using nurses trained for roles in prevention of illness. Throughout the period, CNA continued to press for more emphasis on education of the public and prevention of illness through community nursing.

Membership in 1920 in the national association stood at 13,038 and membership in all the provincial associations was 8,038; in 1930, after fees were increased to 75 cents from 50 cents, CNA membership dropped to 8,023, with membership in the B.C. association about 2,000.[17] One important issue raised by the Canadian Nurses Association was government health insurance. As early as 1921, President Edith Dickson had introduced the idea of establishing such a system and it was supported at CNA throughout the 1920s. However, a federal government committee that looked into the matter in 1928 and 1929 concluded that health insurance should come under provincial jurisdiction. Consequently, by the end of the 1920s, provincial governments were looking into health plans. The B.C. legislature had appointed a Royal Commission to do so. In a 1930 speech, given under the auspices of the B.C. Department of Health and the UBC Department of Nursing and Health, Burnaby Medical Officer J.W. McIntosh, who taught in the nursing program, outlined current proposals for health insurance in the province. He noted that the federal government would give "moral and financial" support for an insurance program provided it were developed with the provinces and run like the old age pension plans, which had been introduced in 1927. The B.C. plan proposed to pay for care from both doctors and nurses.[18]

Specific nursing issues continued to be raised in nursing organizations during this period, including financial stability of *The Canadian Nurse*. Her increasing work in B.C., as Registrar and Inspector of Schools of Nursing, forced Helen Randal to give up her unpaid position as editor in 1924. CNA then hired Jean Scantlion Wilson as its first paid, full-time executive secretary, and she also became editor for the journal until 1933. The costs of financing CNA and the journal were hotly debated issues during these periods.

The most important issue for organized nursing was, however, the state of nursing education across the country. Committees of CNA, and its precursors, for years had stressed that nursing education programs needed improvement. In B.C., the Graduate Nurses Association had established the first minimum standards for schools of nursing in 1924[19] and had persuaded some small cottage hospitals to close their programs. As well, through the work of Helen Randal, many smaller hospitals arranged to send their students to larger institutions for affiliation in specialty areas. In 1926, the association's right to set standards for the schools was upheld by law.[20] Although it was not yet the official arbiter of standards, the association had set a minimum curriculum for schools. It also was able to ensure that students entering hospital programs were between 19 and 35 years of age, had a doctor's certificate indicating good health, and had completed Grade 10.[21] VGH had one of the highest standards in the province for its students. Although it was possible for any hospital school to be affiliated with the UBC Nursing program, at this time VGH was the only school that met all requirements for affiliation. Students entering the UBC program had to meet the University's general requirements, which were high school graduation (junior matriculation (Grade 12) or its equivalent), plus the hospital requirements (physical fitness and smallpox and other immunizations not required of university students in general).

Standards varied from school to school, with small hospitals in various parts of the country, especially rural areas, still opening schools merely to acquire staff. In B.C., where the association had established some standards, hospitals could open a school if they had 25 beds ("*beds*, mark you, *not patients*," as Ethel Johns had once declared furiously[22]). Ontario, for example, in 1929 had at least seven schools in hospitals that had fewer than 25 beds.[23] Criteria for admission of students also varied widely; some schools demanded senior matriculation and some allowed students with only Grade 6[24] – as long as they were healthy and strong! Nursing leaders were outspoken about these conditions and had long demanded changes.

In 1926, the Council of the Canadian Medical Association also expressed concern about the quality of the education of nurses from some of these programs and called for a meeting with the Canadian Nurses Association and the Canadian Hospital Association. Mabel Gray attended this 1927 meeting, representing B.C. The consensus at the meeting was that action should be taken "to secure accurate and detailed knowledge of nursing in Canada from the standpoint of the nurse, the doctor and the public."[25] As a result, the Canadian Nurses Association, under President Mabel Gray, and the Canadian Medical Association agreed to sponsor a scientific study, with CNA eventually providing 70% of the funding.[26] A joint study committee was established and the six members (three nurses, three doctors) decided on a major survey.

The committee wanted a "specialist in education" and their choice was George Moir Weir, professor and first head of the Department of Education at UBC. George Weir had conducted a survey of education in B.C. in 1925, and was a respected educator and researcher. He also had some knowledge of nursing education as Ethel Johns had recruited him to teach courses in the final year of the UBC Department of Nursing from the time it had opened in 1919. The overall objective was that the survey should provide "a constructive plan for the improvement of the nursing service in Canada."[27]

The survey was conducted from November 1929 to July 1931, with the report released in February 1932. This outstanding report helped change the face of nursing education across Canada during the 1930s and has remained a classic in nursing literature. One of its most frequently cited conclusions is that nursing education ultimately should be offered "only by the university,"[28] with the universities awarding "degrees in Nursing, as in Arts, Law, Engineering, Pharmacy, Agriculture, Medicine, or any other field of learning."[29]

THE DEPRESSION

On the 10th anniversary of the Nursing department, things were looking
rosy. Then, in October 1929, the New York stock market crashed – heralding
an economic depression that affected the entire world. Canada was one of the
countries most affected by this Great Depression, as it is called, largely
because of reliance on export of resources. At one point, more than 30% of
the labour force was unemployed, and one in five had to depend on government relief for survival.[30] By December 1929, the effects were being felt in
B.C.'s mining, lumbering, and fishing industries, and Vancouver had large
numbers of unemployed men. During the winter, the federal and provincial
governments began opening "relief offices" in centres across the country; in
Vancouver, breadlines began forming.[31] Personal health care deteriorated
and soon medical reports of scurvy and other dietary deficiency diseases
were common.

The Great Depression lasted throughout the 1930s, ending only with
World War II. Peak unemployment in Vancouver was reached in 1932.
Unemployment was high among nurses as well. Although hospitals were
using more graduates, many nurses still were employed for private duty or for
work in homes, and this means of employment almost immediately stopped.
Hospitals, including the Vancouver General, were also facing financial difficulties; growth in the city had put increasing pressure on VGH, but many
patients could no longer pay for care or for private insurance. Applications to
the VGH nursing school declined, largely because of the total unemployment, but also because of poor, crowded living conditions for student nurses
at VGH.[32]

Single women, a group that included many nurses, were particularly hard
hit in the depression years. During the 1920s, numbers of working women
had increased slowly. By 1931, 14% of the provincial labour force was female,
including about 22,000 women in Vancouver. Of these, just over 4,000 were
classed as "professional," which included nurses, teachers, and legal secre-
taries. They earned, on average, about two-thirds to one-half of what men
earned; this percentage dropped even more sharply when the Depression
began – from 63% (1911) to 56% (1931).[33]

In 1931, the federal government directed funds to "relief camps," where
men were hired at meagre wages to work on projects such as highways and
airports. B.C. had 237 camps, with accommodation for more than 18,000
men (about one-third of all Canada's relief workers).[34] More than one-tenth
of Vancouver's population was on city relief. However, only 155 women were
on the city relief rolls compared to more than 4,500 married and 5,200 single
men.[35] Because single women were declared ineligible for relief, these 155
were widows or deserted wives with dependents. City relief was finally
granted to unemployed single women in 1933, and 900, including many
nurses, went onto the relief rolls that year.[36]

An editorial by Jean Scantlion Wilson in *The Canadian Nurse* in 1932 described ways the Depression was affecting nurses, noting that expansion and development of programs would have to be "retarded for a time" because of financial conditions.

> There is an equally inevitable increase in the need of the people for the service we [nurses] can give, since poverty and destitution have always in their wake a never-ending line of physical ills. To secure more service for a needy people, with a much reduced budget from which to supply it, is the difficult task facing many nursing organizations today.[37]

Jean Gunn, superintendent of nurses at Toronto General, wrote an article for *The Canadian Nurse* in 1933 in which she described unemployment of nurses in Toronto, noting that this was typical of other Canadian cities. She said that at least 50% of nurses listed for private duty, either in hospitals or homes, were unable to obtain work; she also added that many nurses had simply taken their names off the lists because they could no longer afford even the listing service. The average days of work per month was five, with an average income for these nurses of about $300 a year.[38]

The growing union movement continued to press for improved working conditions. This was the period of growth of "socialist parties" such as the Canadian Commonwealth Federation (CCF), forerunner of the New Democratic Party, which worked in government circles for improved wages and working conditions. Some of these changes even spilled over into the nursing field. A private member's bill introduced in the B.C. legislature in 1937 called for regulation of nurses' hours and led to the appointment of a government advisory committee on labour conditions in hospitals. The Vancouver General, St. Paul's, and some other hospital schools of nursing in B.C. had achieved some improvement in standards for their students, such as 10-hour shifts, with a minimum of split shifts, and 1½ days off a week. The committee found, however, that graduates averaged 55 hours a week, with night shifts usually averaging 70 hours a week. Nurses generally worked 5½ days a week, although six-day weeks were not uncommon; student nurses frequently worked split shifts.[39] The committee recommended an eight-hour day and a maximum 96-hour fortnight for graduates, but these recommendations were never acted upon.

In 1930, the Vancouver Graduate Nurses Association had been able to bring about a 10-hour shift for its private duty nurses, with a recommended pay schedule of 50 cents an hour. If a 12-hour shift were needed, this could be arranged for the hourly rate, but 24-hour shifts were considered as 14-hour duties and the recommended payment was $7.[40] As the Depression deepened, however, salaries decreased and a typical private duty nurse was paid about $5 for a 12-hour shift, with pay scales recommending $6 for 24-hour private

Figure 3.5

Margaret Kerr (BASc(N) 1926),
public health nursing instructor and
later assistant professor, 1929-1944.
In 1944, she left UBC to replace Ethel
Johns as editor of *The Canadian Nurse*,
a position she held until her retirement
in 1965.

duty, with an extra $1 for every additional patient.[41] In 1933, the Vancouver
Graduate Nurses Association adopted the eight-hour day, but pay now
dropped to $3 for this shift.[42] Conditions in smaller hospitals throughout the
province were even worse. Finally, in April 1939, nine nurses of a staff of 12 at
St. Joseph's Hospital in Comox went on strike. The nurses wanted eight-
hour shifts, two weeks annual vacation, sick leave, improved meals, and a
laundry allowance of $2.50 a month. After two weeks, the hospital board
agreed to the nurses' demands for eight-hour shifts and a vacation of two
weeks each year.[43]

   Although the Weir Report in 1932 had identified some terrible conditions
in nursing education, the depth of the Depression set back implementation
of most of its recommendations. The UBC nursing program, however,
soldiered on. During the 1920s, the program had granted 37 degrees and
awarded 83 diplomas; during the 1930s, it granted 74 degrees and 154
diplomas.[44] This growth justified the need for increased faculty.

   Margaret Kerr (BASc(N) 1926) was appointed as instructor in the fall of
1929. Of Scottish and Irish ancestry, she was born in Amherst, Ontario,
where she took her schooling. She attended normal school in Vancouver,
and then taught in Kaslo, B.C., for two years before she entered the
Nursing program at UBC. She was an excellent student, and Ethel Johns,
director of the program at that time later said that the fact the program
"survived at all during the first stormy years is due in a large measure to
students like Margaret Kerr who had the vision, the courage, and the
endurance to see it through."[45]

Figure 3.6 Margaret Kerr and Mabel Gray at the graduation tea for the Class of 1933, held at the Dragon Inn in West Vancouver.

After graduating from UBC in 1926, Margaret Kerr worked for two years as a school nurse in Nanaimo. She then obtained a master of arts degree from Columbia University under a Rockefeller Fellowship and was hired at UBC. She was appointed mainly to teach the public health portions of the course; Mabel Gray continued with the teaching and supervision courses. Esther Paulson (DipPHN, 1934) recalled that "Miss Gray and Margaret Kerr were opposites – one dignified and reserved and [one] casual and friendly, thus complementing each other to the advantage of the students."[46] Despite cutbacks at the University related to the Depression, the growing number of nursing students meant that this new position remained in place.

ADVANCES IN KNOWLEDGE AND TECHNOLOGY

Growth in science and technology continued during this period, despite the Depression. For example, the radio and the automobile were two advances that greatly changed Canadian lifestyles. Scientific knowledge related to health care also progressed and nurses were hard pressed to keep up with rapid advances in the sciences and their effects on nursing care. By the mid-1930s, the "microbe-fighting sulfa drugs" were being prescribed for such conditions as respiratory infections, childbed fever and other infections known to be caused by bacteria.[47] Although these drugs greatly advanced treatment of infections, they were highly toxic, and students in the mid-1930s recall having to observe patients closely for symptoms of life-threatening side-effects, such as rash, jaundice, altered urinary output, cyanosis, and dizziness. Astute observation formed a large part of the nursing role, for these were new drugs and were on the leading edge of the medical armamentarium of the time and laboratory analyses were limited. About this time, nurses were routinely allowed to take blood pressures and give intramuscular injections, procedures that previously had been done only by doctors.[48]

Nursing texts and journals of the time reflect the contemporary research in, for example, genetics, bacteriology, and infectious disease control. The scientific principles of asepsis had advanced to the point where nursing of communicable diseases had changed enormously. No longer were student nurses assigned to live in separate isolation buildings with a patient or patients with one particular disease. Instead, application of aseptic measures and "concurrent disinfection" led to use of individual units (private rooms or glassed-in cubicles) within a ward.[49] Strict isolation technique, including gowning procedures, needed to be understood, but nurses even then were beginning to question the scientific value of such traditional practices as wearing masks and gloves, and to undertake their own experiments to determine the usefulness of these items in specific situations.[50]

Ursula Whitehead, a clinical instructor at VGH, wrote an article describing new canvas slings devised to improve nursing care of patients in plaster-of-paris body casts. These slings, devised by Olive Shore, the assistant superintendent of nurses, and Gwen Clements, head nurse of the ward, were improvements on prototypes described in the *American Journal of Nursing*.[51] Grace Fairley, director of nurses and principal of the school at VGH, described the introduction of new teaching devices, such as "rubber arms" and "placebo tablets" used to teach student nurses how to prepare and administer hypodermic injections, which was still a relatively new nursing procedure.[52] As well, lantern slides were the newest audiovisual aid for nursing instruction and presentations.

Government funds for education were cut because of the Depression, especially in its early years. A "crisis" had arisen at UBC in 1932, which led the Senate to move a motion of non-confidence in the President, L.S. Klinck. Part of this dispute related to a battle over establishment of a Department of Home Economics. Women's groups in Vancouver had actively promoted such a program. In 1929 – just before the Crash – the provincial government had approved a $20,000 grant for two departments: Home Economics and Economics. Twenty-five women registered in the former. It was soon apparent, however, that no further moneys would be forthcoming and after one year the home economics program was closed and UBC did not resume funding for such a department until 1942.[53]

Nurses of the time were urged to appreciate "modern methods and treatment of cancer" being introduced in the 1930s. Smoking as a causative factor of lung cancer was known about and was taught to nurses, who were to educate the public about prevention and importance of early diagnosis.[54] Another concern in the mid-1930s that involved nurses was distribution of information about birth control. In September 1936, an Ontario nurse, Dorothea Palmer, was arrested for distributing such information, but a trial acquitted her and made such information "legal."[55]

Improvements in psychiatric care were also occurring. George Weir, who in 1933 became provincial secretary and minister of education in the new Liberal government, spoke to a graduating class of nurses and predicted "even wider fields for the future – a future which would include more public health nursing, more psychiatry, and more preventive work."[56] Nursing educators across Canada were placing increasing emphasis on "mental hygiene," as it was called. In 1935, a few students at VGH were assigned to the Provincial Mental Hospital at Essondale for psychiatric nursing experience.[57] By 1938, all UBC students had a two-month affiliation there.

In a interview on her career in public health nursing, Geraldine E. Homfray (later Langton) (BASc(N) 1931) describes an incident that showed how public health nurses in Saanich dealt with mental hygiene in the early 1930s:

Emphasis on mental health hadn't come to the fore then. We handled it by giving people reassurance, talking things over, but there wasn't any referral to a mental health clinic.... One night, a policeman phoned the health centre to tell us that someone coming down from Nanaimo had passed two adults and two children, naked, walking along the highway.... Being a community-oriented centre, the police thought "Who should know but the nurses?" ... We proceeded and got in touch with the health office and organized this particular family because they were known to us [the family, especially the mother, had been debilitated by whooping cough].... The husband decided through some religious quirk that he had to sacrifice his eldest son for whatever wrongs they had done.... This story [attracted] a great deal of community attention. We immediately flew into action. We knew the children were going to come to us [at the health centre, which also housed the nursing staff], and the mother, because there was no other place to take them.... We ran a tub full of warm water, put mustard in it to warm up those cold bodies, put on milk to make hot drinks for the kids. The children calmed down quite readily, but the mother arrived on the scene and was in a dreadful condition.... and was quite irrational.... We felt we had to get in touch with this woman's mother.... The father had been put in jail, the only safe place he could be taken.... I would like to mention that the staff at the health unit and the volunteer group of helpers rallied to the cause and it was a most marvellous effort of coordinated action.[58]

The nursing staff continued to house the family and obtained clothing until the grandmother could come from the Mainland and have them move in with her. Both parents eventually were admitted to the provincial mental hospital at Essondale.

MULTICULTURAL TENSIONS

An awareness of the importance of multicultural nursing, although it was not called that, was also beginning to surface. Articles such as one in *The Canadian Nurse* in 1933 stressed that public health nurses needed to know and understand the background of "foreign born" Canadians, and, especially, to assist these patients to establish a healthful diet in Canada.[59] However, racial discrimination was common. The Missionary Sisters of the Immaculate Conception had opened a four-bed "oriental home" in Vancouver for sick immigrants in 1921, and by 1928 this had grown to a hospital of 32 beds.[60] Other hospitals also admitted non-white patients. However, when the Vancouver General received a request in 1920 to admit young Canadian girls of Japanese origin into the school of nursing, some VGH graduates and students objected and the Board did not take any action. In 1932, the VGH Board again approached its director of nursing, and Grace Fairley took up the matter with the VGH Alumnae Association. After hearing presentations from such speakers as Henry Esson Young, the association resolved that "Orientals should be admitted to membership" even though none yet had graduated from VGH. This paved the way for Oriental students to be admitted to the VGH school and one Chinese nurse immediately took the hospital's postgraduate course in obstetrics and one Japanese-Canadian student entered the three-year course at VGH.[61]

Figure 3.7   Public Health Nursing Diploma Class of 1938.

Louise Lore (later Yuen) was the first Chinese nurse to enter the UBC program, completing her public health nursing certificate in 1938. She was also the first Chinese student (although Canadian born) to graduate from the VGH program, in 1936. She took the public health course at the request of the Vancouver Metropolitan Board of Health (formed in 1936) "because they felt the need for a public health nurse who could speak Chinese fluently (due mostly to the high incidence of TB among Chinese)."[62] After she completed the course, she found that Metropolitan Health could not hire her because "the City had an ordinance (or bylaw) against Orientals on the payroll. Special arrangements were made through other organizations for me to work ... but paid under a newly formed Chinese Health League.... It was not satisfactory as there was no support from the Chinese Benevolent Association and I was also much underpaid. After two years I left and went back to VGH on general duty."[63] She eventually returned to Metropolitan Health and was paid by the TB Christmas Seal organization, but her salary remained below that of city public health nurses until 1946, when she finally went on the city payroll at regular pay. Just a few months later she left to be married, and soon took her bachelor of arts degree in the United States.

Ruth Akagawa appears to have been the first student of Japanese origin at UBC; she received her certificate in public health nursing in 1938 and Yasuko Yamazaki was the second graduate from the same course in 1939. Margaret

Duffield, district supervisor for the Victorian Order of Nurses in Vancouver, supervised the field work experience of many of the UBC students and in an article on "Nursing Care for Racial Groups" in 1941, she stressed the importance of attracting nursing students from minority racial groups. She described the services offered to and the health needs of the Chinese and Japanese communities in Vancouver and praised the work being done by these first nurses of Asian origin.[64]

Discrimination certainly was not over, however. When the relief camps and relief offices had opened at the beginning of the Depression, "Orientals," including Canadian-born citizens of Asian descent, received only a fraction of the assistance given to others. University graduates of Asian descent found it difficult to obtain jobs during the Depression. Chinese, East Indian, and Japanese Canadians did not obtain the right to vote until federal legislation was passed in the late-1940s.

CHANGES IN THE PROGRAM

Under Mabel Gray's direction, UBC initiated a six-year, double-degree program beginning in the 1930-1931 session. Under new guidelines from RNABC, students entering hospital schools had to be at least 19 years old. The double-degree program allowed the Nursing department to admit students at age 16, who otherwise would have been too young for hospital affiliation. The double-degree students spent three years, rather than two, at the University before taking the hospital clinical portion of the program. Upon completion of the hospital portion (the end of the fifth year in the program), they received a Bachelor of Arts and a hospital diploma. Following the final year on campus, they received the degree of Bachelor of Applied Science (Nursing).

Both the regular combined-course program and the double-degree program were lengthened by a year in the 1934-1935 session. The Department decided that the shorter clinical portion should be increased to the full three-year program given to VGH students; the university students would have the regular academic vacations and would enter the hospital program along with the VGH September class. This longer program continued until 1951, when the double-degree program also was discontinued.[65]

In 1935-1936, because of budget cuts, UBC placed limits on enrolment of first year students in all faculties, including Nursing, which was to be limited to 15. The enrolment list of the department for that year, however, showed 21 entering the program, but these likely included some arts and sciences students who might not plan to proceed in Nursing. Attrition was a major factor, especially during the Depression. For example, of the 10 students who registered for first year in 1929, only three graduated, although there were five in the graduating class, including some students who had entered earlier. For

Figure 3.8   Nursing faculty, 1937. L-R: Margaret Kerr, Mabel Gray, Fyvie Young.

the 1936-1937 year, the calendar description for Nursing indicated a change, and first year nursing students registered under Arts and Science and did not officially enter the Nursing program until second year; this continued until the 1946-1947 session.[66]

In 1932, Hibbert Hill was granted leave of absence from UBC because of ill health and for the next three years, until his death, Mabel Gray carried the full administration of the Nursing program. In 1936, C.E. Dolman, who had taken his medical and advanced education in England before coming to Canada, was appointed acting head of the Department of Nursing and Health as well as acting head of the Department of Bacteriology and Preventive Medicine. He soon became head of Bacteriology although he remained acting head of Nursing and Health. It appears his relationship with Mabel Gray was a collaborative one. One student from this period recalls that C.E. Dolman taught the nursing students bacteriology during their preclinical years on campus and described him as "young and handsome, [with] marvellous diction and vocabulary."[67]

The nursing faculty on campus soon numbered three. Fyvie Young (later Heale), the daughter of Henry Esson Young, had received her UBC nursing degree in 1931. She then took her master of arts degree at Columbia, and returned to UBC to join Margaret Kerr and Mabel Gray. She was hired under a Rockefeller Foundation grant given to UBC and began teaching during the 1937-1938 session with a course called Practice of Public Health Nursing. The Foundation's grant, given for three years, enabled the Department to secure a well-qualified supervisor to visit all the field work agencies to assist them to plan the students' field work. Fyvie Young remained on faculty until the end of the 1939-1940 session; at that time the funding ended, but the University assumed financial responsibility for a position that continued the tradition of regular supervision of field work experience.

The two (or three, for the double-degree program) preclinical campus years were described in the UBC calendars as giving students "an introduction to general cultural subjects and a foundation in the sciences underlying the practice of nursing."[68] As well, the calendars noted that the clinical period at VGH was "planned to afford a wide experience and training in the care of the sick, and to develop the skill, observation, and judgment necessary to the efficient practice of nursing."[69] Mabel Gray vigorously opposed suggestions from some nursing leaders that science courses should be adapted and specially arranged for nurses:

They are of the opinion that in the fuller courses much of the content has no application to nursing or that the student fails to see and make the application. Since the beginning of the modern nursing era, one great weakness in the theoretical instruction of nurses has been that all knowledge approaching the scientific in nature has been administered in 'tabloid' form. As a direct result of this method of instruction, the nurse in general has failed to acquire a scientific point of view and has failed to apply scientific methods to the solution of nursing problems. If this weakness is to be overcome, and if, later, the teaching of the sciences in nursing schools is to be undertaken by nurses, then these nurses must receive the fullest preparation possible for this work.[70]

Instead, Mabel Gray encouraged preclinical students to take full science courses and, in the final campus year, she brought in highly qualified and prominent guest lecturers from other University departments and from leading health care institutions. Part-time and honorary lecturers in the late 1930s included Henry Esson Young, now in his late seventies but still head of the provincial health department, Gregoire F. Amyot, Dr. Young's protege who succeeded him following his death in 1939, and J.W. McIntosh, senior medical health officer for the Metropolitan Health Committee; they taught communicable diseases (including venereal disease) and preventive health.

Other part-time lecturers listed in the calendars included: Anne Cavers and Florence Walker of Vancouver General School of Nursing, who taught in the teaching and supervision courses; Arthur L. Crease, for whom Crease Clinic at Essondale (later Riverview) was named, who taught mental hygiene; and Laura Holland, Zella Collins, and Mary MacPhedran, who would now be called social workers and who taught "social case work."

During the clinical portion of their program, UBC students had a sort of special status not accorded to VGH students because UBC rotations were controlled by the University. UBC students were ensured rotation to services that could take only limited numbers, such as the outpatient department, psychiatric services at Essondale, tuberculosis nursing, and the Victorian Order of Nurses. These were required experiences for the UBC students whereas VGH students had less opportunity to have them. Both groups of students had the same basic clinical experiences – medical, surgical, gynaecological, pediatric and orthopaedic, neurological, infants, operating room, eye, ear, nose, and throat (EENT), obstetrical, communicable diseases, and diet kitchen; however, length of time for UBC students in any one rotation was specified by UBC faculty. This practice occasionally led to some resentment on the part of VGH students who might spend long periods in some areas according to service needs.

During their three years in hospital, however, the UBC students had a strong feeling of belonging to VGH and always proudly proclaimed their graduation from both programs. Classmates often were unaware that some of the group were taking the UBC program. In an interview with alumnae from the UBC class of 1940, one individual stated that several in her class had not known she was with the UBC program until graduation ceremonies, when she wore her academic gown and mortarboard over her VGH uniform. "I always felt resentful for having to wear those things for that graduation because I wanted to wear them for the university graduation.... I wanted to have my nurse's cap on for my hospital graduation."[71]

Although student experiences were better controlled during this period, students still carried out the majority of the cleaning in a unit and a fair bit of the cooking and food service for those patients who did not receive a "full diet." Dorothy Tate (later Slaughter) (BASc(N) 1933) recalled her second day on the ward, when students were "presented with a tray, a basin, and cloths, and taught to clean.... We learned to wash beds between patients and were taught how to bathe patients, too, but it was just cleaning that very first day. There were no lectures, just taught to clean, and we cleaned."[72]

Students in hospital also still provided much of the service, although there were more graduate staff employed at VGH. However, students usually were in change of wards on evenings and nights, with perhaps a supervisor available on call: "I can remember working as a student nurse in the evenings on Ward F [likely about 30 to 36 pediatric and women's surgery patients] and

Figure 3.9   Anatomy class at Fairview, Vancouver General Hospital,
circa 1935. Students were required to wear full uniforms to class.
Note long-sleeved uniforms with white cuffs.

there were only two students on the ward – one for the big ward and one for
the corridor. We just ran and ran and ran."[73]

Nursing classes during the hospital years were held in an old hospital
auditorium, which had been used by UBC before the move to the Point Grey
campus. In fact, all the old buildings at VGH were put to use by the
Hospital's Board of Directors. The vacant building used by the mining
department was turned into dormitories for nursing students and became
known as Laurel House, and another adjacent building was turned into a
temporary residence for nurses, called West House.[74] Accommodations for
the student nurses remained less than ideal throughout this whole period,
despite regular demands for a new building by Director of Nursing Grace
Fairley and fund-raising efforts by VGH nursing students.[75]

A UBC student of this period described her VGH residence life: "I was [at
first] in a four-bed dormitory in West House. The first thing that we were
told was that we had to have our blinds pulled during the day because they
either didn't want us looking into the men's treatment room in the VD clinic
[across the street] or didn't want the men looking into our dorm.... In West
House, we were put in a tiny room under the stairs. You couldn't get to one
bed without climbing over the other bed. That's where the two of us were for
some time before we moved to the Old Home."[76]

Alison Reid (later Wyness) (BASc(N) 1934) also recalled "the old house,"
as she called it. "I was in a two-bedroom room which was on the ground
floor. We had a window right there, so I spent half my nights hauling kids in

Figure 3.10

Home visiting uniform worn
in the 1920s.

so they wouldn't lose their 10 o'clock leave." She said she herself did not
come in through the window, but she "took pity on them."[77]

The students were responsible for either making or having their uniforms
made. Dorothy Tate Slaughter recalls seemingly "thousands of yards" of
sheeting that had to be made into aprons and bibs. The basic uniform was a
white bib and apron over a blue dress and black shoes and stockings. The
rotation with the Victorian Order of Nurses – "the VON experience" – was a
highlight for most students. They wore their basic blue dress and the black
shoes and stockings and added a black tie. Beth McCann (BASc(N) 1940)
remembered that they also wore a borrowed hat and navy blue coat for this
experience. "It fit some people and didn't fit others."[78] One UBC alumna
recalled her experience during a "coffee klatch" interview session: "I have
distinct memories of my VON student days because they delivered babies at
home then. I can remember spending the night waiting for this lady who was
going to deliver. Then she called and we finally went out and this baby was
delivered. We received the placenta in the salad bowl, which I thought was
really something after coming out of the hospital and seeing it all done the
way it should be done."[79]

During the final year on campus, the students also spent rotations in field
work, many of which they recalled in alumnae questionnaires.[80] Helen
Saunders (BASc(N) 1940) recalled field work experience in public health in
the Chilliwack area where she visited some Mennonite families who followed
the old practices of living in clean quarters in the huge barns along with the
animals. Louise Lore (later Yuen) (BASc(N) 1940) spent her field work

Figure 3.11   Esther Naden (BASc(N) 1924), charge nurse at the
Saanich Health Centre where many UBC students had their field experience.

experience in Duncan, and she recalled that the Health Department there
was housed in an old funeral parlour and she and her classmate were billeted
in the "casket room." Phyllis Dorothy Scouler (later Soanes) (BASc (N) 1938)
also went to Duncan but recalled most vividly the visits to a logging camp at
Youbou, which was accessible only via small boat for a long trip up Lake
Cowichan.

Esther Paulson (DipPHN 1934) spent her field work experience at Saanich
and recalled going on visits with Jennie Hocking (DipPHN 1933). Jennie
Hocking had recently joined the Unit, under charge nurse Esther Naden
(later Gardom) (BASc(N) 1924). Esther Paulson recalls that "Jennie never did
turn out to be a good driver and, at that stage, she was not good at all. We
started off one day and she stepped on the accelerator and we took a leap
forward into the ditch with the health unit car. The firemen had to come and
get us out of there."[81] Esther Paulson's classmate in this field experience was
Helen McArthur (later Watson), a University of Alberta student who was
taking her final year at UBC.

> We were billeted in the home of a Scottish lady. She had been the first Scottish
> typist in her youth – very proud of it. She was an unmarried lady and her home
> was a typical little one-storey Victorian cottage, a lot of photographs and
> doillies around. We had a bedroom ... with two iron bedsteads, two straight
> chairs, and a table between the two. We had our breakfast and supper with her
> and we went to the nurses' residence for dinner [at noon], our main meal. She

[the landlady] was not used to the appetites of two healthy young women. We had a good breakfast – good Scottish oatmeal porridge and toast – but the suppers were sparse, usually a poached egg on spinach or something very simple. We would be so hungry that [we] would get on the bus and go all the way into Victoria to get some more food.[82]

Helen MacArthur was one of 14 students who were enrolled at the University of Alberta but who came to UBC to take the final year of their Alberta programs in the UBC Nursing department, graduating from Alberta with a Bachelor of Science in Nursing. Little can be found in the records about this innovative degree affiliation program, which ran from 1933 to 1941. Kathleen Lord (later Birdsall), one of the first three to come, recalled that "since the University of Alberta did not give courses for the fifth year of the degree course, we had to go to another university and [we] chose University of British Columbia, which turned out to be a very happy choice."[83]

NURSING INSTRUCTORS

During both clinical years and on-campus years, students were fortunate to have high quality nursing instructors. The VGH directors of this era did a great deal of the teaching during the clinical portion of the course, and UBC students remember them vividly, including Kathleen Ellis, who had become VGH director when Ethel Johns moved full time to UBC in 1922. Kathleen Ellis was a 1915 graduate of the Johns Hopkins Hospital in Baltimore, but had returned to her native B.C. for her early career, then was assistant to the superintendent of nurses at Toronto General before coming to VGH. During the VGH years, she was active in provincial and national nurses' associations, and was president of RNABC from 1927 to 1929 and instrumental in ensuring that the Weir Report went ahead. In 1929, when she was leaving VGH, the Hospital held its first "white graduation." This was the 30th anniversary of the VGH School and marked the largest class of students in VGH history to that time – 106 nurses plus six UBC students and 16 affiliates from other smaller hospitals in the province.[84] Kathleen Ellis, who was resigning as director of nurses and head of the school, led the procession of students all dressed in their new white graduate uniforms and carrying flowers.

    She was first vice-president of CNA at the time of her resignation from VGH. She then went abroad to take post-graduate studies in public health nursing at Bedford College, London, under the auspices of the League of Red Cross Societies. When she returned to Canada, she became advisor to nursing schools and secretary-treasurer/registrar of the Saskatchewan Registered Nurses Association. In 1938, she became the first director of the new nursing department at the University of Saskatchewan, Saskatoon, a position she held until retirement in 1950. During World War II, she was "loaned" to the Canadian Nurses Association to serve as emergency nursing advisor because of the serious shortage of nurses; she also acted as CNA General Secretary during this period.[85]

As director and head of VGH, Kathleen Ellis taught the nursing students and arranged their rotations and would have been a major influence and role model for students of the 1920s. She was assisted in the teaching program by Margaret Fraser and Anne Cavers. During this period, two grateful patients donated a nurses' library at VGH, in which Margaret Fraser spent many off-duty hours organizing and cataloguing books. Anne Cavers, who is remembered by many UBC graduates, had attended normal school in Alberta and taught for some years before entering nursing. She graduated from VGH in 1927 and immediately was hired for the teaching staff, a position she held for 20 years. Following retirement in 1947, she wrote the first history of the VGH school of nursing, *Our School of Nursing 1899 to 1949*.

Kathleen Ellis was followed as director of nursing at VGH by Grace Fairley, who also became an influence on students who knew her. She was born in Edinburgh and educated at the Edinburgh Ladies' College and School of Home Economics before graduating in nursing from Swansea General Hospital in Wales and taking postgraduate studies in Glasgow. She moved to Montreal in 1912 and was lady superintendent of the Alexandra Hospital. She was active in American, Canadian, and Quebec nursing and hospital associations during this period and was instrumental in the founding of the School of Nursing at McGill University in 1920. While at VGH she continued her professional involvements and was president of RNABC from 1935 to 1938 and president of CNA from 1938 to 1942 and vice-president of the International Council of Nurses.

Grace Fairley hired many more graduate nursing staff and made many improvements in the curriculum of the VGH program during her tenure. She expanded VGH's affiliations to include two-month rotations at the tuberculosis sanatorium at Tranquille and at the provincial mental hospital at Essondale. She also arranged experiences with the Victorian Order of Nurses and Metropolitan Health Board so students had some experience with home nursing as well as hospital care. VGH during this time also offered a number of postgraduate courses in obstetrics, pediatrics, surgery, operating room, and dietetics; these were intended for graduates specializing in these areas. Grace Fairley improved the scope of nursing education to such an extent that more nursing instructors were required. Among those she appointed as clinical instructors were Evelyn Bowman, Agnes J. Macleod, Evelyn Mallory, and Alison Reid (later Wyness) (BASc(N) 1934), one of the first UBC degree graduates to be hired as an instructor at VGH. Agnes Macleod, who later served overseas as a matron of armed forces hospitals and after the war

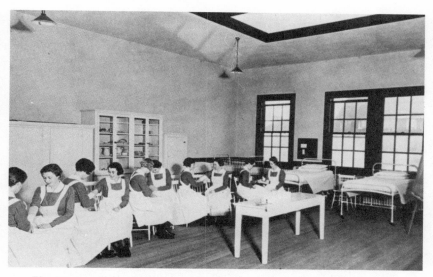

Figure 3.12   Probationers practising bandaging in a demonstration room
at the Vancouver General Hospital. UBC students had a probationary period
at VGH in the summer between first and second years.

became the first director of nursing service and matron-in-chief for all the
hospitals of the Department of Veterans' Affairs, was the first instructor of
"nursing arts." She tried to instill a respect for principles underlying care
rather than focussing on memorization of technique. She and Evelyn Mallory, who later became director of the UBC Nursing program, were both
graduates of Teachers College, Columbia University, and their appointments
represented the growing awareness of the importance of education for nurses.
These two instructors, who remained lifelong friends, particularly emphasized the process of intellectual inquiry among nurses.[86] A UBC alumna
recalls Evelyn Mallory as a clinical instructor at VGH: "I can still see Miss
Mallory rolling bandages. She was so crisp and that uniform had the flared-
out skirt from the Winnipeg General."[87]

Grace Fairley herself taught ethics to the nursing students and, along
with her instructors, developed a philosophy for the school that emphasized
the patient as a person and a member of a family. The patient was the focus,
rather than the disease or technique. The philosophy stressed that students
must not be robots and work by rote, but were expected to question and not
just follow orders. Alison Reid Wyness had great admiration for Grace
Fairley, recalling that "she was ... very friendly with the Montreal people
and Miss [Jean] Gunn in Toronto.... They more or less ran nursing
in Canada."[88]

Figure 3.13   Nursing Undergraduate Executive (NUE), 1933.
L-R Top: Dorothy Tate, President; Dorothy Skitch, Treasurer;
Mabel Gray, Honorary President; Asenath Leitch, Secretary; Alison Reid,
Vice-president. Bottom: Eileen Davies, Hospital Rep; Ethel Rolston, Lit Rep;
Violet Forrester; Vida Carl.

GRADUATES FROM THE PERIOD

Despite the Depression, the Nursing program at UBC continued to enrol bright young women, many of whom went on to distinguished careers that changed nursing and health care in the decades that followed. Among these were Margaret Kerr (BASc(N) 1926), Marion Miles (later Pennington) (BASc(N), 1932), Esther Paulson (DipPHN 1934), Lyle Creelman (BASc(N) 1936), Monica Frith (later Green) (BA 1939, BASc(N) 1940), and Elizabeth (Beth) McCann (BA 1939, BASc(N) 1940).

Margaret Kerr taught in the department, first as an instructor and later as assistant professor, from 1929 until May 1944. Her students liked and admired her and, although she was a large, imposing, forceful, heavy-set woman, she tried hard to create an informal and collegial atmosphere in her classes. For example, uncharacteristically for the time, she urged students to call her by her first name. She influenced many students to take an active role in nursing politics and, when she retired from her nursing career in 1965, three former presidents of CNA were proud to claim that they were "F.S.O.M. – former students of Margaret."[89]

Two of these CNA presidents were among the University of Alberta affiliate students who were influenced by Mabel Gray, Margaret Kerr, and other UBC nurses during their final year. Helen Griffin McArthur (later Watson), president of CNA 1950-1954, returned to Alberta from UBC in

1934 to begin a distinguished career that culminated in many honours and awards. She received a Rockefeller Fellowship to obtain her master's degree from Columbia; her thesis became the basis for an advanced practical obstetrics course that began at the University of Alberta in 1943. She was director of the University of Alberta School of Nursing from 1940 to 1943, then became director of public health nursing for Alberta and the first National Director for Nursing Services for the Canadian Red Cross, a post she held for 24 years. She also served internationally, with one highlight of her career being service in Korea as special representative of the League of Red Cross Societies. Isobel Black (later MacLeod), president of CNA 1964-1966, received her degree from University of Alberta after her year at UBC. She had a distinguished career that also led to international work. Among her many senior positions was director of nursing and principal of the School at the Montreal General Hospital.

Like all UBC nursing faculty in these periods, Margaret Kerr took an active role in nursing organizations, and, for example, was president of the Registered Nurses Association of B.C. and chair of the public health section of CNA. She strongly believed in sharing information with the nursing community and published many articles during the teaching segment of her career. When she left UBC in 1945, it was to become editor of *The Canadian Nurse*, succeeding Ethel Johns. At that time, the subscription list had grown to a respectable 5,000, but Margaret Kerr immediately began lobbying for subscriptions to the journal to be part of all nurse registration fees and soon the provincial organizations had agreed to this method of payment. As editor, she was also deeply involved in activities of the provincial associations and was one of the nursing leaders who recognized the importance of involving French-speaking nurses in the national association. She expanded the bilingual scope of the journal during her period as editor and the magazine began carrying articles in French. By 1965, when she retired, the journal had become well-known internationally and her opinions were sought by editors around the world.[90]

Esther Paulson was another graduate from this period who influenced nursing and health care, especially tuberculosis nursing in B.C. and Canada. For the first five years following graduation, she was in a new position in the "welfare field service" in the East Kootenays. This new service combined public health nursing and social welfare and had been introduced by George Weir, who was then provincial minister of health. This field service provided care where organized health services were not yet available. Esther Paulson then began moving into what would become her major career area and became a recognized expert and consultant in tuberculosis care. Although now treatable, the disease then was rampant, affecting and sometimes killing young people, particularly women, in their twenties. During her years with tuberculosis control, B.C. became the first province to require tuberculosis

Figure 3.14

Esther Paulson (DipPHN 1934) recognized for her knowledge of tuberculosis nursing.

experience for all its student nurses. Eventually, she became the senior nurse administrator for the division of tuberculosis control in B.C., then in 1952 was appointed director of nursing for the new tuberculosis hospital, the George Pearson Centre in Vancouver. She was active in RNABC, CNA, and Canadian Public Health Association affairs throughout her career and served as president of RNABC from 1951 to 1953.

Lyle Creelman became one of the best-known Canadian nurses in the world. She was born in Nova Scotia, but grew up and took her schooling in Richmond, B.C. She completed normal school in Vancouver and taught for three years before deciding to enter the UBC Nursing program, from which she graduated in 1936. She worked in public health in Revelstoke, B.C., for two years, then received a Rockefeller Fellowship to attend Teachers College, Columbia University, for her master of arts degree. She then returned to Vancouver, where she was supervisor of school nursing and, soon, supervisor of public health nursing for the Metropolitan Health Unit. During this period, she was also elected president of RNABC. In 1944, at the invitation of the United Nations Relief and Rehabilitation Administration (UNRRA), she was appointed chief nurse in the British-occupied zone in Germany. She described the many problems in an article for Canadian nurses, saying:

> The most urgent [problem] was the task of caring for the millions of people of many nationalities who had been displaced from their homes by actual war; had fled before the enemy; had been offered the alternative of compulsory work in Germany or starvation; had been the victims of political or religious pressure;

or had been part of the huge deliberate transfer of populations that, particularly in Poland and the Baltic States, had been carried out for political reasons.[91]

Following the two-year period with UNRRA, Lyle Creelman returned to Vancouver, but was soon on leave from the Metropolitan Unit to carry out a survey of public health services in B.C. for the provincial government. This led to her involvement in 1948 in a major study of Canadian public health services, in collaboration with J.H. Baillie. This study, funded by the Canadian Public Health Association, led to publication of the Baillie-Creelman Report in 1950; the resulting relevant recommendations had "a positive effect on the provision of public health nursing and public health."[92] The Baillie-Creelman Report became a required text in many public health nursing courses across Canada.

In 1950, Lyle Creelman was invited to become a nursing consultant in maternal and child health for the newly formed Nursing Unit of the World Health Organization, eventually becoming its Chief Nursing Officer, a position she held until 1968. She was recognized around the world for her clear judgment and administrative ability. As part of her mandate, she recruited well-prepared nurses, including some from UBC, such as Marion Miles (later Pennington) who did public health nursing in Abbotsford before joining WHO. Lyle Creelman directed work on many international projects and promoted the development of WHO's regional offices.[93] For her work, she received many awards, including an honorary doctorate from the University of New Brunswick, recognition from the RNABC, CNA, and Canadian Association of Public Health, and a Canada Centennial Medal and Medal of Service of the Order of Canada from the Government of Canada. In 1992, her alma mater also awarded her an honorary doctorate, the first graduate of the UBC Nursing program to be so recognized.

Several other UBC graduates worked with UNRRA, including Mary Henderson (BASc(N) 1929), who had worked with the Provincial Public Health Service and the Metropolitan Health Services.[94] In 1939, she received the Florence Nightingale Memorial Fellowship, which allowed her to study for a year in London, England. Just after her arrival there, however, World War II began and overseas students were advised to return home. Mary Henderson then went to the University of Toronto School of Nursing for a year of postgraduate study in administration and supervision of public health nursing. She returned to Vancouver in 1941 to continue to work with Metropolitan Health and as an instructor in nursing in the UBC program during the war. Near the end of the war, she, Lyle Creelman, Heather Kilpatrick (BASc(N) 1931), and Frances (Frankie) McQuarrie (BA 1935, BASc(N) 1936) were part of the little group that went, first to Washington, D.C., for two months training, then overseas with UNRRA. Mary Henderson was assigned to El Shatt camp, near Port Said at the entrance to the Suez

Canal, where there were approximately 26,000 Yugoslav refugees; she supervised the public health nursing program in the camp. She recalled that public
health care made quite a difference and that within a few months they could
actually see the improvement in health and a decrease in admissions to the
camp hospital.

Monica Frith (later Green) joined the provincial public health service
immediately after graduation, working in various units around the
province.[95] In 1944, she attended the University of Michigan and obtained a
master's degree in public health and, upon her return, became Consultant
Public Health Nurse for the province. In 1948, she took over from Dorothy
Tate Slaughter and became the third director of nursing for the provincial
public health service. During her 28 years as the chief nurse for the province,
she introduced many new services and saw an enormous expansion during
the 1950s. For example, several experimental projects to test the value of
home care nursing were carried out under her supervision, although such
programs were not implemented until the 1970s. The school health program
for the province was completely revamped in 1962 under her direction. Many
innovative procedures, such as the rheumatic fever prophylaxis program,
became routine parts of the provincial service after being researched through
trial projects, and a minimum basic health service for all schools was introduced for the 350,000 school children in the province. During this time,
Monica Frith (Green) was active in provincial and national associations and
served on provincial, national, and international committees. In 1967, she
was named honorary president of the American Public Health Association
and the following year was made an APHA Fellow. After she retired, she
wrote *Through the Years with Public Health Nursing*, an interesting, informa-
tive, thorough, descriptive book that chronicles the development of public
health nursing in B.C. She has received numerous honours and awards from
the public health community.

Elizabeth (Beth) Kenny McCann was also one outstanding graduate in this
period and an advocate and promoter of university schools of nursing. More
of her story is told in Chapter 5, but soon after graduation she joined the
UBC nursing faculty and remained at UBC throughout her entire career,
influencing UBC nursing students for more than 35 years. One of her
classmates recalled Beth McCann's unfailing enthusiasm and vitality and said
the class greatly admired her positive outlook even when the student experiences were long and overwhelming. "I used to think, 'My goodness, I wish I
could be more like that.'"[96]

During this period, more students elected to take the teaching and supervision courses in their final years, and by the end of this period UBC graduates
were also beginning to influence teaching in B.C. and other provinces.
Pauline (Polly) Capelle (BASc(N) 1939) taught in the UBC nursing program
from 1944 until she retired. Another of the teaching and administration

students from this period was Helen Saunders (BASc(N) 1940), who won the public health nursing award but eventually went into teaching and was a clinical teacher and operating room supervisor at VGH for many years. She received her master's in nursing from the University of Washington in 1962.

Alison Reid (later Wyness) taught at the VGH School of Nursing for five years from 1936 to 1941. After graduation, she attended the CNA meeting that year in Toronto. She went there partly to help find a position, because jobs were hard to come by at the time, and she was offered at general duty position – at $35 a month, plus room and board – at the Ottawa Civic Hospital, "the first outside graduate to be put on staff there."[97] Unfortunately, after about a year, she was diagnosed with tuberculosis and returned to Vancouver for a three-month period of absolute bed rest at home. She then was hired at VGH, becoming head nurse, clinical supervisor, and clinical instructor until her marriage. Frances McQuarrie taught at the Royal Columbian Hospital and at the Vancouver General before going with UNRRA and in 1948 was appointed supervisor of instruction at the University of Alberta School of Nursing.[98]

The Queen's University course in nursing, which was approved in 1942, was greatly influenced by the UBC program of the Mabel Gray period.[99] Dorothy Ritches was the first director at Queen's, and the first instructor to be hired into the program, in 1947, was Jennie McMartin Weir, a University of Alberta graduate who completed her fifth year in the public health program at UBC and who had gone on to take her master's degree in public health nursing at Teachers College, Columbia University. In 1950, after a year as acting director, Jennie Weir was appointed to succeed Dorothy Ritches and served as director for 16 years, resigning to take a full-time teaching position at University of Toronto. Jennie Weir also was active professionally in Ontario and nationally, serving on the executive committee, including a term as president, of the Registered Nurses Association of Ontario, and as president of the Canadian Association of University Schools of Nursing (CAUSN). Another later administrator at Queen's also was influenced by her UBC years: Alice Baumgart (BSN 1958) was director of the Faculty of Nursing at Queen's, from 1977 to 1987; she then became Vice-Principal (Human Services).

Irene Stewart (DipPHN 1934) was one of many nurses from Alberta, such as Marjorie Maynes (DipPHN 1937) and Janet Munroe (later Reynolds) (DipPHN 1935), who came to UBC to take the public health nursing certificate during this period. Irene Stewart returned to Alberta and had a series of appointments in smaller and larger districts in northern Alberta, then in Nakusp and Summerland in B.C., before joining the staff of the Calgary Health Unit from 1954 to 1961. After she retired, she compiled and edited *These were Our Yesterdays: A History of District Nursing in Alberta*.[100]

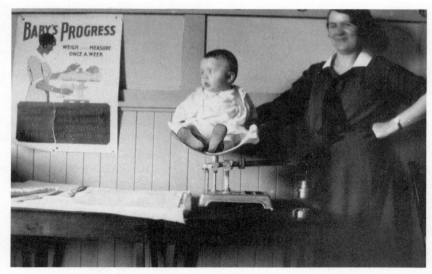

Figure 3.15　Marg McPhee (DipPHN 1933) at a well baby clinic.
The emphasis was on health teaching and child care.

Figure 3.16　Alice Beattie (DipPHN 1938) in front of the Cowichan Health
Centre, Duncan, in 1939. By the 1940s, cars were needed because of the amount
of equipment (including baby scales and a stove and pot to boil water)
that needed to be carried.

Naturally, the majority of graduates from this period went into public health nursing in British Columbia. Among the many nurses graduating in this era who made major contributions are: Ruby McKay (DipPHN 1935) who became director of B.C.'s child welfare branch; Eleanor Scott Graham (BASc(N) 1936), who worked for the Metropolitan Health Committee and the B.C. Provincial Department of Health and then was appointed in 1947 to the experimental Metropolitan School of Nursing in Toronto[101]; Dorothy Priestly (DipPHN 1937), who was the first public health nurse in Prince Rupert[102]; Frances Lyne (later Hobart) (BASc(N) 1927), who went on to become a school nurse in Kelowna; Heather Kilpatrick (BASc(N) 1931), first provincial director of nursing for the Provincial Health Department (from 1940 to 1944) and who left to work with UNRRA[103]; Marjorie Staniforth (later Wisby) (BASc(N) 1941) and Isabel Louks (later Foster) (BASc(N) 1940) who were instrumental in 1943 in forming the B.C. Public Health Nursing Council to work for better salaries and conditions for public health nurses[104]; and Anna Larson (later Mason) (DipPHN 1938) who was a public health nurse in Penticton from 1944 to 1975 and "was highly regarded in her public health nursing role and also in related community activities.... She became a key person in local planning for health resources, including homes and recreation facilities for senior citizens."[105]

An earlier graduate in this period was Kathleen Snowden (DipPHN 1927), who became the first public health nurse in Keremeos and Cawston in south central B.C. Her story was written up by the Okanagan Historical Society.[106] At first, she made her rounds to the 500 residents in her district on horseback or foot, but she soon realized that she needed a car. She borrowed $300 from the Public Health Department and bought a two-door Ford sedan; in emergency situations, the car became a makeshift ambulance. Despite a donation of $10 from the Women's Institute, the car remained a constant drain on her small salary. She shared a small house with a teacher, and in emergency situations patients or family members would call on her for care at all hours.

Unfortunately, the School of Nursing does not have a list of UBC Nursing graduates who served with the forces during World War II, although Bertha Jenkins (DipPHN 1928), Marion Miles (later Pennington) (BASc(N), 1932), Jean Dorgan (BASc(N) 1934), Mabel Olund (BASc(N) 1935), Asenath Leitch (BASc(N) 1938), Isabel Mungen (DipPHN 1939), Helen Saunders (BASc(N) 1940), Catherine Perkins (DipPHN 1940), and Elizabeth Jeffery (DipPHN 1942) were among those who did. Bertha Jenkins became the first school nurse in Cranbrook following her UBC year and also did public health nursing in various locations throughout the province, serving as supervisor in Duncan in 1930 to 1932, before she enlisted in the Royal Canadian Army Medical Corps in 1942. She saw service at various points in Canada and on the hospital ship *Letitia*. Following her discharge, she began a career in

Figure 3.17   Marjorie (Staniforth) Wisby (BASc(N) 1941), a public
health nurse in the Peace River district following graduation. She is shown here
with a MUMPS sign. Children with communicable diseases were quarantined
and a sign was placed in the window of the home.

administration, serving as matron in hospitals in various communities in
B.C.[107] Marion Miles (later Pennington) joined the RCAMC in 1943 and
served in Washington, D.C., and in Saskatchewan. She later served for two
years with UNRRA as nursing supervisor for the Displaced Persons camps in
Germany, then took postgraduate study in New York. In 1949, she was
appointed assistant director of the school of nursing at Dalhousie University.[108] Catherine Perkins served in England, France, Belgium, and Holland
with No. 8 Canadian General Hospital. After her discharge, she took a

certificate course in public health supervision at McGill, then was appointed assistant supervisor with Metropolitan Health Committee in Vancouver.[109] Mabel Olund, Isabel Mungen, and Asenath Leitch served with the Royal Canadian Air Force.[110] Jean Dorgan, when she returned from wartime service, went to the University of Toronto and obtained a master's degree in social work and was head of the Department of Mental Hygiene in Ottawa for many years.[111]

END OF THE MABEL GRAY YEARS

Ethel Johns had seen the birth of a new approach to professionalism for nursing with the opening of the UBC Nursing program in 1919 and had been the midwife who delivered the lusty infant into the world. Mabel Gray, the second nursing head, faced the arduous task of nurturing the program through its formative years and providing a healthy and stimulating environment for its growth and development. This was complicated by both the economic boom during her early years and the great economic depression of the 1930s. Then, in the final stages of her tenure at UBC, she faced the turmoil of the outbreak of World War II.

Mabel Gray retired from UBC at the end of the 1940-1941 academic year, although she was only age 61 and there are no indications of health problems or other reasons for early retirement. Her retirement left the department with no qualified faculty for the teaching and supervision courses and, because senior nurses were being called into the armed forces, this created a major shortage of teachers. Evelyn Mallory, who was Registrar of the Registered Nurses Association of B.C., and educational advisor to schools of nursing, was drawn in to teach the UBC courses as a part-time lecturer and eventually took over Mabel Gray's position.

At least part of the reason for her early retirement may have been Mabel Gray's lack of academic qualifications. Although she was nominally the "head" to all those outside the University administration, she was classed only as an assistant professor. C.E. Dolman was still acting head of the department. Margaret Kerr and Fyvie Young were nursing faculty, as was Geraldine Homfray (later Langton). Both Margaret Kerr and Fyvie Young had preparation at the master's level and Fyvie Young's Rockefeller Fellowship had been given specifically to try to bring about closer integration between theory and practice at UBC. Geraldine Homfray, a classmate of Fyvie Young, had at least one year (1938-1939) of post-baccalaureate preparation (possibly a master's degree) at the George Peabody College for Teachers in Nashville, a prestigious college later affiliated with Vanderbilt University. The program under Mabel Gray had not changed much although the younger faculty considered that it needed to be carried "a big step further...."

Figure 3.18   Public Health Nursing Class of 1938 with faculty members
Mabel Gray, director, Margaret Kerr, and Fyvie Young.

There were specialists coming in, ... many more clinics available that you could talk about. The areas were already equipped with many more facilities, so you had to incorporate that."[112]

Whatever caused Mabel Gray to leave so precipitously, she remained in Vancouver and continued to be active in various nursing organizations. For a time, she became chair of the Nursing Bureau of the Vancouver Graduate Nurses Association, which helped place private duty nurses, and became involved with the Vancouver Local Council of Women. She loved gardening and outdoor sports and took up golf and lawn bowling and learned to drive a car. She died in Vancouver in 1976 at age 96.[113]

Students of the period had been highly positive about the program in the Mabel Gray years and graduated with a philosophy of nursing that reflected some of her ideals and that of her growing group of faculty. Elizabeth Copeland (later Merrick) (DipPHN 1938) was a pharmacist before she entered nursing. She wrote about the UBC program and emphasized that the memories of her course were "warm and happy, with the sense of accomplishment.... I think we all had a sense of purpose and a desire to learn and found the course challenging.... We felt, too, a responsibility to maintain the good reputation the School held."[114]

Geraldine Homfray recalled that the UBC graduates of her time went into the community "filled with enthusiasm.... that the University had set us off on a great track with considerable ability and inspiration.... Following up with this idea that the professional training encompassed the theory of community education, we set about making many contacts.... Our first objective was to make ourselves known to as many people as possible." For example, they contacted local organizations, such as the committee for the local fair where the nurses set up a display for community education about nutrition. They were on their own in the community and had to use their "thinking skills" and make decisions to resolve health care problems in the area. People in the districts respected the nurses "and in some ways the nurses felt they had to rise to meet that respect. Your goals were set a little higher because of that." She summed up her excellent interview on her life as a UBC graduate with the comment: "If I had to live my life over again, I would certainly go into the same field of work – public health nursing."[115]

An article on Mabel Gray's retirement appeared in *The Canadian Nurse*, written by Ethel Johns, who earlier had left the same position at UBC because she did not have the necessary academic qualifications. Although it does not comment on the reasons for Mabel Gray's retirement, the article stresses her broad practical background for the position she held and the many obstacles that she had to overcome, adding: "That she did overcome them is due to the courage and tenacity that are so characteristic of her and to a lively sense of humour which has helped her to deal effectively with situations that might have been baffling if they had been taken too seriously."[116]

CHAPTER FOUR

The Evelyn Mallory Years
1941-1967

Figure 4.1

Evelyn Mallory, 1941-1967.
In 1941, appointed special lecturer;
in 1943, associate professor and head of
Nursing. School status was granted in
1951 and Evelyn Mallory was promoted
to Professor and Director of the School
of Nursing, a position she held until
retirement in 1967.

The Evelyn Mallory years span the longest period for any director in the history of the UBC Nursing program. During these years, the program came of age, and achieved new measures of independence and recognition. The initial growing phases were over, and the program developed as a strong and vibrant entity within the university community. During the first part of this period, Nursing achieved independent status as a School within the University, and this set the stage for its further evolution as a leader in Canadian nursing. By the end of this era, the School was ready to open its master's program.

Because the Evelyn Mallory period covers 26 years, it encompasses many major social, political, cultural, economic, educational, scientific, and technological developments as well as the changes occurring in the Nursing program itself. These tend to fall rather naturally into three main periods, including the early part, which saw Evelyn Mallory work during World War II and the post-war period to achieve transition from department to school. The second period relates to the major influences of the 1950s, during which the generic degree program grew in stature and the UBC-VGH combined program ended. The third period, during the 1960s, focusses on evolution of graduate education in nursing at UBC.

EARLY LIFE OF EVELYN MALLORY

Harriet Evelyn Mallory was born in Barrie, Ontario, in 1902. The Mallory family had moved to Ontario with the United Empire Loyalists.[1] Georgie Jewel Mallory had married a cousin, Caleb Mallory, and the couple had three children, although only two girls survived childhood. Margaret Katherine Mallory was the first born (1898). A second child, a boy, died early in life. Sometime during the girls' early teenage years, their father was killed in a railway accident. Georgie Jewel Mallory married again, to a Robert Urquhart, and the family then moved to Winnipeg.

Evelyn Mallory received her early nursing education at the Winnipeg General Hospital – as did the two previous nurse leaders of the UBC Nursing program – and graduated from its three-year program in 1925. She then became instructor and assistant superintendent at the Winnipeg Children's Hospital for two years, leaving to attend Teachers College, Columbia University.[2] In high school, her sister Margaret had excelled in mathematics and sciences, so the young Evelyn had chosen other subjects "to avoid comparisons." When she attended Columbia, she found she excelled in chemistry and bacteriology, to the point where she "skimped on nursing courses." At the end of the first term, because finances were low, she was planning to leave the program, but was offered a teaching assistantship in sciences that enabled her to remain for the three years. As well, she worked part time in nursing. She received her bachelor of science degree in 1930.

On her return to Winnipeg, she had to take a year at home, on medical advice, she later said, "to rest her eyes." Although she made no further mention of this in interviews, she wore thick, tinted glasses throughout the rest of her career. After a series of short-term clinical nursing positions in Winnipeg – "these were depression years and both jobs and money were scarce" – she made a trip to Vancouver. A visit to the Registered Nurses Association of B.C. was rather discouraging; Helen Randal, the Registrar, advised her to go back to Winnipeg. Evelyn Mallory reported later that she had been told "to go back where you'd come from; there were not enough jobs for B.C. nurses, let alone an 'outsider'." However, she went to see the Director of Nurses at the Vancouver General Hospital. Grace Fairley had been a major advocate for and founder of the McGill School for Graduate Nurses when she was in Montreal,[3] and so also considered Columbia University graduates "outsiders." However, she was looking for well-qual:fied instructors for her growing teaching staff and wrote to Isabel Stewart at Teachers College, who responded, "You have a cracking good one right there!"

Evelyn Mallory taught at VGH from 1932 to 1935, mainly teaching anatomy, chemistry, and bacteriology, frequently using laboratory experiments. She arranged for the student nurses to attend autopsies as part of their anatomy and physiology studies. UBC students from the Mabel Gray era recall Evelyn Mallory as an extraordinarily good teacher during her VGH stay.[4] She left VGH on an invitation to become assistant director of nursing, then director, at the Winnipeg General; during this time, she also served as president of the Manitoba Association of Registered Nurses. She returned to B.C. in 1941 when she was asked to succeed Helen Randal as Registrar for the Registered Nurses Association of B.C.

When Mabel Gray retired in the summer of 1941, her departure left the UBC Nursing department without a qualified person to conduct the teaching and supervision course. Because many nurses had enlisted to serve in World War II, there was a great shortage of nursing teachers. Public health nurses had been declared essential services in B.C. by Gregoire Amyot,[5] the provincial health officer, and were not allowed to be recruited for the war effort; their public health workloads were expanding because physicians also were going overseas. Margaret Kerr was promoted to assistant professor during this time, and Mary Henderson had recently been given a new position that was intended to create a stronger integration of the student program for both UBC and VGH. As well, she and Geraldine Homfray Langton were responsible for teaching the much larger public health component. These three instructors did not feel qualified to take on the teaching and supervision portion of the program in addition to their other duties, so the course had to be dropped for one year.

There were 63 students enrolled in the program in 1941-1942, including 11 in the public health certificate course and 6 in the final year of the degree program, all of whom had to take the public health option. In 1942-1943, the numbers grew to a total of 98; this included 10 out of 12 in the final year of the degree program taking the public health option, and 27, by far the largest class to date, in the public health diploma course. However, Evelyn Mallory agreed to take a part-time position as a special lecturer so the teaching option could be offered again; she had 2 degree candidates and 5 certificate students that year. However, as she was still full-time Registrar, she considered that "neither job was properly done."

In spring of 1943, she was interviewed by UBC President L.S. Klinck for a full-time appointment as associate professor. She was not impressed by his interview and the fact that his main concern was with discipline of students at UBC. She recalled that she told him Nursing "had no discipline problem as our students had chosen their courses and wanted them." Her interview with C.E. Dolman, still acting head of the Department of Nursing and Health as well as his several other appointments, went considerably better. He recommended her appointment and approved her stipulation that she be able to take summer study at Columbia. Her salary started on July 1, and she spent the summer "auditing any courses I wished with the blessing of Isabel Stewart, who had succeeded Adelaide Nutting as director of Teachers College." She started full time at UBC in September 1943.

The bombing of Pearl Harbor in Hawaii on December 7, 1941, brought the United States into World War II and caused Canada, already two years at war with Germany and Italy, to declare war with Japan. The entire Western world was now preoccupied with the war effort, and British Columbia itself was considered vulnerable to attack by the Japanese; forces were mobilized along the coast, gun batteries were erected to protect the harbours, and, for a time, blackout restrictions existed in coastal cities. Overnight, the province climbed out of the Depression and the economy strengthened. Wartime industries, already working hard, went into over-time production and began to use all available supplies and labour. For the first time since the start of the Depression, the need for workers outstripped those searching for work.

The declaration of war with Japan led Canadians to an almost paranoid concern about the activities of Japanese Canadians, most of whom (about 22,000) lived in B.C.[6] More than half of these were Nisei, born in Canada, and most spoke English and had been educated with other British Columbians; many had university degrees. Immediately following the declaration of war with Japan, the Canadian authorities seized all fishing boats (about 1,200)[7] belonging to anyone of Japanese descent. Japanese schools and newspapers voluntarily closed, but anti-Asian feelings, often high in B.C. and particularly so at this time, were not satisfied. In January 1942, the Canadian government moved to evacuate all male "enemy aliens" (Japanese, German, and Italian) from sensitive areas, such as coastal ports, but public pressure continued for a complete evacuation, as was being carried out in the United States. Then, in February, the government decided to remove all persons of Japanese ancestry both from a 250-mile strip along the Pacific coast and from the Trail area, where there was a smelter considered essential to the war effort.

Only a handful of scholars spoke out against the measures, which discriminated in general terms only on the basis of race regardless of whether the individuals were thoroughly Canadian in outlook.[8] Eileen Williams (BASc(N) 1936) was a school nurse at Lord Byng public school in Steveston, B.C., at this period. She wrote an intriguing article for *The Canadian Nurse*

in 1941 describing her wonderful experiences in a school where 400 of the
500 students were Japanese. In a compassionate article on what in the 1990s
would be called multicultural nursing, she described the community and its
residents before the orders came for evacuation of the Japanese.[9]

Most Japanese British Columbians had their properties confiscated and
sold. They were forced to evacuate to camps in the interior of British
Columbia or to Alberta and Manitoba where some lived in camps, surrounded by barbed wire, and worked on sugar beet farms or on road building
projects. Only in 1949 were people of Japanese ancestry allowed back to the
west coast[10] and only a few received compensation. Trenna Hunter, who had
graduated from UBC's public health nursing certificate program in 1940 and
who had started working part-time toward her nursing degree at UBC,
worked with Japanese who were being evacuated. She was employed at the
time with the Metropolitan Health Board and Lyle Creelman, who was the
nursing head of that department, asked her if she would work in the
internment camp at Hastings Park. She was subsequently loaned by Metropolitan Health to the B.C. Security Commission.[11]

> My first glimpse of the Japanese was looking into the housing building, which
> was an old livestock building which had just been evacuated by the army. They
> had left behind the normal housing for the army ... the frame beds, and the
> kitchen facility, and of course the washrooms and that sort of thing. Row upon
> row of the beds with the little Japanese families being allotted one or two or
> three beds, to accommodate the size of the families. It just seemed to be a sea of
> people and confusion.[12]

At first, Hastings Park had only about 2,000 Japanese, with the highest
number later going to 3,200. Trenna Hunter first helped organize the living
accommodations and found "matrons" to be in charge of buildings. She then
turned to setting up a hospital area. "When you think about it, it's like a small
town; all the time there's somebody sick." The Japanese women assisted with
sewing and the men with carpentry, developing movable walls so that ward size
could be adjusted according to the numbers of male and female patients.
Equipment was obtained from Shaughnessy Hospital, which received new
equipment and passed along its discards to the internment camp. Just as she
finished setting up the hospital, W.H. Hatfield, who was medical director of
B.C.'s tuberculosis control program at the time, came and said: "This will do
just fine. This will be the TB hospital. We have to move 150 patients out of our
present accommodation because there is so much feeling about the Japanese
occupying scarce beds that we must get them moved."[13]

Trenna Hunter faced the prospect of setting up another hospital, but
decided simply to wall off the original area for tuberculosis and continue the
hospital ward beyond that. This upset some of the Japanese, who were

concerned about the possibility that "germs will come over the top of the wall." She then faced a teaching job in helping them to understand about asepsis. Those patients with tuberculosis were rather happy to be in the camp where they were closer to relatives and friends and had somewhat more freedom than was usually allowed in TB hospitals. The other hospital beds were mainly filled with children, geriatric patients, and some mentally ill patients who previously had been cared for within the family circles. "This camp was set up really for the old people and the children," she recalled. "The able-bodied men were sent to work on the Hope-Princeton road." Although the men and women were segregated into separate buildings, she tried to set aside a section where elderly couples could remain together and look after each other. The biggest problems were childhood contagious diseases – chicken pox, mumps, and both together, although fortunately there was no measles outbreak. Nutritionists from the health department also were drawn in to oversee the nutrition in the camp and to help teach the residents.

About eight Japanese graduate nurses who lived in Vancouver came into the camp to care for patients in the hospital and the few Japanese doctors practicing in Vancouver came out from their offices to donate their time. According to Trenna Hunter, the Japanese in Vancouver were not forced to leave during the first part of the evacuation period; those moved were mainly from Japanese communities up and down the coast.

A few Japanese students at UBC were given deferments and allowed to continue their studies or to transfer to other schools in Canada. Japanese students enrolled in nursing schools also faced discrimination. Kirstine Adam (later Buckland and Griffith) (BASc(N) 1945) recalled that she had a Japanese student as a roommate in the VGH residence at the beginning of their training. Grace Fairley, director of nursing at VGH, arranged for her to transfer to the nursing program at the Montreal General Hospital without any loss of time. Trenna Hunter also recalled receiving a call from Grace Fairley and agreed to take a Japanese nursing student into the hospital at the Hastings Park camp to give her lessons there as field work experience so that the student could graduate from VGH. "We had the smallest nursing school in the world – one student for six months."

By 1941, more than 250,000 Canadian men and 2,000 women were in the forces; this figure was to more than double by the end of the war. Because of the growing shortages of workers, women were entering the work force in great numbers. The west coast ports especially were involved in shipbuilding and aircraft production and, for the first time, women were being hired at good salaries to work in heavy industry; "Rosy the Riveter" became a role model. Although wartime restrictions prohibited strikes, unions became stronger. Organization of unions and the rise of the socialist political parties in B.C. had progressed, albeit slowly, during the Depression; now unions and their workers were in positions to demand better salaries and working conditions. By May 1946, the VGH graduate nurses joined Local 180 of the Hospital Employees Union – and demanded increased pay and shorter hours; minimum pay was $140 a month.[14]

In 1943, the RNABC had formed a committee to look into socioeconomic matters and, in 1946, the association began a comprehensive labour relations program. Many of the nurses did not trust unions and wanted nursing control and involvement. RNABC thus set up a Labour Relations Committee, which negotiated annual collective agreements with the individual hospitals or agencies. During the next 10 years, many major gains were achieved, including increases in salaries and vacation time, the 40-hour week, yearly pay increments, grievance procedures, and a voice in working conditions.[15]

Populations in B.C. cities, especially Vancouver and Victoria, grew rapidly during the war years, leading Victoria's medical health officer to note that practically every available space with a roof was being used.[16] By 1944, Vancouver, Victoria, and New Westminster, among other cities across Canada, were designated "over-populated cities" and people had to prove they had available housing before they could move there.[17] Civil defence units were set up and volunteer inspectors would check the blackout curtains in local neighbourhoods. Victory bonds and victory gardens, shortages, leg makeup (because stockings were unavailable), paper drives, and metal resalvaging were the order of the day. Rationing was imposed, first on gasoline and butter, then on sugar, liquor, coffee, and tea, but few complained; rationing cards and coupons were cheerfully accepted, especially when radio news reports brought the dreadful conditions of the war zones into living rooms.

Kirstine Adam (later Griffith) recalled that the blackouts "were a real headache" because of the big curtains that had to be pulled across the high windows in the large 21-bed wards in the Heather Pavilion at VGH. All the beds had to be shifted so that they were six feet from the walls so the nurses could get at the curtains. "Of course there were no street lights and we used to go down to Nick's, which was the soda fountain on the corner of Broadway and Heather.... I can still remember falling over my feet on the curbs and everything else, as there were no street lights. Everything was blacked out and we weren't allowed to use flashlights."[18]

Throughout the war, enrolment at UBC remained at a steady 2,400.[19] Students already enrolled in the University at the beginning of the war had been advised by the National Research Council to remain in their courses as they would be able to contribute better to the war effort on graduation. Military training on campus became popular and soon there was compulsory military training for all physically fit male students. In 1943, at the request of the Women's Undergraduate Society, a compulsory war work program was instituted for undergraduate women as well.[20] During the 1942-1943 session, each physically fit woman undergraduate on campus was required to take one hour a week of physical military drill; this proved to be the beginning of compulsory physical education on campus.[21] Women students organized voluntary Red Cross work as well and lined up for courses in first aid, home nursing, day nursery, map reading, and motor mechanics. In the 1943-1944 session, Margaret Kerr, who had written a teaching manual on first aid instruction that was published in *The Canadian Nurse*,[22] taught 144 women at UBC in a first aid training course, which Dean of Women Dorothy Mawdsley praised as "outstanding."[23] A modern Armoury (in use on campus until 1993) was erected, the gift of the UBC Canadian Officers' Training Corps (COTC); these student officers had waived their pay allowances so the building might be achieved.[24]

Another important event occupying Nursing faculty at this time was the formation of a Provisional Council of University Schools and Departments of Nursing; "provisional" and "departments" were soon dropped and the Council (or CUSN, as it was known) developed throughout the 1940s and was the precursor to the Canadian Association of University Schools of Nursing (CAUSN). UBC was a founding member of the Council in 1942 and UBC Nursing faculty, including Evelyn Mallory, Beth McCann, and Ruth Morrison, were among the early leaders. Evelyn Mallory, the second president for the years 1948-1952, succeeded Kathleen Ellis, a former director of nursing at VGH who was then with the University of Saskatchewan nursing program.[25]

During the 1942-1943 year at UBC, the Department of Home Economics was re-established and strong public representations were made to the Board of Governors for new departments, schools, or faculties for pharmacy, physical education, and physical medicine. At the same time, some courses in arts and sciences had to be discontinued or deferred because of declining enrolments or because instructors had left to join the forces. L.S. Klinck, who had served as president since 1919, announced his intention to retire and a search began for his replacement. In 1944, Norman ("Larry") MacKenzie took over. That same year, R.E. McKechnie, UBC's chancellor, age 83, died suddenly in May from an infection incurred from a cut obtained while he was performing an operation. Both McKechnie and Klinck had been good friends and strong supporters of the Nursing program, having worked hard for it to be established at UBC in 1919. Eric Hamber became the new chancellor.

Toward the end of the war, there was once again increased interest in the role of public health and, across Canada, increasing demands for well-prepared public health nurses. At UBC, restrictions on enrolment for the Nursing program were lifted and in 1942-1943 the number of registrants in the public health nursing courses increased by 50 per cent over any previous year. The problem was to provide suitable field work experience for this large number of students. Geraldine Homfray Langton, who was instructing in the

UBC program, and Isabel Chodat (later Petrie) (BASc(N) 1935), senior health nurse with Metropolitan Health, wrote an article for *The Canadian Nurse* describing UBC's innovative plan for field experiences. Students were sent to only one or two placements, but for longer periods and under the mentorship of a staff nurse. In a new course, called Introduction to Family Health Service, they were assigned four families in which they assessed "the medical, behaviour, social and economic aspects of family health."[26]

There were changes, too, in the Nursing faculty at this time. Mary Henderson left at the end of the 1943-1944 academic year to accept an appointment as a supervisor of public health nursing with the United Nations Relief and Rehabilitation Administration (UNRRA). There she worked with many other UBC nursing graduates, as mentioned in Chapter 3. Margaret Kerr also left UBC to take over as editor of *The Canadian Nurse* from Ethel Johns, who was retiring. She was replaced by Pauline (Polly) Capelle, who held a double degree from UBC (BA 1938, BASc(N) 1939) and who had recently been the Supervisor of Nursing with the Division of Venereal Disease Control with the Provincial Board of Health.

By early 1945, the end of the war was predicted; Germany surrendered on May 7 and Japan on September 2. Mary Hicks (later Cumming) (BASc(N) 1945) recalled that Miss Gray, who had retired in 1941, entertained the eight members of the graduating class at a tea party. "It turned out to be V-E [Victory in Europe] Day. The brave soul drove us along Granville Street in all that mob."[27] In the spring of 1945, in an effort to prevent wars in future, 46 nations, including Canada, sent representatives to San Francisco to form a world body and, after nine weeks of work, the United Nations was created.

A significant piece of social legislation was passed by the Canadian Parliament in 1944, when the House of Commons approved the Family Allowances Act; this introduced a monthly "baby bonus" for all children under age 18. Canada now had an old age pension scheme and a baby bonus, and, once again, compulsory insurance to help protect citizens from the high costs of illness was being discussed.

WARTIME CHANGES IN NURSING

The wartime shortages of workers in every field affected nursing as well. Many nurses were serving overseas, but now women had other chances for employment and nursing schools had to compete with other sectors to attract applicants. Many schools of nursing followed a recommendation by the Canadian Nurses Association that courses be "accelerated" and, in early 1943, the Vancouver General reduced the length of its program to 28 months from 36.[28] As well, senior students at VGH were allowed to live away from the residence, if they could obtain written permission from their parents. For the VGH students, courses in preliminary and first year terms were reduced;

many repetitive service experiences, such as cleaning rubber gloves, were cut, so educational standards were not affected. In the senior year, the students were given more responsibility, their stipend was increased, and they were called "staff students." For the university students in the degree program, the theory remained unchanged and their practice was condensed into 30 months, with the last two months as "staff students."[29] Federal government grants to schools of nursing, administered by CNA, allowed schools such as VGH to hire additional instructors.[30] As well, because of the need for staff, hospitals had to try to attract married nurses back into the work force. Because of demands of homes and families, hospital authorities no longer could require these women to live in residences. Many single graduates also took the opportunity to move out of hospital dormitories. However, living costs for these nurses now were much higher, so they began to demand higher wages and shorter hours.

Grace Fairley, who was still director of nursing at VGH, had been elected president of the Canadian Nurses Association in 1938. With the outbreak of the war, she was appointed Matron-in-Chief of the Royal Canadian Army Medical Corps. Although the position was largely honorary, it involved considerable administration as well as support for recruitment of nurses for overseas duty. Canadian nurses quickly volunteered for service, but although hundreds sought to enlist, the Medical Corps at first could take only a few because of a lack of field hospitals overseas. As a result, about 300 Canadian nurses joined the South African Nursing Services so they could get into the war zones earlier.[31] As most of Europe had fallen to German forces, the Allied wounded were cared for mainly in Britain under the British medical command. Soon, however, Canadian nurses began to be sent to England and many staffed emergency hospital quarters set up in England's stately homes. After the Allied forces again achieved bases in Europe, Canadian field hospitals became recognized internationally for their excellent front-line care. As in World War I, nurses were revered as heroines. By the end of the war, more than 3,000 Canadian nurses had served with the forces both overseas and in Canada.[32]

Canadian nurses also were concerned about care of nurses who had become prisoners of war both in Europe and in civilian prison camps in Hong Kong and Singapore.[33] The first head of UBC's Nursing department, Ethel Johns, at this time editor of *The Canadian Nurse*, was appointed to the U.S. National Nursing Council for War Service.[34] As CNA president, Grace Fairley expressed concern that standards of care not deteriorate during the war years because of the shortages of nurses. The use of nursing assistants (called "non-professional workers") re-emerged during this era and both Britain and the United States began programs for these aides.[35] Medical orderlies and ambulance attendants had proven practical in field hospitals in the war areas, and nursing aides soon were being tried in hospitals across Canada as well, as Evelyn Mallory described in an article in 1942.[36]

NURSING AT UBC TO 1951

During the war years, enrolments in Nursing at UBC grew steadily. Although numbers in the degree program did not increase markedly, those in the one-year certificate programs, both teaching and supervision and, especially, public health, more than doubled compared to the Mabel Gray years. Immediately following the war, however, enrolments in Nursing, as in other departments of the University, exploded. As the war drew to a close, the Canadian government provided financial assistance for education for returning veterans, and universities across Canada, including UBC, declared their doors open to all qualified veterans. During the last year of the war, disabled veterans were returning and enrolling in courses and, at the end of the war, many service personnel, including nurses, took advantage of this assistance to take their degrees during the late 1940s. In 1943-1944, registration in Nursing was 67; in the 1944-1945 session it was 112; in 1945-1946, it was 128; in 1946-1947, it was 145, of which 52 were Department of Veterans' Affairs students.

Tuition fees for first year nursing students in 1943-1944 were $173, which included the registration fee of $5, two sessional fees of $75, an Alma Mater fee of $13, and a "caution fee" of $5. This latter, which was not unique to Nursing, was a fund to cover possible breakage of laboratory equipment. Students were advised that costs for a year on campus – including board, living accommodation, travel expenses, and tuition fees – would be about $700.[37]

Students of this period were extraordinarily proud of their UBC program and many of the graduates from the wartime years continued on to graduate education and remained active in nursing throughout their lifetimes.[38] Dorothy Ladner (BASc(N) 1944) obtained her master's in public health from the University of Pittsburgh in 1965. She spent most of her working life in public health. She said that she became "committed to prevention" during her work with children in her hospital experiences at UBC and throughout her career believed that prevention should have greater priority. Among her career moves was a period as executive director of the Lower Fraser Valley Cerebral Palsy Association. She later operated a children's care unit that eventually became the Variety Club's treatment centre. About her student years, she recalled studying in the locker room in the basement of the old Science building because the Library was so crowded. She particularly liked the opportunities for working closely with students in other science disciplines, despite the overcrowded facilities.

Margaret M. Campbell (later Jackson) (BASc(N) 1942) appreciated the program's "broad base in the sciences." She recalled that at the time it seemed a long course, but it "proved a solid and valuable base on which to build subsequent working and educational experience." She went on to take her master's in public health at the University of Michigan, Ann Arbor, in 1949.

One of her classmates in the master's program was another UBC graduate, Mary Ross (BASc(N) 1943). She became coordinator of the community health nursing unit in Burnaby from 1952 to 1976. She recalled that during her campus years and immediately after the students did a great deal of volunteer work for the war effort, such as Red Cross blood donor clinics, civil defence exercises, and teaching first aid.

Janet C. Pallister (later Bailey) (DipPHN 1942) worked as staff nurse and supervisor in various health units in B.C. following graduation. She then went to McGill and later joined the Alberta Department of Health, where she eventually was Director of Public Health Nursing for that province for 14 years until her retirement in 1976.[39]

Use of blood transfusions had increased greatly during the war. The first blood donation from Vancouver to be sent overseas occurred in 1941. The war accelerated the introduction of new medical advances, including the discovery of the Rh factor and the trial of new drugs. Penicillin was the "wonder drug" of the war years and saved thousands of lives that might formerly have been lost to infections. Near the end of the war, streptomycin was discovered and became the second major drug, especially because it was effective against the tubercle bacillus. Cortisone as an effective treatment for arthritis was another of the amazing discoveries of the immediate postwar period. In 1949, the "artificial kidney" machine was introduced into Vancouver's major hospitals and, because of the discovery of heparin, dialysis, which had been first suggested in 1913, finally became a practical treatment for patients with reversible acute uremia.[40]

The students of the early 1940s recall their years in residence at VGH as strict and confining. Marjorie Eileen Staniforth (later Wisbey) (BASc(N) 1941) recalled the strict policy regarding late leaves and remaining in residence. One day when she did not go on duty until late afternoon, she got up early and went home, only to be accused of sleeping away from the residence. "Even though I explained, my word was not good enough. In that era, the student had very little status of any kind." She also recalled one of her classmates getting into trouble because she recommended that the uniform have short sleeves so that those removable cuffs would not have to be put on whenever a doctor was present.[41]

Kirstine Adam (later Griffith) remembered that there was no allowance for sick time for students in those days and that you had to make up every day off ill before you could graduate. Mary H. Wilkinson (later Carty) (BASc(N) 1946) recalled, too, that students had few late leaves and so some slipped in and out the fire escape doors when they had a chance. She summed up this strict policy as "incredibly stupid discipline for mature students."[42]

Memories of clinical placements in these years were particularly vivid. Stories of the psychiatry rotation at Essondale reveal intense memories of the poor treatment regimes of the era. This was a period before introduction of tranquillizer medications and patients received mainly custodial care. Trenna Hunter summarized these experiences as "gruesome." Kirstine Adam (later Griffith) related the story of the first death she saw as a student. "An 18-year-old girl died in my arms from TB." During her senior year, she worked in the Infectious Disease Hospital (IDH) wards and remembers the first antibiotics given at VGH. She was responsible for supervising intravenous antibiotics for syphilitic patients. On another ward, most of the patients had kidney complications resulting from administration of sulphonamide drugs; no one had realized that the new sulfa drugs formed crystals in the urine if patients were not forced to drink enormous volumes of fluids. Surgical experiences also were often heavy as patients were confined to bed rest for long periods postoperatively. When Kirstine Adam had her appendix removed, she was not allowed out of bed even on the sixth day. She also recalled that hernia patients were nursed flat on their backs with no pillows and were not allowed to sit up for seven days following surgery and not allowed out of bed for 21 days.[43]

The increasing enrolments at the end of the war placed great strain on university facilities, including the Library, which was seriously overcrowded. The military organizations in B.C. donated army and air force "huts" that had been used in camps during the war. The huts were transported to UBC and provided 37 new classrooms for 4,000 students, including nursing students. Other huts were set up as "temporary" quarters for laboratories and support services, such as reading rooms, student club offices, and "snack shops."

Evelyn Mallory recalled that, before the move to the huts, Nursing had to compete for space in the old Science building. Nursing's single assigned classroom was in almost constant use, but Robert H. Clarke of the Chemistry department constantly booked his classes into it "without any consideration for Nursing." Evelyn Mallory made an impassioned written plea to the administration for more accommodation. Some funds were obtained through the Pan American Sanitary Commission to assist with the Nursing request. The Department of Nursing and Health moved in 1946 from its overcrowded quarters in the Science building to the "Orchard Huts."

When the department moved into the huts, Nursing was given its own secretary for the first time. Marjorie Longley replaced Isobel Todd, who had been the part-time nursing secretary for 16 years. Describing the move years later, Evelyn Mallory said that Nursing "got the only secretary, the only typewriter, and ... the only old Ford available in the city – war shortages being a cramping feature of life."[44] A serious fire in the early morning hours of November 25, 1948, threatened the Orchard huts when the Psychology classrooms, in the huts just behind Nursing, burned to the ground. The Nursing huts were scorched and flooded by fire hoses, but otherwise undamaged. Four days later the Nursing faculty were able to use the offices and classrooms once again.[45]

Figure 4.2　In 1946, Nursing moved from the Science building, renamed Chemistry, to the Orchard huts, former army barracks. These facilities were crowded and inadequate, but students found postwar campus life exciting.

Figure 4.3　Class of 1950 in front of one of the Orchard huts.
L-R: Shelagh (Wheeler) Smith, Dorothy (Byers) Logan, Vera Wood,
Ada George, Beryl Robinson.

Lorna Horwood, who was teaching in the program at this time, credited the close quarters in the huts with creating opportunities for Nursing. The architecture students were in an adjacent hut and the Nursing and Architecture faculty developed joint activities for their students. For example, they worked together on design of modern maternity wards and other such projects.[46] Students of this period were encouraged to establish professional links and to take an active professional role, including writing for the nursing journals. Several UBC students published in *The Canadian Nurse* during this time. For example, Elizabeth Scoones (BASc(N), 1947) wrote up her student experience with the VON for the student page in 1945, stressing the value of home visiting experience for all nurses.[47]

Despite the crowded and inadequate facilities, students recall that the program was exciting and stimulating. "Because of the people – war veterans attending UBC were very adult – the facilities mattered little and the atmosphere was everything," Betty Pullen (later Hall) (BSN 1952) remembered. "The opportunity to learn was of higher priority than fancy buildings – people (students and staff) ranked above the physical plant," said Caroline Livingstone (later Stacey) (BASc(N) 1950).[48] Students recall the emphasis on a broad liberal education, with introduction to the new Canadian novelists and poets, such as W.O. Mitchell, Robertson Davies, and Earle Birney. Eric Nicol was on campus and had written a play for the UBC Players' Club. UBC Professor Freddie Wood and Joy Coghill, respectively husband and friend of Beatrice Johnson Wood (one of Nursing's first three graduates), were making drama history in Canada.

A "Nursing D" program was initiated in 1945-1946 to make it easier for graduate nurses to obtain degrees. They had to have university entrance qualifications, but the program enabled them to complete their degrees in three academic years on campus. Those who had taken either the public health or teaching and supervision certificate were given credit for some of these courses and were able to complete the degree program in two years.

In 1949, the Senate approved introduction of a Department of University Extension, which began organizing correspondence and evening courses.[49] This allowed students in other parts of the province to take credit courses toward their degrees. Nursing students also could take advantage of this new opportunity. This move proved to be the beginning of the distance education programs of the 1980s and 1990s.

Housing during the postwar period was extremely scarce. The influx of veterans, including many couples with children, filled any possible accommodation, including tent and trailer sites set up on campus and on Little Mountain and Lulu Island. This emergency dormitory housing led to pressures for better accommodations on campus, especially for single women. The Fort Camp and Acadia residences, including three buildings for women, opened at the end of this period.

Figure 4.4   The F.F. Wesbrook building opened in 1951 on the corner of
University Boulevard and East Mall. Named for UBC's first president, it housed
Bacteriology, Preventive Medicine, the School of Nursing, Student Health
Services, and a 26-bed infirmary, mainly for students.

Figure 4.5   Students' common room in Wesbrook; note the sparse furnishings.
This was a favorite meeting place for lunch or bridge and sometimes for study.
The Nursing Undergraduate Society raised funds to try to improve it.

Between 1945 and 1951, a massive building campaign was launched at UBC, leading to 20 new permanent buildings, including a new North Wing of the Library. The F.F. Wesbrook Building, which opened in 1951, was named for UBC's first president and housed Bacteriology, Preventive Medicine, Nursing, and a centre for the UBC student health service that included a 26-bed hospital. Five new faculties emerged during this time, including Law (1945), Graduate Studies (1948), Medicine (1949), Pharmacy (1951), and Forestry (elevated from a department in 1951).[50] As well, Nursing and three other departments (Social Work, Physical Education, Architecture) lobbied for and achieved independent status as Schools.[51]

The move to "schools" rather than "departments" occurred because the University wanted to recognize those fields that had professional relationships and field work experiences with outside agencies. As well, there was a need for the University to give stronger status to the heads of these departments, although technically the heads still reported to the dean of one of the few UBC faculties. UBC has a long tradition of keeping its faculties few in number, in contrast with other universities in Canada.

Nursing's move to school status was also prompted by several other events. For example, the Registered Nurses Association of B.C. was anxious for the program to develop links with other hospitals and develop a central teaching program, as originally had been suggested in the Ethel Johns years. Grace Fairley had retired in 1943 as director of nursing at VGH and Elinor Palliser was her replacement. Elinor Palliser had graduated from the Johns Hopkins School of Nursing in 1921 and had certificates in teaching and in administration of nursing schools from McGill. As well, she had worked as instructor or as assistant superintendent in large Ontario hospitals. Both Evelyn Mallory and Elinor Palliser had ideas, sometimes conflicting, about development of their respective educational programs.

Evelyn Mallory was extremely active in nursing politics at this time and was conversant with the professional goals for university nursing education. She had been honorary secretary of the Canadian Nurses Association in the mid-1940s and in 1946 became second vice-president, and she was president of RNABC from 1945 to 1949. As well, the newly-formed organization for university programs for nursing was beginning to work on standards for curriculums and to talk about the importance of nursing faculty fully controlling the clinical portions of programs.

In 1949, a Senate committee, under Walter Gage, dean of Arts, was appointed to consider the whole matter of university nursing education at UBC. This 31-member committee had representatives from the Senate and administration, the Department of Nursing and Health, other university departments, the nursing profession, hospitals, and the public. Several of the nursing representatives were UBC graduates, including Monica Frith, director of public health nursing for B.C., Esther Paulson, supervisor of nursing,

TB Control, Trenna Hunter, director of nursing for the Metropolitan Health Committee, and Muriel Upshall, UBC Student Health Services.[52]

Other organizational arrangements were going on in the University at the same time. C.E. Dolman became head of a reorganized Department of Bacteriology and Immunology. He had anticipated the need to have a nurse as head of the Nursing department and he recalled in an interview years later that the new president, Norman MacKenzie, also believed that Nursing should be headed by a nurse. C.E. Dolman recalled that he often wondered why it took Nursing so long to get academic qualifications and noted that nurses held seminar after seminar to examine "what was nursing?" He wondered why nurses kept questioning the importance of their profession.[53]

The new Faculty of Medicine, under Dean Myron Weaver, opened in 1950, and had, as one of its many departments, Public Health, with Lawrence E. Ranta replacing C.E. Dolman as head. The possibility was raised that Nursing should be under the umbrella of the Faculty of Medicine rather than remaining in the Faculty of Applied Science. The medical men were shocked and surprised that Nursing did not want to come under Medicine. Lorna Horwood, a Nursing faculty member at this time, told Beth McCann that she recalled that a member of the Senate committee stated: "Lorna, it never occurred to me that you wouldn't want to come under medicine.... It has just been assumed."[54] Strong support for Nursing's independence from Medicine was given by the RNABC member, Alice Wright, and other influential members on the committee, including Sally Murphy Creighton of the UBC Senate; as a result, the School of Nursing remained under the Faculty of Applied Science.

Because of reductions in budgets in 1949-1950, Evelyn Mallory had planned a one-year unpaid leave; she was granted a bursary from the W.K. Kellogg Foundation to complete her master of arts degree at Columbia. Before she left, Evelyn Mallory submitted a brief from the faculty to the committee, outlining weaknesses of the existing program; as well, she remained in close touch with the committee.

After a year of study, the Senate approved recommendations brought forward by its committee:

1. That the Department of Nursing and Health be reconstituted as a semi-autonomous School.
2. That a qualified nurse be appointed as a full-time Director of the School.
3. That the distinctive degree of Bachelor of Science in Nursing [BSN] replace the degree of B.A.Sc.(Nsg) formerly conferred on graduates in Nursing.[55]

As well, the School was authorized to review arrangements with Vancouver General Hospital and to explore and consider with other appropriate and

Figure 4.6   School of Nursing faculty, 1954, taken in front of the
old faculty club. L-R: Evelyn Mallory, Ruth Morrison, Margaret Duncan,
Beth McCann, Polly Capelle, Lorna Horwood.

interested agencies both new programs for graduate nurses and the development of a more effective comprehensive basic program.

During the committee sessions, there was brief discussion about the
possibility of Nursing becoming a faculty in its own right. One reason the
idea for a Faculty of Nursing did not gain support was lack of academically
qualified faculty.

Evelyn Mallory was just back from receiving her master's degree, but
several other of those in the School of Nursing had not yet received even this
preparation. The lack of faculty members prepared with master's and doctoral degrees was not unique to Nursing at UBC. At the time, there were no
master's programs in nursing in Canada and few even in the U.S. The W.K.
Kellogg Foundation, which had been established by the breakfast food
magnate in 1930, began directing considerable funding in the late 1940s and
early 1950s to assist in the preparation of nurses for university faculty
positions.[56] UBC Nursing faculty received between $10,000 and $11,000 in
Kellogg fellowships or other financial assistance in the late 1940s; the early
awards went to Evelyn Mallory ($3,900), Margaret Duncan, Pauline Capelle,
and Beth McCann.[57] Other financial assistance from Kellogg to UBC Nursing faculty included fellowships in the early 1950s to Lorna Horwood and a
second one to Beth McCann. These grants enabled faculty to achieve at least
master's level preparation. Many academic critics were quick to point out
that this level of preparation still was not equal to that required for faculty
members in other university departments.

THE SCHOOL OF NURSING IN THE 1950S

Evelyn Mallory's new title was Professor and Director of the School of Nursing and, beginning in the 1952-1953 year, the basic program took five years once again. Students needed the equivalent of first year Arts and Science before entering the four-year program in the School of Nursing (one year on campus, two years in hospital, and a final year on campus). The faculty at UBC assumed greater responsibility for clinical components during the first year in Nursing (that is, the second year on campus) and some subjects previously taught during the preliminary term at VGH were incorporated into this year. A nursing laboratory was established in the new Wesbrook building and an introductory "nursing arts" course introduced. As well, students returned to campus at the end of their first year at VGH for introductory courses in human growth and development, public health nursing (including some home visiting), and history of nursing. The School was attempting to have greater control of its students throughout the program, including the clinical years.

Changes were also made in the final year of the program for those entering in September 1954. The final year "options" of either teaching and supervision or public health were discontinued and a general program was taken by all students. This included field work in public health, in teaching and supervision, and in a new four-week administration experience in a small hospital. This latter continued until 1961. The philosophy of the School was that the degree program should prepare a well-grounded professional nurse with a solid liberal education. Graduates were to be able to practice both in care of the sick and in promotion of physical and mental health, and care for families as well as individuals either in homes and hospitals or through other community agencies.[58]

During this time, the School initiated evening classes for graduate nurses to provide greater flexibility and attract working nurses. Evelyn Mallory had long been concerned about the need to move nursing education into tax-supported educational institutions. As president of RNABC, she had spoken vigorously about the need for expansion of nursing education programs and the need to look beyond hospitals "as the only right and possible way" for students to be prepared.[59] Under her direction, the UBC School established a policy whereby graduate nurses could enrol as part-time students under certain conditions. In 1951-1952, three part-time students registered for an evening course; in 1952-1953, there were 35.[60]

One big change for students when they entered the hospital portion of the generic program in the 1950s was improvement in residence life. The new student nurses' residence at VGH opened in December 1950 (and was finally completed in 1952) – with private rooms rather than dormitories or double rooms. With the increased residence accommodation, the VGH school became the largest in Canada, and VGH, which was going through a

Figure 4.7   The new eight-storey student residence at VGH opened in
1950 on the southwest corner of 12th Avenue and Heather Street. It had single
rooms for 575 students and contained the VGH School of Nursing offices, library,
classrooms, and other facilities. Since 1940, classes had been held in the old
UBC Auditorium. Students moved out of the old nurses' homes with strong
feelings of nostalgia. In 1993, the residence closed permanently and was
scheduled for demolition.

Figure 4.8   Senior Tea, for students who had received their black bands and
white shoes and stockings, was held in one of the lounges in the residence at
VGH. This is a picture of the class of 1958 with Beverly DuGas, Director
Nursing Education, pouring. The tea was a tradition and these rites
of passage were important events in the lives of the UBC students.

building boom, opened several new buildings and additions and became the largest hospital (in numbers of patients) in Canada.[61]

Vancouver itself had continued to prosper during the postwar years as demands increased for B.C.'s natural resources of lumber, fish, coal, aluminum and other metals, and water (for hydroelectric power sold to the U.S.). Although the war was over, new tensions grew between the Soviet Union and the United States in what became known as the "Cold War." Even UBC considered courses in civil defence. A 12-hour course in Nursing Aspects of ABC Defence, the responsibility of Pauline Capelle, was taught to students and faculty alike as part of a provincial civil defence program.[62] The North Atlantic Treaty Organization (NATO) was formed in 1949 at the start of a period of strong anti-communist feeling, led in the U.S. by Senator Joseph McCarthy. Vancouverites also were caught in the hysteria over possible invasion or nuclear war between the U.S. and the U.S.S.R. and Canada's first backyard nuclear bomb shelter was built in 1950. That year was also the start of the Korean War (June 1950 – July 1953), to which Canada sent troops and nurses. A Canadian field hospital remained in Korea following the war, as part of United Nations' forces. Canada also sent nurses to Europe with the NATO program and established its first army base in Germany in 1953.

Vancouver grew during the 1950s, especially in new suburban areas on the North Shore and in the former farm areas of the Fraser delta in Richmond, Delta, Surrey, and Langley. The automobile became the most important method of transport. In 1952, a new provincial political party, the Social Credit Party under W.A.C. Bennett, crept into power in a minority government. In the 1955 election, Social Credit became entrenched, largely on promises of improved road, rail, and ferry transportation throughout the province. With a campaign involving the building of bridges and highways, including the Deas Island Tunnel, the party capitalized on the whole wave of international economic prosperity and a commitment to free enterprise; British Columbians had a decade of "the good life."[63]

Health insurance programs had long been suggested in B.C., despite strong opposition from the medical community, and had even been supported by a referendum in 1937. Coalition governments of the 1940s in B.C. began to enact legislation leading to hospital insurance. In 1949, the B.C. Hospital Insurance Service program, based on individual contributions, was passed, but became an administrative nightmare. In 1952, the Social Credit government replaced premium collections with a tax base, supported by a sales tax, thus ensuring universal coverage. When in 1957 the federal government enacted a national hospital insurance program, in which it would pay half the costs of hospital care, B.C. became one of the five founding provinces. Although medical coverage was not yet assured and most families required private medical plans, hospitals for the first time had stable budgets provided through the provincial ministries. Although this was not the intention of the government plans, the move resulted in more emphasis on hospital-based care and decreased emphasis on public health and community care. Money suddenly poured into hospitals, a change in focus that greatly affected the education of nurses.

This focus on clinical, hospital nursing had begun in the 1940s, prompted by shortages of hospital nurses during the war. At that time, the Canadian Nurses Association and the Canadian Red Cross Society had funded a special demonstration school in Windsor, Ontario, to determine whether clinical nurses could be prepared in shorter programs. The Metropolitan School prepared diploma nurses in two years rather than three because the school was under educational control and students were not used to provide service in return for their education. This proved a prototype for the move to two-year nursing programs in community colleges throughout Canada, although the first two-year programs in B.C. did not open until 1967.

The federal hospital insurance plan was not the only new social legislation. In January 1952, a new federal Old Age Security Act provided universal pensions for those aged 70 and older and the Old Age Assistance Act provided pensions to needy people aged 65 and older.

A serious epidemic of poliomyelitis, formerly called infantile paralysis, broke out in B.C. in 1954, eventually leading to 787 cases and 26 deaths.[64] As there were no preventive measures or any effective treatment, nurses faced challenges both during acute phases and in continuing rehabilitation. Most patients developed some form of paralysis and often had muscle spasms during the acute period. "Hot packs" (compresses), massage, and muscle stimulation were routine aspects of nursing care. Severe cases were nursed in "iron lung" machines, which were required for those with respiratory paralysis. Whole wards of polio patients confronted UBC students taking their Infectious Diseases Hospital rotations. Immunization was not available for the 1954 epidemic, but in 1955 Canada began a mass immunization program using a new vaccine developed by Jonas Salk. In 1956, more than 100,000 persons in B.C. were vaccinated in a massive public health program aimed especially at school children. By the end of the 1950s, vaccination was available for all those under age 19 and the end of polio was in sight. In 1962, the Sabin oral polio vaccine was developed and replaced the earlier injections.

Other scientific advances during the 1950s included introduction of television. The Canadian Broadcasting Corporation (CBC) began its television service in 1953. In the same year, scientists finally determined the structure of deoxyribonucleic acid (DNA), which in 1944 a Canadian scientist had identified as the carrier of hereditary material in cells; this discovery paved the way for great advances in understanding of the processes of life. A major advance in nursing care at the beginning of the 1950s was introduction of postanesthetic recovery rooms (PARRs); patients went to these special care units rather than returning immediately to the ward and requiring a nurse, usually a student, to

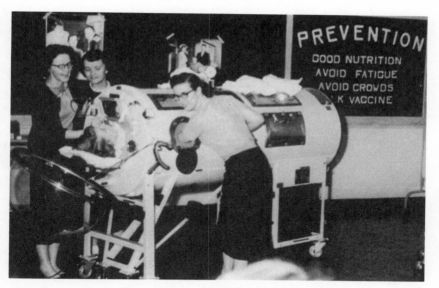

Figure 4.9   School of Nursing Open House, 1955. The theme was prevention of poliomyelitis. Note student in the iron lung. Salk vaccine was available in Canada in 1955 and a mass immunization program was undertaken. Over the years faculty and students have participated in Open House events. Thousands of school children and the public visit the campus.

stay at the bedside. Doreen Pope (BASc(N) 1950) recalled being the first student in the PARR when it was first set up at VGH.[65] A new "heart-lung machine," to maintain heart and lung functions during heart operations, allowed VGH to begin open heart surgery in 1956. In 1959, VGH opened the $8 million, 10-storey, 504-bed Centennial Pavilion; it had 18 ORs and new main kitchens as well as six floors of acute care beds.

STUDENT RECOLLECTIONS OF THE 1950S

The struggle between the UBC and VGH administrations over curricular changes of the 1950s went largely unnoticed by students, who were not, at that time, consulted about such matters. Class sizes had grown fairly steadily, with the degree program admitting about 20 students on average during the early 1950s and during the later part of the decade averaging about 40. This growth further strained UBC-VGH relations. UBC students at VGH were aware of some jealousy over the fact that they were receiving a fuller educational program, with strong support from their own UBC faculty and preferential rotations that gave better integration of theory and practice. These feelings usually were not directed toward individuals, but were divisive within classes. However, the degree students "carried on," and, later, most

Figure 4.10   UBC students assigned to the milk lab at VGH were
required to make infant formula and glucose water. It had to be siphoned
into baby bottles.

students reflected that UBC faculty had been highly protective and determined to make the best of the final years at VGH.

Although the educational program was much better controlled than in
earlier periods, students during the 1950s still gave large amounts of service to
the hospital. For example, students working nights in their maternity rotation were assigned to the "Milk Lab," where they had to prepare large
volumes of formula for the newborns. Women during the 1950s were far more
apt to bottle feed rather than breast feed and students were charged with
sterilizing bottles and, using the hospital's recipes, preparing formula and
glucose water, and siphoning these into bottles. This was a time before
prepared infant formula, total parenteral nutrition (TPR), and enteral diets.
Students provided service in the diet kitchens during the evenings by making
sandwiches and "evening nourishments" (such as eggnogs and milkshakes)
for patients who were on therapeutic diets and needed extra calories.

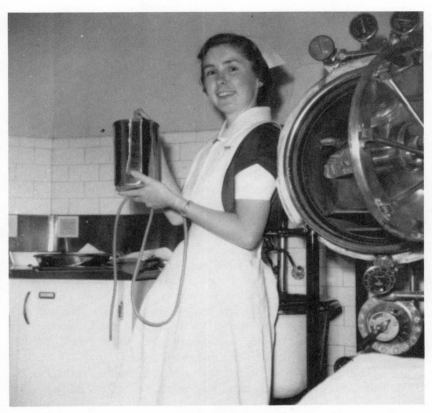

Figure 4.11   Elizabeth Robertson (BSN 1958) in the service room,
Heather Pavilion VGH. Note the autoclave on the right. Students had to
wash and sterilize equipment such as dressing trays. On busy shifts,
this meant staying late to tidy up.

Students also spent long hours working in central supply and service rooms
washing and sterilizing equipment and supplies, such as dressing trays,
tracheostomy sets, catheters, glass syringes, and equipment for patients'
lockers (stainless steel – or, in older wards, enamel – bedpans, basins, and
kidney dishes). Housekeeping staff were more common, and were responsible
for the cleaning of floors and bedside units during day shifts, but sterilization
and infection control were considered nurses' responsibilities and were too
important to be delegated. Beth Walton (later Fitzpatrick) (BSN 1955)
recalled checking the steel needles for burrs. "There seemed to be more stress
on the equipment because you had to use it again and you had to know what
every part was for.... We had to do a lot of cleaning of equipment and
cleaning of the environment.... I still go into a patient's bedside unit and

think 'this needs to be cleaned up.' You have to restrain yourself from cleaning up their bedside tables."[66]

Although instruction about nursing care was based on principles, students still had to follow some rather rigid rules. For example, rules for bed making were strictly enforced by VGH teachers and staff, and students recall one VGH instructor who used to get underneath the bed to be certain the corners were mitred correctly.[67] Leaving the bed casters sticking out, rather than carefully turned in so that the bed was more stationary and so staff would not trip over them, was a mortal sin.

Many of the medications had to be mixed or diluted and many intramuscular injections were drawn from stock bottles. Hypodermic injections were prepared by the nurses on the floors. Narcotics (morphine and codeine) were in tablet form and had to be dissolved in distilled water, using a spoon over an alcohol lamp. The solution was then drawn up in a slippery glass syringe. Near the end of the 1950s, disposable equipment was beginning to be used, but was considered too expensive for general use.

Students also had to learn "fractional dosages" so they could adapt standard doses to meet the needs of smaller or weaker patients and children. All measurement was in the apothecary system of grains, drams, and ounces, although the metric system was just being introduced into hospitals and nurses had to learn both and how to switch from one system to another. Ada George (BSN 1950) had become "the materia medica instructor" at VGH and was famous for her drug quizzes and math drills.

The operating room was one of the most memorable experiences for students of the 1950s. Students recall long evening practice sessions on OR set-ups, draping, and sterile techniques during off-duty hours. Nevertheless, despite the routine, graduates frequently say that they really learned the principles of asepsis and sterile technique. Beth Walton remembers "the thrills in the OR and having a chance to scrub with famous surgeons such as Rocke Robertson and being first assistant for abdominal perineal resections."[68] On the other hand, Alice Baumgart (BSN 1958), later a president of CNA, recollects "some of the nonsense that was perpetrated upon us." When she was taking her OR experience, a prominent surgeon, the father of a classmate, brought in some reference material for her student presentation. She was "reamed out for presuming to approach a senior surgeon for information.... From that moment on, I understood how dysfunctional the hierarchical boundaries could be."[69]

Despite the civilizing influence of the introduction of tranquilizers and other psychotropic agents, psychiatric nursing rotations continued to appal many of the UBC students. Elizabeth Robertson (BSN 1958), who later was a faculty member at the University of Alberta and then at UBC for several years, recalled seeing her first electroconvulsive therapy (ECT), also called electric shock treatment. She described it, at the

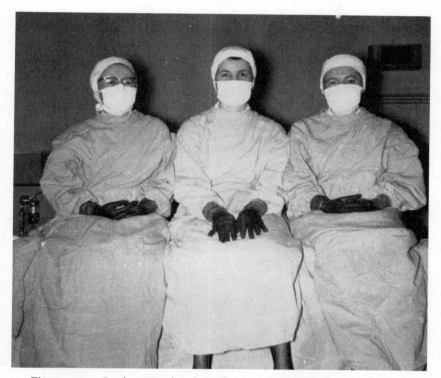

Figure 4.12   Students in the class of 1958 scrubbed and ready for their operating room experience. UBC students spent hours in the evenings practicing draping and OR setups for the next day.

time, in a letter from Essondale back to her classmates at VGH, as "barbaric."[70]

Ann-Shirley Gordon (later Goodell) (BSN 1960) termed her rotation at Essondale as "horrendous."

> I hated it. We had very poor preparation. My first day in the unit we were being oriented by some nurses from Essondale. A group of us were told to go into that room and help them, so we went in not knowing what we were doing and they had a person on a table and each of us were told to hold an arm and leg. What they were doing was shock therapy and I had never seen a grande mal seizure in my life. I had no idea of what was going on. It was a nightmare experience for me.[71]

Ann-Shirley Gordon Goodell also recalled her pediatric rotation. "I loved afternoons, because I always liked it when families came in. The routine was different. We had more time to spend with families.... and [I] believed that

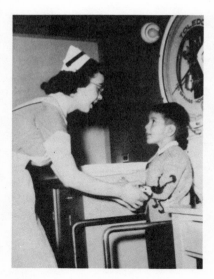

Figure 4.13

Pediatric experience for Arlene Aish (BSN 1958) in the Health Centre for Children. In the early years, this experience was at the Infants Hospital on Haro Street and Heather Pavilion. In 1954, the Health Centre opened in the renovated Semiprivate Pavilion on 12th Avenue.

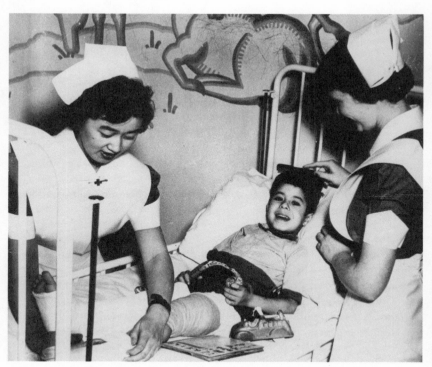

Figure 4.14   Pediatric nursing in the Health Centre for Children. This was a memorable experience for many students.

what we were doing was so wrong. We were telling parents to go home and leave their children and *not* visit because they upset their children when they came in.... Today that's just unbelievable." She did her graduating essay – a major, thesis-like nursing study given as a one-unit course during this era – on "The Psychosocial Adjustment of Children to Hospitalization." When she graduated, she wanted to continue this study on play therapy and went as an assistant head nurse to a pediatric hospital in Cincinnati that offered such programs. She married there and remained in the U.S. for 22 years, taking her master's degree in nursing with emphasis on pediatrics. When she returned to Canada, it was to become the nursing director of British Columbia's Children's Hospital. She later became Executive Director of the B.C. Division of the Multiple Sclerosis Society of Canada and, in 1992, began pursuing doctoral studies at UBC.

When Ann-Shirley Goodell was in her fourth nursing year, she and her classmates taught the first group of UBC students at St. Paul's as part of their teaching and supervision course. "That was quite challenging.... Here we were, fifth year students, learning to teach in a whole new milieu with a group of students who were going through the initiation of being the first group in a different environment to take their clinical practice. It was a good experience."[72] Student field work experiences during their final years included teaching and supervision, public health, and a small hospital experience. The three one-month experiences were given in January, May, and June. For the small hospital experience, most of the students went to the West Coast General Hospital in Port Alberni,[73] although in later years Surrey Memorial Hospital also was used for this rotation. As a result, the January period meant that many of the students were away from campus and missed non-nursing courses, which could not be rescheduled. Because of this, the School of Nursing once again began to look into curriculum changes.

During the 1950s, the School began taking a major role in the UBC "Open House," which was held once every three years to publicize the value of the University to the community. Waverlie Watson (later Warila) (BASc(N) 1949) recalled that her class ran a babysitting service during Open House. "We were swamped with customers. This was before Day Care ... and we didn't expect so many parents to leave their children with strangers."[74] The Class of 1955 showed off the new nursing arts lab in the Wesbrook Building and the Class of 1958 borrowed an "iron lung" from Pearson Hospital and used it to show the public the technology used in treatment of poliomyelitis, which, thanks to the new vaccines, was now almost under control. But Ann-Shirley Gordon Goodell recalled another epidemic, just a year or so later. "We had practically obliterated polio. Then in my last year at University, when I was working as a float at VGH, we had a polio epidemic of the people up north. A lot of people had refused the vaccine and then we had this horrible epidemic.... I remember it being so terrible because there was so much guilt involved. Whole families would come in with polio.... I can remember ... when the power went off at VGH and having to pump [use a manual device to keep the lung going] two iron lungs at the same time and how eerie it was."[75]

The collapse of the new bridge over the Second Narrows to North Vancouver was another memorable event for students at VGH on June 17, 1958. Eighteen workmen and one diver were killed and many others injured.[76] Those students not on duty but in residence were put on standby to assist with care in the Emergency Department. Ann-Shirley Gordon Goodell recalled that she was on the sun roof of the residence and heard all the ambulances racing to the hospital. The students could see the broken span from the sun roof.[77]

INFLUENTIAL FACULTY

Nursing faculty recruited by Evelyn Mallory proved to be distinguished and influential nursing leaders. The UBC School of Nursing, along with McGill and the University of Toronto, had one of the leading university nursing programs in Canada and its teachers had prominent roles at national and international levels. Senior faculty of the School in the 1950s, in addition to Evelyn Mallory, included Pauline (Polly) Capelle, Elizabeth K. (Beth) McCann, Ruth M. Morrison, Lorna M. Horwood, Margaret Duncan (later Jensen), Margaret Street, and Margaret Campbell. Brief descriptions of four of these teachers illustrate the quality of leadership given to students during this time.

Pauline Capelle was a 1939 graduate of the UBC program.[78] She was born and raised in Burnaby and her father was in the merchant marine corps. Her mother died when Pauline was young, so she helped raise her younger sister. The young Pauline was determined to have a university education and, as money was in short supply, worked at house-sitting and baby-sitting for room and board during her university years. Following graduation, she went to work with the provincial health department as a nursing supervisor with the Department of Venereal Disease Control. She was one of the first nurse specialists in this area and, on behalf of the public health nursing section of the CNA, provided an introductory article for *The Canadian Nurse*.[79] In the article, she noted that nurses had not accepted VD control as a responsibility, despite the fact that venereal diseases were the most prevalent diseases of the day in Canada. While with the department, she was, among other things, responsible for the educational programs for both undergraduate and postgraduate students. Although she wished to join the army during the war, public health nurses were considered essential home services. During this early part of her career, she was an active worker with CNA and RNABC and

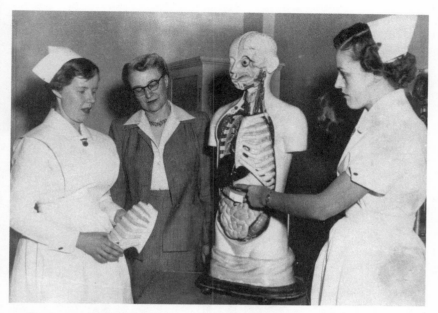

Figure 4.15   Evelyn Mallory with Barbara (Blackwood) Kozier (BSN 1955)
and Laurie Larsen (BSN 1955).

its Vancouver chapter, and she was a strong supporter throughout her career, serving on the executive and on many committees.

Near the end of the war, Evelyn Mallory offered her a position on faculty as instructor and supervisor of public health nursing. Early on, Pauline Capelle recognized that if she wished to remain on faculty she would need a master's degree. Her first choice would have been master's preparation in public health, but Ruth Morrison had joined the faculty and was considered senior in that field. Evelyn Mallory recommended postgraduate work in pediatrics because the School needed someone with preparation in that area. So, in the early 1950s, Pauline Capelle took a year's leave to attend the University of Chicago. While there, she studied under and began a life-long friendship with Florence Blake, one of the early American researchers in pediatric nursing. Florence Blake offered Pauline Capelle a job when she graduated but, out of a sense of loyalty to UBC, she turned it down. She is remembered by many of her students as their teacher for Human Growth and Development. She remained on faculty at UBC until her retirement in 1971.

Ruth MacIntyre Morrison was appointed as assistant professor at UBC in 1946. Born in Dartmouth, Nova Scotia, her first job, for a short period, was as a newspaper reporter in Halifax, but in 1921 she entered the Toronto General Hospital School of Nursing and began her nursing career as a supervisor at the Moose Jaw (Saskatchewan) General Hospital. In 1928, she

Figure 4.16   Graduation day, 1950. L-R: Elinor Palliser, Director of Nursing
Vancouver General Hospital, 1943-1952; Shelagh Wheeler (later Smith), president
NUS; Ruth Morrison, professor School of Nursing, 1946-1965. This picture was
taken on the steps of the Main Library. Graduating students wore the gown
over their VGH graduation uniforms.

joined the Saskatchewan Department of Public Health and spent nine years in
rural and urban public health before joining the Victorian Order of Nurses in
Sackville, N.B., and later the Nova Scotia Department of Public Health. She
served on the boards of the Saskatchewan and Nova Scotia Registered Nurses'
Associations. She attended the University of Minnesota for graduate study, first

for the baccalaureate degree in nursing and then the master's of public health degree before coming to UBC. After coming to UBC, she took a leave of absence in 1950-1951 to attend Teachers College, Columbia University, to obtain her master's degree in teaching and supervision in public health nursing. At UBC, she taught mainly public health nursing, but was active in provincial and national associations, serving on executive committees and representing nursing on a number of government committees as well.

She, along with Evelyn Mallory and Beth McCann, was influential in keeping alive the Council of University Schools of Nursing (later to be renamed the Canadian Association of University Schools of Nursing) during its "provisional" years in the late 1940s. She served as its president for two terms in the late 1950s.[80] She is credited with convening "one of the most creative meetings of the group" in 1957, when, travelling to the Atlantic provinces on another matter, she arranged to hold a "cross-country meeting" with as many members and faculty as possible on her return journey. She organized an initial meeting in Halifax then made train stops in Montreal, where she achieved a quorum of 15 members, London, and Saskatoon. Although air travel had begun in the 1950s, train travel across the nation was still more common – and considerably cheaper – and nursing leaders were always seeking ways to stretch scarce dollars.

In 1951, Ruth Morrison was appointed a member of the World Health Organization's Expert Panel on Nursing, one of the first faculty members at UBC to be involved with WHO during the Evelyn Mallory years. She was also involved with provincial and national public health associations. She wrote several articles on public health nursing during her career, including one identifying the changes in public health nursing in the curriculum at UBC in the early 1960s.[81] Her students recall her as an interesting, approachable, outgoing, and positive person. She frequently took on the social responsibilities required of faculty for Evelyn Mallory, both because she liked to do such things and because she was good at it while Evelyn Mallory was not. She retired from UBC in August 1965 after 19 years on faculty. Anne Wyness (BSN 1965) recalled that Ruth Morrison gave her students a lecture on "planning for retirement," noting that she began planning too late and pensions for female faculty members were "a pittance."[82]

Lorna Horwood joined the UBC Nursing faculty as assistant professor in public health in September 1948. She was originally appointed to replace Pauline Capelle, who was on study leave. Born in Ottawa, Lorna Horwood graduated from the Toronto General in 1931 and took a postgraduate course at the Toronto Psychiatric Hospital, then a nursing teaching certificate from the University of Toronto in 1934. Following appointments as superintendent of nursing in two psychiatric hospitals in Ontario, she turned to public health. In 1941, she became an "industrial nurse," recognizing early the importance of occupational health as a specialty for nurses, something she taught her students at UBC. She took a public health certificate at the University of Toronto, and had just completed her bachelor of arts degree at Queen's University when she was hired at UBC.

With her background in psychiatric nursing as well as public health, she seemed ideal to Evelyn Mallory, who wanted to see improvement in the psychiatric nursing portions of the program at UBC. Although VGH and UBC student nurses began going to Essondale for mental health nursing experience in the late 1930s, psychiatric nursing education had remained separate. The psychiatric program usually was a two-year rather than a three-year program and had much lower entrance standards; the graduates could only work in psychiatric institutions. In the late 1940s, Canadian schools of nursing began requiring a psychiatric rotation for all students, and in 1950 the National League for Nursing in the United States began requiring accredited nursing programs in that country to include psychiatric experience. The Crease Clinic at Essondale was opened during Lorna Horwood's years at UBC, and she later recalled that the Provincial Psychiatric Hospital was making marked improvements in care of the mentally ill.[83]

Soon after her arrival, she convened an RNABC committee to set up an "institute" (or short continuing education program, as it would later be called) for industrial nurses, who were just beginning to be employed by industries in B.C. Throughout her time at UBC, she was active in RNABC, serving on many committees and as a member of the board of examiners, and in CNA, as well as in many other women's organizations. She was especially active in the University Women's Club and served as a representative to the Vancouver Branch of the United Nations' Society. In 1952-1953, she received a Kellogg Foundation Fellowship and went to Teachers College, Columbia University, to take her master of arts degree. In 1957, Lorna Horwood resigned to accept a position with WHO; she had applied much earlier to WHO and international nursing had always been her goal. Throughout her years with WHO as a nursing consultant in mental health, she kept in touch with the UBC School and made several official visits, such as those from Taiwan and from Thailand.

Margaret Duncan (later Jensen) (BASc 1946) served on the UBC faculty from 1950 to 1963 and was one of the most popular teachers of this period. Evelyn Mallory described her when she was leaving as "the best qualified member of the staff."[84] After her graduation from UBC, she was hired as a clinical instructor in medicine at VGH and was there for three years. She then received a Kellogg Foundation Fellowship on the recommendation of the School so she could attend the University of Chicago to take a master's degree in nursing with emphasis on maternal child health. On her return she joined the faculty and took over the hospital liaison duties previously carried out by Beth McCann. She taught nursing arts for the first year classes and maternity nursing in clinical areas as well as helping to supervise small hospital administrative experience for final year students. Most students of this period recall Margaret Duncan warmly and fondly. She, Beth McCann, and Margaret Campbell were the faculty members closest to the students and they gave strong support and mentorship.

Beth Walton (later Fitzpatrick) (BSN 1955) thinks she was in one of the first classes to be taught by Margaret Duncan at UBC and described her as "a unique teacher."[85] For example, Margaret Duncan was not afraid of admitting to students that she too had made mistakes; she would even make them in class, then sit back and ask the students to criticize her – something that surprised them. "We thought she was perfect," Beth Walton remembers. Margaret Duncan's strong influence and role modelling affected Beth Walton's career. After a period as an instructor at UBC, Beth Walton decided to pursue nurse midwifery, as Margaret Duncan advised this "would be the way of the future." Beth Walton took her midwifery in Boston and then her master's degree in nursing at Yale; she then became director of the Preparation for Childbirth Program at Yale New Haven. A few years later, she joined a private practice with three obstetricians who wanted a nurse midwife in their office. "I probably was the first nurse midwife to work in private practice in the United States. There may have been some others around the same time, but it was the early seventies that the movement began.... There was an article ... about midwifery in private practice in *Medical World News* and ... my picture's on the cover." Beth Walton married about this time and went to teach at Southern Connecticut State University for 11 years. In the 1990s, she returned to British Columbia and taught part time in the UBC program once again.

Margaret Duncan's vision of obstetrical nursing of the future led her to become the first of the UBC faculty to seek doctoral study in nursing and in 1962 she went to the University of California for further study, with an emphasis on maternal child care. While she was in California, she married. She returned to UBC for one year to fulfil her contract related to the leave of absence, then moved to California, where she began teaching in the School of Nursing at San Mateo State College. Later in her career, she wrote several textbooks on maternal child nursing that became standard textbooks and went through several editions.

Margaret Street was another of the faculty recruited by Evelyn Mallory. She first had a one-year appointment in 1952-1953, but at the end of that year was invited to go to Calgary General Hospital as clinical coordinator. She then became associate director of nursing at Calgary General and during this period took part in the CNA project, headed by Helen Mussallem, to evaluate hospital schools of nursing in Canada. In 1961-1962, she took her master's degree at Boston University, then was invited to rejoin the faculty at UBC to take charge of the new diploma program in Administration of Nursing Units.

Figure 4.17

Margaret Street, faculty member from 1962 to 1972. She helped plan the Health Sciences Centre Hospital at UBC. In 1972, her book, *Watch-fires on the Mountains: The Life and Writings of Ethel Johns*, was published.

Margaret Street had a distinguished career before coming to UBC.[86] Born in 1907 in Toronto, she grew up in Winnipeg and graduated with a bachelor of arts degree from the University of Manitoba, then took her teaching certificate and taught in Manitoba high schools before she entered nursing. Her diploma in nursing was from the Royal Victoria Hospital in Montreal. Following graduation, she taught nursing in various schools and in the late 1930s was an assistant night supervisor at the Vancouver General Hospital. She returned to Montreal in the early 1940s to take a certificate in teaching and supervision at McGill School of Nursing. While a student there, she submitted a paper to Ethel Johns, editor of *The Canadian Nurse*, something that was to have a major influence on both their lives in later years. During her early career, she held senior positions in provinces across Canada; she was Registrar in both Manitoba and Quebec and was president of the Alberta Association of Registered Nurses. She was active in nursing organizations and had strong and extensive networks with other nursing leaders, such as Mabel Hersey and Gertrude Hall.

These qualifications made her an excellent choice for the faculty at UBC and she was soon drawn into administrative chores. UBC was anxious to have a university hospital, so she and Evelyn Mallory were funded by the dean of Medicine to tour university hospitals in the United States and prepare a report. This led to Margaret Street's appointment to the planning committee for a proposed Health Sciences Centre Hospital to be built on campus. Her involvement with the hospital during its planning and early development stages was extensive and she can be credited with initiating the nursing plans for the hospital, including the foundations for its emphasis on degree-prepared nurses and an all-RN staff. She was listed as an assistant to Evelyn Mallory and, during the final years of her 11-year tenure, taught the administration courses in the new master's degree program in nursing. She retired in 1972 and retained close links with the University and the School of Nursing as a professor emerita until her death in 1993.

While at UBC, Margaret Street renewed her acquaintance and became close friends with Ethel Johns, who was living in retirement in Vancouver. Following Ethel Johns' death in 1968, she was asked to assist with the review of Johns' papers and decided she should write a biography of this first director. The result was publication in 1973 of *Watch-fires on the Mountains: The Life and Writings of Ethel Johns*, which is considered an outstanding biography of a Canadian woman. From proceeds of the book, she endowed the Ethel Johns and Isabel Maitland Stewart Scholarship Fund for the UBC School of Nursing. Margaret Street received many honours for her outstanding contributions, including investiture into the Order of Canada by the Governor General in Ottawa ceremonies in 1982.

Evelyn Mallory continued to seek faculty members with experience in specialized clinical fields, such as Elizabeth (Betty) Cawston (public health), Helen Shore (public health), Margaret Neylan (psychiatric nursing, continuing education), Helen Niskala (medical-surgical), and Sylvia Holmes (obstetrics). Faculty numbers grew from four nurses in 1943 to 18 in 1965. In addition, she employed a number of young instructors, all recent graduates from the UBC program, to supervise clinical portions of the students' experiences at St. Paul's or in the field work areas. Several of these young instructors went on to become major nursing leaders, including Alice Baumgart (BSN 1958), Jacqueline Chapman (BSN 1958), and Rose Murakami (BSN 1962).

AN INDEPENDENT PROGRAM BEGINS

Some of the problems that led to the move from department to school status in the early 1950s continued to plague the relationships between UBC and VGH. The most important of these related to control of the experiences for UBC students, which led in the early 1960s to a split with the Vancouver General and to arrangements for student clinical rotations at St. Paul's Hospital.

Although administrators of both VGH and UBC nursing programs tried hard to resolve difficulties, increasing enrolments in both programs created major problems. Resources for clinical experiences, especially for clinical field experiences such as psychiatric and public health field work, were stretched to their limits, and the UBC administrators believed that these experiences were essential for degree preparation. VGH administrators objected because the UBC students received priority for these experiences.

Furthermore, UBC students were returning to campus during summers for special courses, which reduced their service time on wards. As well, because UBC instructors now were at VGH to assist and supervise the UBC students, the differences in the quality of education were increasingly visible.

Evelyn Mallory summarized some of these difficulties in a 1958 report on the split with VGH.[87] "Instead of having a program planned specifically in relation to their background and needs, students are 'fitted into' a plan designed for the Hospital's 3-year students.... Increased enrolment in the University program has made this 'fitting in' process a much more difficult one." A committee was set up by UBC President Norman MacKenzie but, after several attempts, it was unable to reach agreement. "The VGH staff ... were firm in their stand that there must be no differences in the instruction and experiences provided to the two student groups. This would wipe out priorities ... for degree-course students which had been in effect for years and would require the withdrawal of University instructors now working in that part of the program." As a result, although UBC again offered some further compromises that VGH rejected, the University decided that its School of Nursing should take control of all four years of its program and seek clinical arrangements with other hospitals.[88]

In another report, Evelyn Mallory reiterated the concerns that led to the split with VGH. "It was decided, with considerable reluctance on the part of all concerned, that the University should seek elsewhere for a clinical practice field for its basic-programme students, and that no more University students would be admitted to the Vancouver General Hospital."[89] The last class to complete the combined course graduated from VGH in August 1960 and from the University in October 1961. For years following the split, relations between UBC and VGH schools of nursing remained strained.

Fortunately, St. Paul's Hospital had approached UBC in 1957 about participating in the degree course. In these discussions, Evelyn Mallory had indicated that the UBC School would not want an arrangement similar to that begun with VGH more than 35 years earlier. "While the type of program in 1920 was a forward step then, it is no longer considered good educational practice in respect to a degree course in Nursing."[90] When the split with VGH occurred, however, the University and St. Paul's were able to work out a new agreement that sent the UBC students to St. Paul's for the majority of the clinical work during the second and third years of the four-year program (after either first year in Arts and Sciences or Senior Matriculation). The faculty at UBC were completely responsible, however, for the student work at St. Paul's.

UBC students took their clinical experiences at St. Paul's and the contract gave the hospital's administration some specific responsibility related to admission and general supervision, such as a preliminary interview with the hospital's administrator. A joint faculty committee, with representatives from

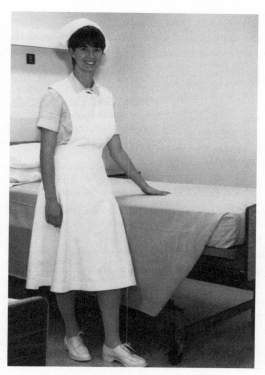

Figure 4.18   Distinctive UBC uniform, circa 1960, modeled by
Patti Stevenson, NUS president, 1992-1993. This uniform was worn for the first
time by the class of 1962. It was a pink and white striped cotton dress with a
one piece apron and bib. The cap, so the story goes, was designed by Alice
Baumgart (BSN 1958) who folded it out of a serviette over dinner. After a few
years, the dress was worn without the apron. During the early 1970s the starched
pink and white uniform was replaced by a plain white one.

Figure 4.19

UBC School of Nursing pin designed
by students in 1958 and used as the
graduating pin from that time.

both schools, was set up to ensure communication and liaison, and there was considerable exchange of information. However, the UBC students were seen as distinct from St. Paul's students throughout their program. They did not graduate from St. Paul's at the end of the third year and did not qualify for registration until the end of the fourth year at UBC. For the first time, the students were identified by their own uniforms, caps, and pins. The graduation pin had been designed by students and first used in 1958. The cap was developed when the students entered St. Paul's and the story is told that Alice Baumgart (BSN 1958), who was an instructor at the time, folded it out of a serviette over a dinner with other faculty.

Rooms for up to 20 UBC students were available in the St. Paul's nurses' residence, for $15 a month for room, board, and laundry. For the first time, however, UBC students could make arrangements to live at home or in other accommodation approved by their parents. Meals for all students were supplied by the hospital in a small separate dining room. However, some students recalled that the food was not especially good; meals were free, but the hospital frequently used donations from local businesses and the quality of these varied. St. Paul's agreed to limit its own enrolment of students if UBC classes grew. In return, the University granted some major scholarships to St. Paul's graduates to enable them to achieve their degrees. Among the first to take advantage of these scholarships were several of the Sisters.[91]

The program now was officially described as "an integrated program which includes preparation for staff level positions in public health nursing as well as work in hospital. It also includes preparation for teaching and a consideration of the fundamentals of ward management and supervision."[92]

The first group of 20 second-year students from UBC, wearing their newly designed pink-striped uniforms with white bibs and aprons, entered St. Paul's in May 1959. They were accompanied by two UBC clinical instructors, Alice J. Baumgart (BSN 1958) and Margaret E. Speirs (BSN 1951). All these first students lived out of residence, at least for the summer, because of lack of room. They had locker rooms and classrooms, and the UBC faculty had offices, in the St. Paul's education building. The program was planned for a 44-hour work week, with Saturday afternoons and Sundays off. To facilitate teaching, UBC students were assigned only to day and afternoon shifts, except during certain rotations when they were on 11 p.m.-7 a.m. night duty. This major change to concurrent classroom teaching, rather than "blocks" of instruction, was intended to ensure better integration of theory and practice. However, one former student recalled that this first group was "worked to death" to prove the program was a sound one.[93]

Evelyn Mallory acknowledged that the admission standards for the new program were much more difficult. The five required courses in first year Arts and Science (or Senior Matriculation) included English 100, Chemistry 100 or 102, Math 101 or 120, Zoology 105 or Biology 100, and an approved elective. Nursing students needed a 60 per cent overall average as a minimum, but the actual admission standards usually were much higher. First year nursing continued to follow the earlier lines of heavy science courses (Bacteriology 100, Chemistry 210, and Psychology 100) plus four nursing courses, including an anatomy and physiology course adapted especially for nursing (Nursing 155).

During the second and third years of the course, students took some concurrent lectures on campus, including English 200, Sociology 200 and 301, and some nursing theory. However, most experiences were clinically oriented and based at St. Paul's. Students had rotations to four additional agencies, including a 12-week course at the Provincial Mental Hospital at Essondale and time at the B.C. Cancer Institute (later called the B.C. Cancer Agency). During the early 1960s, admissions to the program had to be limited to a maximum of 30 students a year because clinical resources continued to be in short supply. This problem was not unique to UBC but plagued most of the nursing programs in the Lower Mainland, where numbers of student nurses continued to grow at the hospital schools; all were competing for clinical facilities. In 1962, some UBC students had their obstetrical experiences at St. Vincent's Hospital because St. Paul's did not have enough maternity patients. In 1965, negotiations with the Vancouver General Hospital once again allowed the School to send UBC students there for clinical experiences, especially in the Health Centre for Children.

The fourth year program had been "drastically revised" when the association with St. Paul's began. It was designed to prepare a nurse to give competent professional service in all fields of nursing, including public health, and the final year included preparation for teaching and a study of the fundamentals of supervision and administration. Sociology 320 was the only non-nursing course in fourth year during the early 1960s, but the year was exceptionally heavy with nine nursing courses including field work and a nursing study. This graduating essay, as the students usually referred to it, was a continuation of a special formal paper that had been required of all students throughout the 1950s.

The postbasic degree program (still called Nursing D) for registered nurses who wanted degrees was completely revised to keep its goal the same as that of the basic degree program. Most nurses completed the postbasic degree in three years, although credits were given if they had appropriate senior matriculation or university subjects. The emphasis in those courses taken in conjunction with the basic degree students reflected shifting values in nursing.

The two 10-month certificate courses continued during the 1960s, but these also changed from those offered earlier. Nursing B, the public health nursing certificate course, continued to be given, but Nursing C, the teaching and supervision course that began in the 1920s, was discontinued at the end

Figure 4.20   Aileen Bond (DipPHN 1942), senior public health nurse in
Dawson Creek, Halfway Valley Reserve, in 1949. The public health diploma
program, which began in 1920, was discontinued in 1973.

of 1960-1961. Nursing C now was a diploma in Administration of Hospital
Nursing Units, directed to preparation of head nurses. The first class
attracted seven students. George Veitch McKnight, one of 20 students who
graduated from the program in 1963, may have been the first male student in
any program in the School.

These certificate course changes represented a shifting focus in nursing
throughout the country. Canadian university nursing educators no longer
considered that nursing teachers should be prepared in certificate courses, but
thought they needed at least a basic nursing degree and postgraduate study.
Nursing leaders recognized that nursing, if it were to keep pace with changes
in health care, needed well-prepared teachers. Most hospital schools of
nursing in B.C. had begun to adhere to this philosophy, and teaching staff
usually had diplomas or degrees from UBC. A majority of VGH teaching
staff during the late 1940s was from the UBC baccalaureate program. Both
Helen Mussallem and Beverly Du Gas, who were directors of nursing
education in the 1950s, had master's level preparation.

As Evelyn Mallory pointed out, "There is a tragic dearth of persons
qualified for senior level positions in nursing service and nursing education
and of nurses qualified ... to act as clinical nursing experts (or consultants) to
help effect improvement in patient care. These needs are urgent and can only
be met through graduate programmes."[94]

CHANGES IN NURSING IN THE 1960S

The first half of the 1960s was a period of great growth and prosperity both in Canada and in B.C. Fishing, mining, and forestry, particularly the wood pulp industry, were expanding rapidly and the Columbia River Treaty, which allowed for sale of water to the U.S., was signed in 1961, one of the signs of an economic boom. The population was beginning to expand rapidly; in 1961, the population of British Columbia stood at 1.62 million; this was to double in the next 30 years. All education in the 1960s was changing. The Social Credit government of W.A.C. Bennett was support-ing expansion of postsecondary education throughout the province. The University of Victoria opened its campus in 1963; since 1920, its precursor, Victoria College, had had an affiliation with UBC,[95] but not a campus of its own or the authority to award its own degrees. Simon Fraser University opened in 1965, and other community colleges opened in B.C. centres over the next decade. In 1967, the B.C. Institute of Technology (BCIT), the first of B.C.'s community colleges, opened a two-year diploma nursing program. This shorter, non-hospital program was the first in B.C. to follow the changing pattern of nursing education in Canada and its first director was a UBC graduate, Barbara Blackwood (later Kozier) (BSN 1955). Nursing education was moving into postsecondary institutions with budgets con-trolled by the provincial departments of education, rather than health, and, across Canada, hospital-based diploma schools were beginning to be phased out.

The Canadian Nurses Association seconded Helen K. Mussallem from the Vancouver General to carry out a survey of hospital schools of nursing during the late 1950s. Her report, *Spotlight on Nursing Education*,[96] was published in 1960. It documented a wide disparity in quality of nursing education across Canada and noted that improvements recommended by George Weir in 1932 and in other reports had not been made. Because of the success of the federally assisted hospital insurance plans, hospital care had become the norm and, by 1961, Quebec was the last of the provinces to agree to participate in the national plan. The provincial governments now were beginning to look at medical insurance.

In 1961, the federal government established a broad-based Royal Com-mission on Health Services. As part of its comprehensive mandate, the Commission, under Chief Justice Emmett Hall, hired Helen Mussallem and funded a major study on nursing education, which also examined university preparation of nurses. Faculty of the UBC School of Nursing, one of the 16 university schools across Canada, completed a questionnaire and met with Helen Mussallem. Her report, *Nursing Education in Can-ada*,[97] greatly impressed the Royal Commission, which then recommended, as part of its influential report, that nursing education in universities be expanded. The recommendations were that university degree programs should prepare at least 25 per cent of all graduates, compared with the current 5 per cent, and that master's and doctoral nursing programs were needed in Canada.

After publication of the Royal Commission report, the UBC School of Nursing prepared a brief for the University on implications for the School. Four significant changes that Nursing faculty believed needed to be considered at UBC were (1) a master's program in nursing, (2) a research program, (3) creation of a Faculty of Nursing (rather than a School), and (4) expansion of credit and non-credit courses for working nurses. Action on this final recommendation formed the beginnings of a continuing education program for nurses in the late 1960s and was the precursor for distance education nursing programs or "Nursing Outreach" in the early 1980s.[98] Responses to the suggestion for a master's program were positive and faculty began preparing a brief, which was approved by the Senate during the 1965-1966 term, contingent on funds and qualified faculty being available.

Another important campus event was the opening in 1965 of the Woodward Biomedical Library, a gift of the Mr. and Mrs. P.A. Woodward Foundation and funds from a matching federal government grant. The Nursing Reading Room in the Wesbrook Building had served students of the 1950s and early 1960s, but facilities were inadequate and only a limited number of books, magazines, and reference materials could be accommodated. When the Woodward Library opened, the nursing collection, which was transferred from Wesbrook, was found to be inadequate. Ethel Johns was asked by the nursing faculty to advise the Library, and she donated her own collection and made recommendations for development of an historical collection for the Charles Woodward Memorial Reading Room. The opening of the Library allowed nursing students once again to work in a collegial atmosphere with students from other health sciences disciplines and to have access to a wide range of materials.

In 1966, the School initiated a one-year certificate course leading to a diploma in psychiatric nursing; this coincided with preparation for the new psychiatric care hospital on the UBC campus, the first building of the UBC Health Sciences Centre Hospital. This psychiatric certificate course, under Margaret Neylan, lasted only three years and was to help prepare nurses to staff the new unit at UBC. Hospitals that provided clinical experience for these students included Lions Gate, Royal Jubilee, and Shaughnessy. At that time, the philosophy of organized nursing, including the Canadian Nurses Association and the Registered Nurses Association of B.C. was that psychiatric nursing programs should be closed and that psychiatric nursing should be a specialty area for registered nurses. Provincial governments in central and eastern Canada accepted this move, but in the four western provinces, programs for preparation of psychiatric nursing have continued to be separate from those for registered nurses.

Figure 4.21   The Woodward Biomedical Library opened in 1965 and replaced
the reading room in the Wesbrook building, which was crowded and had a
limited selection of nursing texts. Students now had access to a wide range of
references on nursing and other health disciplines.

Other changes were happening in psychiatric care. General hospitals were
now considered appropriate sites for psychiatric wards. This reflected a
philosophy of care for the whole person, and community mental health, or
preventive care, was considered to be the approach of the future. The
provincial department of Mental Health Services passed an act in 1955
establishing mental health centres that would offer preventive services and
follow-up care. Beverly Mitchell (BSN 1951) was the first supervisor of
nursing for the first community Mental Health Centre, in Burnaby, in 1957.
Care of individuals with psychiatric problems, aided by the new psychotropic
drugs and advances in treatment, could be given in the patient's own
community. The days of the large provincial mental institution were numbered. Typical of these changes was the new emphasis on mental health
programs by the provincial public health service. Pauline Siddons, who
received her certificate in public health from UBC in 1948, was appointed in
1969 as the first provincial nursing consultant in Victoria with special
responsibilities for mental health. She brought into general public health
nursing the new mental health care approaches.[99]
    Toward the end of the Mallory years, the School of Nursing once again
began offering short "institutes" for nurses, including a three-day one on

Psychiatric Nursing with 117 registrants and a three-day one on Rehabilitation Nursing of Elderly Persons with 90 registrants.[100] Such institutes were recommended in a 1966 brief on Continuing Education for Nurses prepared by the School.

In 1966, the federal government passed the Medical Care Act, which extended health insurance to cover medical services (frequently referred to as "medicare"). Canadians now were assured of physician services, but the act also had the effect of making doctors the main access point, or "gatekeepers," to the health care system. Because medical services were seen as "free," the public usually turned to physicians for advice and care rather than to public health nurses in the community, as frequently had been the norm previously. Hospital and physician insurance plans emphasized treatment and acute care rather than health promotion, education, and prevention. Taxpayers' money was funnelled mainly into hospital and physician support; public health care and individual responsibility for lifestyle and health were downplayed and devalued. The cure model, rather than a care model, became the chief focus and the public became increasingly dependent on physician services. This development had serious implications for the type of nursing provided and for nursing education during the next two decades; nursing education was required to provide vast numbers of graduates to meet demands for hospital-based care and to focus on technical support for medical care.

STUDENT RECOLLECTIONS OF THE 1960S: THE NEW PROGRAM

Students of the 1960s were influenced greatly by the switch to St. Paul's Hospital as their clinical location and by the fact that this was a Roman Catholic Hospital run by the Sisters of Providence. During the 1960s, the Sisters, distinguished by distinctive, long, traditional habits, were in charge of the units, although few were directly involved in patient care. Certain religious protocols now had to be included in student orientation. For example, care of the dead and dying was subject to religious edicts and care of the fetus in spontaneous abortion had to involve a baptism. Moral codes of the 1960s were less strict than those of the 1950s (although still considerably different from those of the 1990s). However, the strict beliefs of the Sisters as practiced on the wards often conflicted with these changing mores.

The hospital administration encouraged frugality and nothing was thrown out. Newspaper was used under drapes and to make bags for bedside waste; scrap paper was recycled. A sign posted on one of the wards indicated that "it is a sin to break thermometers."[101] Students were also required to stand when a Sister appeared, even in class, and standing for physicians on the wards also still was expected behaviour in most situations. Anne Wyness (BSN 1965) recalls that St. Paul's own students were indoctrinated into this behaviour while the UBC students were not and frequently questioned the rationale for

Figure 4.22   First capping ceremony held at St. Paul's Hospital for the class of 1962. The UBC School of Nursing had become independent in 1958 when it separated from the Vancouver General Hospital, an arrangement that had been in effect since 1919. The class of 1965 was the last one to have this traditional capping ceremony. After that, students were issued caps on admission. In the mid-1970s, wearing a cap became an option and caps soon became obsolete.

practices, which sometimes led to friction. The UBC students were constantly reminded by their instructors that they were guests in the institution and must behave accordingly.

On the other hand, UBC students also had their quirks, such as the infamous "toe pleat." UBC instructors had long stressed the importance of allowing room for a patient's feet when the bed was made, rather than using rigid, tightly drawn upper covers. Unfortunately, the bed with a toe pleat did not look as neat, and supervisors and staff at VGH and St. Paul's had often pointed this out rather forcefully. UBC students learned to stand their ground on the matter, but often were forced to learn a diplomatic approach, which may have stood them in good stead later.

Anne Wyness' class was the last, in 1962, to have a capping ceremony. When the move was made to St. Paul's, UBC discontinued many of the traditional ceremonial rites of passage, such as differences in uniform from year to year and use of black shoes and stockings at the beginning of the hospital experience. When the capping ceremony was discontinued, students were issued caps along with the uniform and simply wore them throughout their hospital rotations.

The psychiatric experience at Essondale, now called Riverview, continued to be a memorable time and most students appreciated the opportunity to live in a residence. Nancy Symmes (later Frood) (BSN 1964) recalled her experience in recreational therapy with patients at Colony Farm at Riverview and "hanging up our caps while playing volleyball in full dress uniform."[102] Margaret Neylan was in charge of this experience, which included six weeks at Crease Clinic and six weeks in various other settings at Riverview, Woodlands, and Valleyview. Because awareness of forensic psychiatry was beginning at this time, all students also spent an evening visiting Oakalla Prison.

Another new experience introduced for students in the 1960s involved a stint in a physician's office during the obstetrical rotations; students thus learned importance of early prenatal care. Pediatric rotations were also marked by some advances. Students spent time observing play therapy and, as part of a growth and development course, observed children's behaviour through one-way mirrors. Closed circuit television also was being used on campus and Sigurlina ("Dilla") Narfason (DipPHN 1964) recalled being in a sociology class that was so large that students observed the lectures via closed circuit sets in other classrooms, which she thought was a first on the campus.[103] She also recalled the assassination of U.S. President John F. Kennedy on the morning of November 22, 1963, as such a tragic event and at the time such an unusual incident that classes at UBC were cancelled for the remainder of the day. Sheila McDonald (later Tully) (BSN 1965) also mentioned the assassination and recalled that she was in a maternity rotation at St. Vincent's Hospital and that she and her classmates were sent home at noon.[104]

Many students of the Evelyn Mallory era recalled studying under Kasper Nagaele, a professor of sociology and later dean of Arts at UBC. He was especially interested in nursing's roles and had been commissioned by CNA to do a major study of nursing education. During a period of great personal stress, he committed suicide and students of the time recalled being utterly shocked. Anne Wyness said that her class had "adored him as a teacher" and Sheila McDonald (later Tully) (BSN 1965) said "we had learned so much from him and admired him for his caring attitude."[105]

GRADUATES OF THE EVELYN MALLORY PERIOD

Evelyn Mallory's time at UBC covered more than a quarter of a century, so she influenced a large number of students. A rough count of graduates from her era shows that about 675 received degrees (out of a total of 749 nursing degrees awarded since the opening of the program) and about 1,100 received diplomas (compared to 1,254 diplomas since the opening). With such large numbers, perhaps it is not surprising that many went on to become nursing leaders. However, any examination of Canadian nursing and its contributions shows that many UBC nursing graduates of this period went on to great achievements.

A look at the achievements of the "Class of '58," from the middle of the Mallory era, gives an indication of the scope of practice influenced by UBC nurses. In some ways this class may not be typical, but the 43 women in that class, which included 32 "generic students" and 11 "returning RNs," have been extraordinarily prominent in nursing and health care. The class held a 33-year reunion in 1991 and, although six members of the class had died, all the others remained interested in and involved in nursing or health care. Popular sociology would indicate that women who graduated in the 1950s did not pursue careers; this does not appear to be true for UBC nursing classes of the 1950s. Only two of the Class of '58 never practiced nursing, but both became influential community members applying their nursing background. For example, Lloy Pountney (later Jefferson) served on the board of trustees of Lions Gate Hospital for a number of years.

Fourteen class members pursued careers in nursing education and, at the time of the 33-year reunion, eight still were teaching, at least part time, in university nursing programs, including those at Dalhousie, Queen's, Toronto, Calgary, Victoria, and Washington; others had, at one time in their career, taught at the universities of Alberta and Hawaii. Three – Elizabeth Robertson, Jacquie Chapman, and Alice Baumgart – had been on faculty at UBC, and others, such as Janice (Jan) Bell (later Scott) and Glennis Zilm, had been clinical instructors or part-time lecturers. Alice Baumgart, generally considered by her classmates as the most important leader from that class, went into nursing education early as an instructor under Evelyn Mallory. Later, she obtained her master's degree in nursing at McGill and her doctorate in education from Toronto. She taught in the School of Nursing at the University of Toronto before being appointed dean of the Faculty of Nursing at Queen's University. She then became Vice-Principal, Human Resources, at Queen's. A noted writer and researcher on feminism and nursing, she served in many executive positions with provincial and national nursing associations. At the time of the reunion, she was president of the Canadian Nurses Association and immediate past president of the Canadian Association of University Schools of Nursing (CAUSN). In 1993, she was elected member-at-large for the International Council of Nurses. She is co-author of a popular nursing textbook, *Canadian Nursing Faces the Future.*

Others of the class are authors as well. Carol Partridge (later Smillie), who is on the faculty of Dalhousie University's School of Nursing, is co-author of *Community Health Nursing in Canada*, a classic public health nursing text. She also is an active researcher in community health, especially in studies of ways to reduce cigarette use among teenagers. Glennis Zilm, after a few years in bedside nursing, public health in Australia, and teaching in a diploma program, joined the staff of *The Canadian Nurse* under the editorship of Margaret Kerr. She then left nursing for a period to work as a reporter and editor for *The Canadian Press*, the national news service, and served as the science and health reporter on Parliament Hill. Among the major news stories she covered there was the release of Mark Lalonde's report, which helped create new directions for health care. She eventually returned to nursing journalism, then to editing nursing textbooks. She is author or editor of a number of professional documents, many of them for the Canadian Nurses Association.

Jacqueline (Jacquie) Chapman, a professor in the graduate program of the University of Toronto's School of Nursing, is one of Canada's most noted nurse researchers. She began her research early in her career into the study of care of premature babies and their subsequent development, following these babies' development to discover what effects prematurity may have had on them in later years; some of her subjects now are adults with families of their own and she has become their "family friend" as well as researcher. She also was influential in research that led to improvements in care in neonatal nurseries, including the importance of the tiny premature babes having opportunities for bonding with their mothers and the effects of neonatal nursery design on the care of premature babies.

Norma MacKay (later Friedmann), after a career in teaching at the University of Victoria, became influential in design and planning of hospital buildings and works as a planner for new building and hospital expansion with the Greater Victoria Hospitals. She recalled being introduced to hospital planning in a project during her UBC student years and learning there the importance of functional design.

Several class members went into public health, including: Jean Hogg (later Groves, Sordi) who was in charge of the provincial unit in Kamloops; Joan Cousier (later Lansdell), who was second-in-command in Kelowna when she retired after 30 years with the provincial health department; Lorraine Hellier (later Bednar), who was senior nurse in the Leduc-Strathcona health unit near Edmonton; and Audrey Nagano (later Hamaguchi), who after working as an occupational health nurse in Ottawa for many years was with the Department of Veterans' Affairs in Vancouver.

Again, popular sociology studies suggest that those who went into university nursing programs in the 1950s would have gone into leadership positions and not stayed in or returned to bedside nursing. However, several of those at the reunion were proud that they were working, by choice, with patients on a day-to-day basis. For example, Elizabeth Robertson had left university teaching and was working on the "step-down unit" in the cardiac care area at Lions Gate Hospital and was involved in a committee to improve patient teaching. Jan Bell (later Scott), the daughter and niece of two UBC nursing graduates (the Kilpatrick sisters, Elspeth (BASc(N) 1930) and Heather (BASc(N) 1931)), had worked in a variety of positions, including teaching part time in the UBC program, but kept returning to bedside care and was working in the ambulatory ENT unit at VGH. Phyllis Adair (later Killeen), after a brief stint in librarianship, was employed in a surgeon's office and Carol Williams (later Freemantle) was working in a urologist's office. Jean Frances (later Fortier) was working full time on a neurology unit in a Montreal hospital. Sheila Murray (later Jankus) had gone into geriatric care and was a nursing coordinator in extended care.

Pat Scorer was chief nursing officer of the Health Sciences Centre Hospital in Winnipeg when she retired. She was one of the "returning RNs" in the Class of '58 and had come from a senior position in Winnipeg, to which she returned and remained throughout her career. Another of the "returning RNs," Monica McArdle Angus, was active in nursing organizations immediately after graduation and president of the Registered Nurses Association of B.C. from 1969 to 1971. She then pursued doctoral studies in psychology and is in private practice as a psychologist. Joan Alexis Kahr (later Redekop) worked in nursing for a while, then she and her husband began working in China. At the time of the reunion, she was home on leave from teaching English to university teachers and researchers in Tianjin, where they live, not in an "English-type compound" but among the Chinese. She says she uses "her nursing principles" but is not involved in nursing.

This brief survey by no means mentions all the endeavours of the Class of '58, but it does profile contributions students from this period made. Other classes also provided nursing leaders in education, public health, administration, research, and practice. Other recognized nursing leaders in education who received their undergraduate degrees during the Evelyn Mallory years include Marilynn J. Wood (BSN 1959), dean of nursing at the University of Alberta and before that at Anusa Pacific University School of Nursing, and Dorothy Jean Kergin (BSN 1952), director of the University of Victoria School of Nursing from 1980 until shortly before her death in 1989. During Dorothy Kergin's tenure, the distance education degree program for registered nurses grew rapidly; nurses throughout the province were able to take their entire programs through a combination of innovative distance learning courses, some of which involved use of the newly established Knowledge Network and satellite television to take education into remote areas of the province. Before moving to Victoria, she was associate dean of Health Sciences (Nursing), McMaster University. An extremely influential woman, she was active in promoting collaborative relations between nursing education and nursing service; even when she was beginning her career with the provincial public health department in B.C., she was committed to joint appointments between university programs and agencies so expertise could be shared. At McMaster, she was deeply involved in developing an expanded role for nursing in primary care; her research in this area later was incorporated into basic degree programs as part of the physical assessment skills for nurses and firmly established new roles for all nurses. Dorothy Kergin also was involved with international nursing and was consultant to the nursing program at the University of Malawi and a consultant to the Canadian International Development Agency (CIDA) regarding development of nursing in Pakistan. She was president of the Canadian Association of University Schools of Nursing from 1976 to 1980.

Norma A. Wylie (BSN 1957) worked with the World Health Organization and spent seven years during the 1970s in Singapore and Malaya, where she set up basic curricula for nursing schools. Nursing in Asia at that time was almost nonexistent and Norma Wylie helped upgrade the role of the nurse in China, as she later described it, "from the basement to the first floor."[106] On her return from Asia, she taught at the Southern Illinois University School of Medicine, where she was the first woman and first nurse to receive a clinical appointment along with a full professorship with tenure at a medical school in North America. She had moved to Illinois to open a hospice program, but the move also gave her an opportunity to teach medical students, something she had always believed was important. Her experiences in teaching doctors the bedside knowledge that nurses use resulted in a book, *The Role of the Nurse in Clinical Medical Education.* She later took part in an exchange program between SIU and Sun Yat-Sen University in China in the late 1980s.

Lavinia Crane (BSN 1951) was the fourth director of nursing for the B.C. Health Department, following three other UBC graduates who held that position. She took over as director in December 1975 and served until retirement. She had joined the provincial department immediately following her graduation and served in a variety of centres throughout B.C. She took her master's degree in public health, specializing in home care, at the University of Michigan. In 1961 she was appointed Consultant with the Division in Victoria and was given special responsibility for developing the B.C. home care program.[107] After setting up demonstration projects in Kelowna, Vernon, and Saanich, she expanded the program during the 1960s. The Home Care Program, which was just being introduced at this time and was replacing the Victorian Order of Nurses, proved highly successful and cost effective. Under Lavinia Crane's leadership, both as consultant and as director, the provincial department initiated many research projects.

Trenna Grace Hunter (BASc(N) 1944) was director of public health nursing for the Vancouver Metropolitan Health Department from 1944 to 1966, immediately following Lyle Creelman, another UBC graduate (see Chapter 3). During these years, she became deeply involved with national nursing politics and served on the executive for several years before being elected president of the Canadian Nurses Association from 1956 to 1958. During her term in office, she actively supported such trends as the promotion of a code of ethics for nursing and CNA's advisory role to government. She was acutely aware of the need for specialties in nursing and how these might be administered.

Fern Trout (BASc(N) 1944) became well known as a nursing administrator. She worked in a variety of hospital administrative positions in B.C., Quebec, and Ontario. In 1950, she became a "travelling instructor" for the Registered Nurses Association of B.C., a position that called for her travel throughout the province to outlying districts. "I taught anything the nurses wanted. A little bit about modern equipment that was coming at that time, for instance the first kidney machine was in use, a lot about modern medications, and a general updating about techniques."[108] In 1962, she moved to Toronto to take further education in hospital administration, which involved one year on campus at the University of Toronto and a one-year residency in various departments of a hospital; she was only the fourth female to take such a course. In the latter part of her career, she might have been considered a "trouble-shooter," frequently being brought into hospitals throughout B.C. to organize or reorganize the nursing departments, such as at Penticton General, Lions Gate, and Shaughnessy.

Edith Pullan (BASc(N) 1948) became interested in psychiatric nursing following her graduation from the Vancouver General Hospital School of Nursing in 1940 and worked at Essondale in a number of positions. Following her graduation from UBC, she became instructor in charge of the training program for psychiatric nurses then director of nursing at the Provincial Mental Hospital at Essondale in 1951.

Barbara Blackwood (later Kozier) (BSN 1955) was another Nursing graduate who became a well-known author of nursing textbooks. Her first textbook was written with Beverly Du Gas; later texts with Glenora Erb (BSN 1962) on nursing fundamentals went to several editions.

Beverly Witter Du Gas, who became director in charge of nursing education at the Vancouver General in the 1950s and 1960s and later acting associate dean of the Faculty of Health Sciences of the University of Ottawa, was enrolled in the double degree program. However, after completing the clinical portion and receiving her VGH diploma and her Bachelor of Arts (BA) in 1945, she did not return for the seventh year. She nursed in Seattle for a brief period and, because the University of Washington would recognize her BA from UBC, she entered the master's in nursing program there without her nursing degree. She later took her doctorate in education at UBC in 1969. She has been a consultant with the World Health Organization at various times since 1965. She was coauthor (with Barbara Kozier) of a textbook, *Introduction to Patient Care*, first published in 1967. She later became the sole author of this book, which is in its fifth edition in the 1990s and has been translated into five languages and used in 40 countries. She is also coauthor of a 1993 textbook on geriatrics, *Promoting Healthy Aging*.

Figure 4.23

Many UBC graduates pursued careers in teaching. Ruth (Cochrane) Mann (BASc(N) 1947) was an instructor at VGH and is shown here with Helen Mussallem, who also taught at VGH, then was Director of Nursing Education until 1957.

Figure 4.24

UBC graduates continued to fill important roles in public health nursing in B.C. Margaret (Baird) Wilson (BSN 1961) was a public health nurse in Saanich when this picture was taken in 1961. Note the uniform, hat, and typical bag.

Dorothy Byers (later Logan) (BASc(N) 1950) followed Beverly Du Gas as director of the VGH School of Nursing after having taught in the program. She was director from 1965 until her retirement in 1986. She was also extremely active in nursing alumni activities.

Ada George (BSN 1950), after teaching at the Vancouver General for several years, was another of those who went into nursing administration. She was the first director of nursing at Surrey Memorial Hospital, coordinating its planning and opening, and later was director of nursing at Pearson Hospital in Vancouver. Always active in nursing politics, she was president of the RNABC for two terms from 1961 to 1965.

Another of the many UBC graduates who taught at VGH was Vivian Jackson (later Blake) (BSN 1952). She and Grace ("Torchy") Stewart (later Adamson) (BSN 1951), who, incidentally, was a niece of Evelyn Mallory, taught at VGH following their graduations and were well known to many of the students in the 1950s. Following their marriages, both were active in the VGH and UBC nursing alumni associations and various community volunteer groups. Vivian Blake also served on and was chair of the board of directors of the Vancouver General Hospital for a number of years.

Annette Stark (BSN 1960), Colleen Stainton (BSN 1961), and Wendy Dobson (BSN 1963) were among the UBC nursing graduates of this era who became nationally-known nursing researchers. Annette Stark obtained a master's degree in public health and a doctorate in epidemiology and became an epidemiologist researcher. For a period, she also taught in the newly developed Department of Health Care and Epidemiology at UBC. She then became director of health services and policy research and then of health systems programs for the Health Sciences Division of the International Development Research Centre (IDRC) in Ottawa. In 1993, she became head of health research for Southeast and East Asia. Colleen Stainton (BSN 1961), a professor in the Faculty of Nursing at the University of Calgary with a joint appointment in the Faculty of Medicine, has specialized in research in perinatal family dynamics, investigating high-risk perinatal experiences and parent-infant attachment. Wendy Dobson took her master's degree in administration at Harvard and a doctorate in economics at Princeton and became executive director of the C.D. Howe Research Institute, which is an independent, non-profit organization that carries out national research and analysis on economic policy issues. Previously she had served with the Canadian University Service Overseas (CUSO) in India and conducted research in international development.[109]

Another UBC nursing graduate who left nursing to go into a related health sciences discipline was Frances Vera Rigby (later Mervyn) (BSN 1961), who took her master's and doctoral degrees in psychology and became a faculty member with the Massachusetts School of Professional Psychology and was also in private psychotherapy practice.

CLOSING OF THE MALLORY ERA

In 1967, Evelyn Mallory retired. She later stressed that she had given the University ample notice that she would leave, but the administration had not been particularly active in launching a search for her successor. At the end of August 1967, just after she reached age 65, she officially ended her association with the School.

When she left, the University and the Nursing program were considerably different from when she had arrived. Hospital and medical care insurance had spawned enormous change in the way health care was delivered and nursing had grown to keep pace. At the University, the new Health Sciences Centre Hospital was underway, with the first building, the psychiatric hospital, almost ready to open. Emphasis was being placed on greater interdisciplinary participation among the health sciences faculties. The number of Nursing faculty had increased proportionally with the growth in student numbers. The School had achieved control of the clinical portions of the program and the generic program was fully integrated. Recognition of the need for more and different kinds of advanced preparation in nursing had been achieved and certificate courses in hospital unit administration and in psychiatric nursing had been started in recognition of health care needs and needs of practicing nurses. The public health diploma course continued to be offered because public health nursing was still growing in the province, and enrolment in this course continued to be high, with class sizes reaching 50 students. However, the teaching and supervision courses had been discontinued because nursing educators had recognized the need for more than just certificate preparation for teaching. As a climax to Evelyn Mallory's stewardship, the Master of Science in Nursing (MSN) program had been approved by Senate.

Evelyn Mallory herself and the faculty she attracted had an important impact on the students and their beliefs. Most of those from this period who made major contributions to the progress of nursing in Canada and abroad credit the inspiration of the School and the dedication of the faculty with having a major impact on their careers. Questionnaires to alumni asking for memories of these years stress these points, particularly the emphasis on professionalism and professional responsibilities.[110] Frances Vera Rigby (later Mervyn) (BSN 1961) summed up the influences as "the great dedication of our university teachers, who were wonderful female role models, and the wonderful comradeship of our nursing class." Wendy Dobson (BSN 1963) recalled "the sense of innovation, in which the faculty and students felt deeply involved" and rated the program highly, "especially the skills in teaching, administration, and ethical awareness from Evelyn Mallory." She added that the creativity and sense of discovery learned then is "even now, refreshing."

Most students of the period profoundly admired Evelyn Mallory, even if they did not have a close relationship with her. She had a manner and demeanour that did not encourage close ties with students, and even faculty members who knew her well referred to her as "Miss Mallory" or, affectionately, as "Miss M," but never Evelyn. Despite this distance, students recalled Evelyn Mallory with deep respect and appreciated her intelligence, visions for nursing, and deep commitment to improvement of nursing and nursing education. Delcie Hagnes (later Hill) (BSN 1964) wrote that, as a student, she had been somewhat frightened of Evelyn Mallory because "she came across to me as a highly disciplined, hard-working, strict lady"; later she found her warm and approachable.

In any discussions of these years, students frequently refer to Evelyn Mallory's sense of humour. Joan Fisher (later Brumwell) (BSN 1955, MSN 1981) recalled "her wit, and dedication to the School, and her fervour regarding history and teaching." In class reunions, students always recall Evelyn Mallory as coming to the front of the classroom, perching on the corner of the desk, twirling her long beads, and swinging her leg, which frequently was shod with a red, high-heeled sandal. Despite these personal observations, alumni of the period most frequently mention the scientifically based, problem-solving approach to nursing that was typical of the program, and the development of nursing skills based on scientific principles and research. Typical alumni comments stressed the excellence of the program. Anne Stewart (later McCaulen) (BNS 1960) said, "I felt adequately prepared and competent to assume a position of responsibility – which I did." Irene Westwick (later Jones) (BSN 1959) recalled that the concept of "total health care" and the recognition of the interdisciplinary approach were important at this time. Students of this period who went on to become nursing leaders frequently stress that Evelyn Mallory and the other faculty of this period had taught them how to think.

Faculty members held a small retirement tea at Beth McCann's home, because Evelyn Mallory had declined an official retirement party, and presented her with a silver tea service. The choice of the tea service seemed a bit surprising to some, who knew she rarely entertained at home, but it turned out that she had privately advised one of the faculty that this was what she wanted. She subsequently donated the tea service to the School for use at its social functions, and some faculty members later said she likely had this idea in mind when she suggested such a presentation. The Nursing Division of the UBC Alumni later had the silver tray engraved acknowledging her gift to the School.

On her retirement, UBC President John Barfoot MacDonald paid tribute to her many contributions, first as head and later as director of the School: "Outstanding in her profession, Miss Mallory combined her knowledge and experience with patience, industry, and imagination to develop a School of Nursing at this University recognized for its high standards and proficiency."[111]

Figure 4.25

Evelyn Mallory continued to teach until
her retirement in 1967. She was always
referred to as Miss Mallory (never
Evelyn) or, by close friends and
colleagues, as "Miss M." She was
admired for her dry wit and her
extensive knowledge of nursing.

Following her retirement, Evelyn Mallory remained briefly in Vancouver
in the house she shared with her mother. The two soon moved to Vernon,
however, where other family members resided. She lived quietly in retirement, rarely attending any nursing functions, although her home was always
open to faculty and students who visited the area. She did appear at one
special function, a well-attended, surprise dinner in her honour hosted by the
Nursing Alumni Division at the faculty club. Margaret Street recalled that
Evelyn Mallory was delighted with the event and "was simply glowing with
happiness at the honor."[112] Speeches were given highlighting her contributions to nursing and to the School and she received flowers and many tributes
from former students.

When she was in her eighties, her memory began to fail and she moved into
a nursing home in Vernon. She died July 15, 1993, in her 92nd year. Her
contributions to nursing had been many, but perhaps her most important
legacy was in the dedication, sense of confidence, and commitment that filled
the students she had taught. They went into the world confident that they
could make a difference in nursing and health care and create a better and
healthier future for Canadians. As Margaret Brown (later Patterson) (BASc(N)
1949) recalled, Evelyn Mallory had a "vision for nursing of the future."

CHAPTER FIVE

The Beth McCann Years
1967-1971

Figure 5.1

Elizabeth (Beth) Kenny McCann, acting director, 1967-1971. Beth McCann was a 1940 graduate of the UBC Nursing Program. She became a faculty member in 1947 and remained on faculty until retirement in 1982.

Elizabeth (Beth) Kenny McCann's association with the University of British Columbia's School of Nursing, first as a student, later as a faculty member, for a four-year period as acting director, then as senior professor and professor emerita, spanned more than a half century. During all those years, she saw and participated in numerous changes with unfailing enthusiasm and enduring optimism. Few students, colleagues, friends, or acquaintances can remember Beth McCann without smiling widely and appreciating her friendliness and her devotion to nursing education in general and to the UBC School in particular.

Born in Ioco, B.C., on February 9, 1917,[1] she was the elder of two surviving daughters; another girl born earlier had lived only four days. Her father and mother had moved to Ioco (now a suburb of Vancouver) from Petrolia, Ontario. Both sides of the family were of Irish decent, but both parents were born in Ontario. Her father worked for Imperial Oil and had been transferred to B.C. early in the century to supervise the building of the oil refinery. Her mother had been a teacher for a brief period before the marriage. The two girls, only two years apart, attended school in Ioco until Grade 9, then completed their secondary schooling at Crofton House, a well-known girls' school in Vancouver.[2]

In 1933, the family moved into Vancouver and, at age 16, Beth, who had always wanted to be a nurse, entered the University of British Columbia. Because she was too young to go directly into the Nursing program, she enrolled in the double-degree program, which would take seven years but allowed her to receive both a Bachelor of Arts and a Bachelor of Applied Science (Nursing). In her first years at UBC, she was active in MusSoc, the Musical Society, and was usually a part of the chorus during the annual presentations. Her Arts graduation came in 1939 and her Nursing graduation in 1940, by which time Canada had entered World War II. Although she had wanted to join the Navy, Canada was short of nurses and nursing education programs were considered important on the home front. Following graduation, she became an instructor at the School of Nursing at the Royal Columbian Hospital in New Westminster until 1943, then at the Vancouver General Hospital for one year. In 1945, she took a seven-month course in operating room nursing, and practised for a short time in the operating rooms at VGH. She then took a year off to tour Canada and the United States by car.

On her return, she began what was to be her life-long commitment – the education of nurses at UBC. She was recruited into the expanding faculty just as the University attempted to deal with the mushrooming growth of its programs following the end of the War. She was the first Nursing instructor to work both on and off campus with the University program's students while they were at VGH. During this time, she helped organize a wider field of experience for the students. She also spent a four-month summer term as a W.K. Kellogg Scholar studying nursing education at the University of Washington in 1948.

Both she and her sister Anna lived in the family home near the University gates. Her father died about 1948, and the two daughters and their mother remained in the home, which throughout Beth McCann's life was a well-known gathering place for faculty colleagues and friends and for UBC Nursing students and alumni. Beth McCann loved to entertain, although all the details of the entertaining frequently were left to her sister, who was a hospital dietitian and a magnificent cook. Although they lived together throughout their lives and were close friends, the two sisters had considerably different personalities and went their respective ways. Both liked to travel, although they rarely travelled together. Beth McCann travelled widely throughout the United States during her vacations and also visited Ireland and Pakistan among other overseas trips.

In 1952-1953, Beth McCann took educational leave as a W.K. Kellogg Fellow to attend Wayne State University for graduate studies toward the Master of Science in Nursing degree, returning to the UBC School of Nursing in the fall of 1953 as an assistant professor. While at Wayne State, she was invited to become a member of Sigma Theta Tau, the nursing honorary society, and maintained a lifelong membership. After she returned to UBC, she continued her thesis work, and, in 1959, received her master's degree. In 1961, her application for promotion was approved and she became an associate professor in the UBC School of Nursing.

In addition to her scholarly activities on campus, she was active throughout her career with the professional nursing associations, particularly at the local and provincial levels. She served as vice-president and president with the Vancouver Chapter of the Registered Nurses Association of British Columbia (RNABC) and as chair of its public relations committee as well as a member of other of its committees. She helped launch and, from 1953 to 1955, became chair of the RNABC's Instructors' Group. She was also instrumental in formation of the Nurse Administrators' Association of B.C., a group devoted to improving the standards of nursing administration throughout the province.

One of her many major organizational commitments was to the Conference of Canadian University Schools of Nursing, later known as the Canadian Association of University Schools of Nursing (CAUSN). She was one of a small core membership of about 23 nursing faculty from across Canada during the 1950s who worked hard to keep this group going and growing.[3] She served as secretary-treasurer from 1950 to 1952 and from 1956 to 1958, a time when the young association had few funds to manage; in 1952, when she turned over the funds to the new treasurer, the account stood at $368.52.[4] She was president in 1970-1972, during her term as acting director of the UBC School. By this time, the organization had grown in stature and, during her term as president, she finally convinced CAUSN to hire an executive secretary, on a part-time basis, to manage its business rather than rely on volunteer efforts of the executive. Later in her term, a permanent head office was established in Ottawa so that the group could participate more fully in national policy making and networking.

Beth McCann was appointed professor in 1967. She was the first Nursing faculty member other than a director to achieve full professorial status[5] and she was proud of this distinction. However, she was a practical nurse-scholar and "a people person not a theoretical person,"[6] as her friend and colleague, Chemistry Professor Basil Dunell, described her. The search for a definable academic discipline for nursing, something that plagued nursing (and other female-dominated professions) in academe for many years, was, according to Basil Dunell, "a real problem for her."[7]

In 1967, following Evelyn Mallory's retirement, Beth McCann became acting director, a position she held for four years. The University had been dilatory about seeking a successor when Evelyn Mallory announced she intended to retire, and many Nursing faculty expected Beth McCann would simply take over. According to her nursing colleague, Betty Cawston, she "wanted the job terribly."[8] According to her sister, this was not so; Anna McCann said that Beth McCann had told faculty, "I don't want the job. I'd rather teach."[9] The University then finally began the slow process of searching for a new director. Beth McCann recognized that the School needed a nurse with preparation at the doctoral level if it were to achieve academic recognition within the University.

CHANGES AFFECTING NURSING IN THE LATE 1960S

Canada celebrated its 100th birthday in 1967 with, among other things, Expo 67 in Montreal, which emphasized technological and scientific achievements. During the late 1960s, the economic boom allowed an infusion of funds into exploration – on all fronts, whether of outer space or of inner human space. Pierre Elliott Trudeau was elected prime minister in 1968 on a popular wave of Trudeaumania. However, by 1970 he was facing an increasingly hostile Quebec separatist movement, which culminated in the October Crisis and the kidnappings of James Cross and Pierre LaPorte and the death of LaPorte at the hands of the Front de Liberation du Quebec (FLQ).

In 1967, South African surgeon Christiann Barnard performed the first human heart transplant. And in 1969, the Americans achieved one of the century's greatest engineering feats with the first manned lunar landing, when Neil Armstrong took his small step out of the *Eagle* onto the moon's surface. Many small advances in medical science were keeping pace with these major scientific advances. In Canada, massive government funding was channelled into medical and scientific research. The federal government set up, for the first time, a Ministry of Science, and funnelled more money into the National Research Council (NRC). As well, it separated the Medical Research Council from the NRC and made it an independent Crown corporation with a budget of almost $250 million.

This infusion of funds into medical research further affected the direction of health care in Canada. Medical care insurance had been in place in B.C. and Saskatchewan since 1965, and on January 1, 1968, a federal plan was implemented. These events, coupled with the success of the hospital insurance plan, caused the Canadian public to believe that there could be a cure for all ills, either through a magic pill or wonderful surgery. But this emphasis on medical and hospital care resulted in further decreases in funding for public health initiatives. Unfortunately, funding for medical research did not extend to funds for nursing research. Despite the proliferation of technological advances, such as cardiac monitors, vastly improved incubators for premature babies, and life support systems, nursing care was not valued. Nurses were simply expected to take these advances in stride without any nursing studies into the ways that these new machines would alter their work, affect patient care outcomes, or influence the direction of health care.

Specialized units in hospitals were just beginning. The simple, broad divisions of care, based on the medical categorization of medical, surgical, urology, and other such wards, was beginning to break down. Instead, there was recognition of a need for ambulatory units, extended care facilities, intensive care units, rehabilitation wards, and so on. Although these units were based on needs for specific nursing care, research into nursing needs was not being done nor was there a focus on education for nurse specialists.

Professional nursing at this time may have made a great anachronistic blunder. Just when this explosion of knowledge was occurring, the profession recommended shorter basic courses for diploma students. The move to a two-year diploma program was a delayed response to demands going back to the 1930s for improvements in nursing education. Nursing educators had long wanted to release students from "training programs," where there was a commitment to service. Educators believed that if service demands were removed from the educational period, diploma programs could be shorter than the traditional three years. Unfortunately, the shortening of programs was ill timed, given the explosion of knowledge and the expectations that would be placed on nurses in the latter part of the century.

The shortening of diploma programs did not markedly affect university nursing programs. However, university administrators and politicians had sometimes questioned the need for "basic" four-year and five-year programs that seemed to be preparing what they saw as the "same kind" of nurses now produced in two-year college programs. Lack of research funds directed to these issues and lack of qualified nurse researchers to do the research further exacerbated this problem. It was a Catch-22 situation.

CHANGES AT UBC

The assassinations of Dr. Martin Luther King, Jr., and Senator Robert Kennedy in 1968 stand out in student memories as some of the shocking news events of the time. The Vietnamese War continued throughout this period, as well, and many conscientious objectors from the United States came to Canada. The late 1960s were also years of student unrest. Experiments, mainly by young adults, with consciousness-altering drugs such as LSD and marijuana, were gaining national attention and were raising concerns in universities across Canada. A generation of "hippies" and "flower children" was migrating west and set up camps at Kitsilano Beach and elsewhere on the mainland. Student protests, over almost any "establishment" action, were increasingly common on campuses, including UBC. Some of the protests, even in Canada, were directed toward the Vietnam War.

Kenneth Hare was president of UBC for a short period during this unrest and was followed in office by Walter H. Gage, former dean of Arts. In a 1968 brief prepared by the Alma Mater Society, students demanded a greater voice in government of the University, including participation in academic and administrative appointments, representation on governing bodies, and participation in University development, financing, and housing.[10] Although the administrators began to look into the student requests, they were shocked when more than 1,000 students occupied the Faculty Club for two days in the fall of 1968. Student leaders finally persuaded the students at the Faculty Club "sit-in" to leave to attend a mass student rally. The new administration under President Walter Gage then began to take action on the student proposals for change and for increased student representation on Senate; all departments were encouraged to appoint students to faculty committees. After this one protest, UBC was spared further major unrest, and the Alma Mater Society and student leaders were listened to more seriously.[11]

One result was immediate attention to construction of the Student Union Building (the SUB) and of new student residences, including the Gage Tower, during a major building campaign on the campus in the late 1960s. The innovative new Sedgewick Library, which was built underground in the centre of the campus, and the TRIUMF project (the Tri-University Meson Facility) were in the planning stages. An addition to the Woodward Biomedical Library was undertaken as part of the opening of the Instructional Resources Centre, which was to house the offices of all deans and directors in the health care disciplines in a move to more interdisciplinary cooperation and coordination. One creative curriculum change was the Arts I program, which provided greater flexibility for students and faculty faced with rapidly growing class sizes and a sometimes impersonal environment for first year students. The move was to augment the large classes with smaller seminar groups and tutorials and to develop thematic concepts.

Student enrolments during this period grew to about 20,000, with almost 40 per cent of the students women. Many students were married and 43 per cent of the women students had children; this necessitated accommodation for married students and for day care services on campus. Financial assistance for mature women students was another growing concern.

CHANGES IN THE SCHOOL

The opening of the Psychiatric Hospital, the first wing of the UBC Health Sciences Centre, in March 1969 realized a dream for a major research and teaching hospital on campus. The Centre was planned to allow students from the various health disciplines to study and work together in an innovative modern setting. Nursing had participated fully in this dream and Margaret

Street, of the Nursing faculty, had been involved in design of the hospital, which incorporated many new nursing administration concepts.

All faculty saw the proposed university hospital as a means of breaking down barriers among the various health professions. The heads of Medicine, Dentistry, Pharmacy, Nursing, Rehabilitation Medicine, and Social Work all were to have their offices together in the new IRC building and would try to work together for a better, more collaborative approach to health care. In the hospital, there were to be more joint appointments, with faculty holding part-time clinical appointments and practitioners teaching part time. Nursing faculty members envisioned being actively involved in giving support and education to hospital staff – in all disciplines – and being involved in the administrative planning of the hospital. The hospital itself was envisioned as a laboratory for research, where the most recent advances in care could be tested. The desire was to move away from the "ivory tower" and to see more integration between the University and the hospital community.

Although the Nursing curriculum did not undergo major changes during her period as acting director, Beth McCann and the faculty evaluated the courses and laid foundations for changes in coming years. A complete description of the undergraduate program offered by the School was drawn up and is preserved in the School's Archival Collection.[12] Of particular interest is reference to a "Model of Nursing" to guide the teaching philosophy throughout the four years of the program. The terms used in the brief description of the model, which was then in its early stages, indicate progress toward what would later become a distinctive UBC Model for Nursing.

The curriculum also reflected the move toward more student choice within the program. Students were given more options, especially in non-nursing courses. For example, they could take either English 200, previously a required course, or an option from the humanities. Students in the third year of the basic program also were allowed choices in their field work experiences.

Although the student unrest of the 1960s had not permeated the School of Nursing, the faculty, in line with the administration's pressure to listen to students, began to initiate even more student-faculty interactions. Students were appointed to School committees, such as the curriculum committee. At first, this was on an experimental and non-voting basis, but that soon changed. Students requested changes in summer field work to allow them to work during the summers. The School also listened to requests from registered nurses who wished to attend the University. Summer courses were being considered and discussion was opened on proposals to reduce the length of the post-RN program to less than three full years. Although this change did not occur in the Beth McCann era, this was the time in which its planning began.

All nursing programs across Canada at this time were experiencing a decline in enrolments, as were most universities, and recruitment programs were initiated. President Walter Gage noted the "sudden and unpredictable decline" in enrolments at UBC in his 1971-1972 president's report. The UBC nursing faculty involved students in recruitment drives, especially for visits to high schools, which proved successful. However, Beth McCann noted in one of her reports[13] that scholarships for university nurses were in especially short supply. She and President Walter Gage addressed this need in various ways and a few new nursing scholarships were added to the meagre amounts of funds available for nursing students.

Discussion was also going on in the School about the need for diploma programs. Such discussions frequently involved meetings with the Registered Nurses Association of B.C. and other professional bodies to ensure that community needs were considered. However, enrolments in two of the diploma programs were dropping and employers were expressing a preference for degree graduates. The psychiatric diploma program had not proved successful at all, with only nine completing the course during the three years it was offered, and it was discontinued at the end of 1967-1968. The administration of hospital units course, which had been popular but which was considered to have outlived its usefulness, was discontinued at the end of 1969-1970. The only diploma course retained at the end of this period was the public health diploma course, but it was revamped and renamed the community health nursing course.

On the other hand, in these years the University expanded the role of its extension department and renamed it the Centre for Continuing Education. Its mandate was broadened to include short, non-credit as well as credit courses. As well, a new and exciting Department of Continuing Education in the Health Sciences was established, including a Continuing Education in Nursing program, which was initiated in April 1968. This, in part, reflected the expanding national interest in scientific education, and funds were provided through the National Research Council as well as through the W.K. Kellogg Foundation, although most of this funding was directed to continuing medical education. The Registered Nurses Association of B.C. provided a grant of $5,000 to help start the nursing program and Assistant Professor Margaret Neylan was relieved of other teaching responsibilities, which had included the psychiatric diploma program, to take over development of this new venture.

The first course offered was a program for baccalaureate graduates to assist them to provide continuing nursing education programs within their agencies. The movement to continuing education in the health sciences was an ambitious undertaking. Leaders viewed life-long education for health professionals as an essential component of practice and were promoting continuing education credits as a basis for promotion, salary increases, and even reregistration. At this time, the University was viewed as the logical place for such continuing education programs and the UBC Senate strongly supported such endeavours.[14]

This period had also been marked by an expansion in the University's research programs and in the amounts of money being made available. In the 1971-1972 academic year, some $13 million was spent on research activities at UBC compared with $9 million in 1967-1968.[15] Research was especially focussed on the health science disciplines, but unfortunately the School of Nursing was not yet ready to participate fully. Beth McCann noted in her report to the president for 1967-1968 that Nursing faculty had, to date, been totally immersed in teaching. "We are facing now the need to adjust our loads and attitudes toward making possible a concerted effort to initiate research activities as an integral part of our faculty responsibilities. We are investigating and seeking resources for funding."[16] However, as noted above, federal and provincial government funding was directed mainly toward medical research rather than to nursing. Furthermore, the School of Nursing had only recently attracted its first doctorally prepared faculty members with the appointments of Floris King and Margaret Francis. Floris King was appointed to enable the School to commence the master's program.

THE MASTER'S IN NURSING BEGINS

At the beginning of the 1968-1969 academic year, six students registered for the new Master of Science in Nursing (MSN) degree, the fourth master's in nursing program in Canada.[17] Although the School had not been able to attract external funding to support the program, the Senate and Board of Governors had finally agreed to go ahead. Some financial assistance was offered to students who enrolled in the first class, partly to attract students when the program's opening was announced with only short notice. Dean William Armstrong of the Faculty of Applied Science announced that five scholarships of $1,000 each and five teaching assistantships of $800 each would be available for the students enrolled in the first class; students could apply for either or both.[18] None of the School's records show the source for this money, but it is possible it could have been allocated that year from either the General Scholarship Fund or the Graduate Fellowship Budget. Awards and scholarships in this period were administered mainly from the President's Office and it is possible that this was arranged between President Walter Gage and Beth McCann.

The program was two academic years in length and a thesis was required of all students. The emphasis in the program was on administration or education, with clinical options developed first for nursing in long term illness and soon after in psychiatric/mental health nursing. During the first year, all nursing classes were taught by either Floris King, who taught the research course and nursing in long term illness, or Alice Baumgart, who taught the "core concepts" course. Of the first class, five students elected the education stream and only one selected administration. Margaret Street taught the administration course. Beth McCann taught the nursing education course for one year only; Margaret Campbell was away on education leave at Teachers College, Columbia University, to take her doctorate and took over this course when she returned in 1970. She continued to develop and teach it until she retired in 1988.

The nursing in long term illness course was taught by Floris King and involved four hours of seminar each week and clinical experience, which was arranged for each student in line with needs and interests. A written paper was based on this field experience and students also prepared another major paper and gave an oral presentation on one long term illness studied in depth. The course in methods and techniques of research, also taught by Floris King, was required of all students. Although undergraduates in previous years had been introduced to a need for research and basic elements of research were discussed and included in courses, research as a distinct course had not been part of undergraduate nursing's theoretical base. The research course in the new UBC master's program was aimed at enlarging a core group who might undertake research in the future. Canadian nurses were beginning to be aware of just how important nursing research would become.

As part of this increasing awareness, the First National Conference on Research in Nursing Practice was organized by Floris King and the UBC School of Nursing with a grant from the Department of National Health and Welfare. The three-day meeting, held in Ottawa in February 1971, attracted 380 participants from across Canada and the United States, with several of the UBC nursing faculty playing key roles. The report of the conference[19] noted that until about 1960 few significant research studies on nursing practice had been reported in the Canadian nursing literature. The conference planners recognized the importance of studying nursing practice in clinical settings and of trying to establish what kind of nursing would be needed for the future.

Three of the first six students who enrolled completed the MSN program within the two academic years; two others completed it later and the other never completed the thesis. The first three MSN graduates were Myrna Lindstrom, Ethel McIntyre Smith (later Warbinek) (BSN 1957), and Ann Taylor. In the next two years, only two MSN degrees were given annually, but the number jumped to eight in 1973 and seven in 1974.

THE GOLDEN ANNIVERSARY

A major event of the Beth McCann years was the celebration in 1969 of the 50th anniversary of the School's founding. The year opened with a commemorative service on January 12, 1969, in the Memorial Room of the Woodward

Figure 5.2   A major event to celebrate the School's 50th anniversary in 1969 was a commemorative service in the Memorial Room of the Woodward Library. It honoured Ethel Johns, the first director, who had donated her papers to UBC. Beth McCann is pictured here with Chancellor John M. Buchanan.

Biomedical Library in which UBC honoured Ethel Johns, the first director, who had recently died and left her papers to the University. Chancellor John M. Buchanan welcomed the invited guests, who included Mabel Gray, second director of the School, and Margaret E. Kerr (BAScN 1926), who had been the first full-time faculty member. Part of the event involved presentation to the Library of Ethel Johns' collection of medals and medallions, her library of professional nursing books, and other of her nursing memorabilia. She had died the previous September, and Margaret Street, who was working on her biography, had catalogued the materials for presentation.

The medals and medallions included her graduation medal (1902) from the Winnipeg General Hospital, her Mary Agnes Snively award from the Canadian Nurses Association, a medallion of the Institut Edith Cavell-Marie Depage in Brussels, Belgium, and a medallion, dated 1845, of the Conseil General d'Administration des Hopitaux Civils de Lyon, France. Rae Chittick, who had been director of the McGill University School of Nursing, gave a brief tribute to Ethel Johns, and Beth McCann paid tribute to the first three directors, including third director Evelyn Mallory, who was unable to make the journey from her retirement home in Vernon.

Figure 5.3   Ethel Johns's memorial ceremony, January 12, 1969.
L-R: Beth McCann; Mabel Gray, director, 1925-1941; Pauline Capelle,
faculty member; Florence (Jackson) Barclay (BASc(N) 1939);
Margaret Kerr, former faculty member.

The Nursing Division of the UBC Alumni held a "Florence Nightingale
Birthday Party" and tea on the afternoon of May 1, to publicize the 50th
anniversary. Barbara Baird Gibson (BSN 1955), an assistant professor in the
School of Librarianship at UBC, was guest speaker and gave a presentation
on Florence Nightingale's life.

Figure 5.4   Faculty members at the Ethel Johns' memorial ceremony.
L-R: Polly Capelle, Ruth Morrison, Beth McCann.

On May 9, the School and Alumni hosted a banquet attended by 300 graduates and guests. The guest list was impressive, including Chancellor and Mrs. John Buchanan, President Walter Gage, acting Dean of Applied Science Frank Noakes, and most other deans of the health science faculties. The toast to the University was proposed by Beatrice Johnson Wood (BASc(N) 1923) and the toast to the School by Heather MacRae, president of the Nursing Undergraduate Society. In keeping with traditions of past nursing celebrations, some nursing alumni performed a brief, amusing skit showing "golden vignettes of nursing."

On October 24, the first Marion Woodward lecture was held, as part of the annual Homecoming celebrations, as the final event of the anniversary year. Beth McCann had approached the Mr. and Mrs. P.A. Woodward Foundation, which had been so generous in funding the Woodward Library and the Instructional Resources Centre, for sponsorship for an annual lecture. After some deliberations, an agreement was reached to establish the annual Marion Woodward Lectureship. Although Marion Woodward had never allowed her name to be used in conjunction with such grants, she met with Beth McCann and not only allowed her name to be used, but attended the initial Woodward Lecture, and held a tea at her home.

Figure 5.5

Beth McCann's address at the
50th anniversary banquet held at
the faculty club on May 9, 1969.
The toast to the University was given
by Bea (Johnson) Wood, one of the
first graduates.

Figure 5.6   On October 24, 1969, the School held the first
Marion Woodward lecture. The speaker was Helen Mussallem, pictured here
with Beth McCann and Marion Woodward in the Woodward home.

The first guest lecturer was Helen K. Mussallem, the well-known B.C. nursing leader who was then executive director of the Canadian Nurses Association. The lecture, titled "Nursing Tomorrow," was attended by 300 people. A reception at the Faculty Club for more than 100 honoured guests followed. Helen Mussallem had generously agreed to meet with students and faculty as part of her trip from Ottawa to give the lecture and had also been entertained at an informal faculty dinner the evening before. This began a tradition of the Woodward lecturer meeting with faculty and students as part of the visit. The Woodward Foundation had originally granted $500 annually, but this was increased to $1,000 in 1970 to cover increasing travel expenses and now involves expenses and $500 as the honorarium for the speaker.

On the day following the lecture, UBC Nursing students held an open house in the School's facilities in the Wesbrook Building for visiting alumni as part of the anniversary celebrations and Homecoming festivities. A luncheon, sponsored by the Nursing Division of the Alumni, was held after the open house at Cecil Green Park. The Nursing Division, under president Grace ("Torchy") Stewart Adamson (BSN 1951), had been actively involved in the 50th anniversary celebrations. Among the Division's efforts was the establishment of a Golden Jubilee Scholarship, to be awarded annually to a student entering the final year of the MSN program.

Although this particular Homecoming week attracted more nurses, traditional events also went on as usual. Homecoming for many years had involved the Teacup Football Game, which was played between nursing and home economics students and which always attracted huge student crowds. The 1969 game raised $1,500 for the Children's Hospital (on West 59th Ave., an expansion of the original Crippled Children's Hospital established in 1922).[20] The Teacup games, originally called the Powder Puff Games, had started in the early 1950s as part of various Homecoming stunts, and had been followed by the passing of the hat to raise funds for worthwhile causes. They soon became a tradition, with the donation of a Teacup Trophy in 1954 and frequently with the involvement of B.C. Lions football players as coaches for the two teams. By 1969, it had become, as Beth McCann said, "much more professional that it used to be when we weren't even sure which goal was ours."[21]

FACULTY OF THE SCHOOL IN THIS ERA

Although Beth McCann was holding a watching brief while the search went on for a new director, the faculty of the School grew marginally during her term. She attracted some part-time lecturers, and she continued to seek joint appointments, a relatively new approach in nursing education in Canada at the time. Faculty who remained from the Evelyn Mallory period included Margaret Street, Pauline Capelle, Margaret Campbell, Alice Baumgart,

Elizabeth Cawston, Helen Shore, Rose Murakami, Helen Niskala, Sylvia Holmes, Eileen Campbell, and Margaret Neylan. Among those who joined the faculty at this time were Floris King, Margaret Francis, Helen Gemeroy, Maude Dolphin, Helen Elfert, Ethel McIntyre Smith (later Warbinek), Jessie Hibbert, Helen Olsen, Kirsten Weber (later Hyde), Jo-Ann (Crawford) Wood, and, on a part-time basis, Ruth Elliott and Betty Johnson.

Floris Ethia King had been appointed in August 1968 to coordinate the implementation of the MSN program. The School faculty realized that a doctorally prepared nurse was essential for the program and she was hired soon after completing her doctoral degree in public health at the University of North Carolina. She had been born in Caron, Saskatchewan, in 1927 and her undergraduate nursing degree was from the University of Toronto and her master's degree in public health was from the University of Michigan. She was one of a rare few doctorally prepared Canadian nurses of the time and, in fact, her academic preparation exceeded that of any nurse employed in British Columbia.

In addition to her nursing qualifications, she was an accomplished pianist and artist; she had been a concert pianist for four years in her late teens and early twenties before she entered nursing. Students from the first classes recall her as enthusiastic, although perhaps a bit stressed with the magnitude of the task of introducing a new program. She came to UBC with no previous experience on a faculty. She had practised in public health and had held a senior position as a field program director and nursing consultant with the Canadian Tuberculosis Association. She had not been involved in the early planning stages of the UBC master's program in the Mallory era, when Margaret Campbell, Margaret Street, and Alice Baumgart had been intimately involved in designing the courses and guiding the program through the School Council, Graduate Curriculum Committee, and, finally, the Senate. During her four years at UBC, her main influence was in research. Great emphasis was placed on the MSN thesis, which was required of all students. As a result, Floris King and other faculty were intimately involved in developing and approving research proposals for student theses. She resigned in 1972 to become professor and director of the Dalhousie University School of Nursing.

Margaret Francis also had recently completed doctoral studies, receiving her doctorate in education from the University of Maryland. She had received her basic nursing education in Delhi, India, and, after emigrating to the United States she took her master's degree at the Catholic University of America. She taught in the undergraduate program at UBC and was a warm and caring teacher who was well-liked by her students, many of whom kept in touch with her after they graduated. She was at UBC for only a few years, and left to teach in Dalhousie University's and then the University of Manitoba's nursing programs. She died in Winnipeg in the late 1980s.

Helen Gemeroy was the first nurse administrator to hold a formal joint appointment in the UBC School of Nursing. She had been appointed in 1968 when the Psychiatric Unit, the first wing of the UBC Health Sciences Centre, opened. She came from a joint appointment as a faculty member of the McGill School for Graduate Nurses and director of nursing at the Allan Memorial Institute in Montreal. In addition to her nursing diploma, she held a bachelor of arts degree from Sir George Williams University in Montreal and a master of arts degree from Columbia University. She was hired as associate professor and assistant director of nursing at the UBC Health Sciences Centre, in charge of the Psychiatric Unit.

In working out the new joint appointment, Beth McCann and Helen Gemeroy tried hard to make the collegial relationships that had been envisioned for the Health Sciences Centre work in practice. As Helen Gemeroy recalled in an interview, "We tried to employ, on a staff level, nurses with baccalaureate degrees ... and we also held out for all registered nursing staff."[22] This represented a deliberate attempt to allow a nurse to function as the primary caregiver; one nurse would be responsible from admission to discharge for the care of each patient. This new approach was replacing the team nursing approach to care. In the UBC Centre, it worked relatively well in the psychiatric areas.

Helen Gemeroy also served as a mentor and advisor to many of the faculty members of the School, who appreciated her insights into faculty politics at a university level. As she recalled, "I think UBC suffered from isolation, and the university nursing program had focussed a great deal on community health and public health nursing. In fact, there were very few nurses [at that time] in Vancouver in administrative positions who had gained their advanced preparation at UBC.... I saw great efforts within the School of Nursing to be a colleague with other schools of nursing across the country.... They were a long way away from the more established schools of nursing in Ontario and Quebec, which was a disadvantage in some respects."[23]

Rose Murakami (BSN, 1962) rejoined the faculty in 1970 after completing her master's degree in nursing at McGill. She returned as coordinator for the second year of the generic program. She had taught in the program in the Evelyn Mallory years, mainly in clinical areas at St. Paul's. Because she was committed to clinical nursing practice, Rose Murakami always carried a full load in supervising students in clinical areas in addition to her coordinator activities. An extremely supportive person, her office door was always open to students and junior faculty alike. She had high standards and a deep commitment to quality care. This dedication to clinical practice eventually lured her into accepting a position as director of nursing at the Purdy Pavilion for Extended Care at the UBC Health Sciences Centre. After she assumed this position in 1981, she maintained close ties with the UBC School, first through a joint appointment and by continuing to teach as a part-time professor in the master's program and to supervise master's theses. She also earned a master of science degree from Boston University with a major as a clinical nurse specialist in rehabilitation nursing and a minor in gerontological nursing. She gained a reputation for her expertise in care of geriatric patients and in maintaining their independence even when they were in an extended care facility. From 1987 to 1993, she was an adjunct professor in the School. During this time, the UBC Hospital and Shaughnessy Hospital merged and Rose Murakami became chief nursing officer at the UBC site, then later assistant vice-president for nursing research and education. In the restructuring of management at the University Hospital in 1993, her position was deleted. In January of 1994, she joined the staff of the RNABC.

Elizabeth (Betty) Cawston (BSN 1960) also taught in the Mallory years, then went to the University of Washington to obtain her master's degree in nursing in 1965. She had been a classmate of Beth McCann's during their Vancouver General Hospital courses and then nursed at VGH for 10 years in a variety of capacities including head nurse and supervisor. She also had experience with the Venereal Disease Clinic in the provincial public health program for eight years, during which time she took a diploma in teaching and supervision and then her baccalaureate at UBC. Along with Helen Shore and Kirsten Weber (later Hyde), she taught public health nursing courses initially under Ruth Morrison. During the Beth McCann years, she taught mainly community health nursing. A major portion of her time involved coordination of student experiences with various community agencies, and she became well-known and highly regarded by those in agencies throughout the province. A well-liked and respected teacher, she too had an open-door policy and was known, especially in later years, for her warm support and counselling of individual students. She served on the executive of the Nursing Division of the UBC Alumni for many years.

She became a close friend and confidante of Beth McCann, especially in their later years, and the two planned their retirements together. They toured New Zealand and the South Pacific, then continued an active involvement with the Alumni Division. A woman with a strong sense of humour, Betty Cawston said in an interview following her retirement that she missed, most of all, the contact with students, and some of her colleagues – but that she did not miss committee meetings at all.

Ethel Smith (later Warbinek) (BSN 1957, MSN 1970) joined the faculty in 1970, after graduating from the first class in the master's program. She had taught surgical nursing at VGH for 10 years before returning to UBC for her master's degree, then immediately was offered a faculty position by Beth McCann to teach in second year. She remained on faculty, teaching mainly in second and fourth years and always involved in clinical teaching. Her research areas are aspects of clinical teaching, especially development of a guide for observation of clinical teachers, and history of nursing. She is

Figure 5.7

Elizabeth (Betty) Cawston (BSN 1960), a faculty member and close friend of Beth McCann, taught community health nursing for many years and was a well-liked and respected teacher with a wonderful sense of humour.

actively involved with the History of Nursing Professional Practice Group and the Nursing Division of the UBC Alumni.

One of her teaching assignments during the Beth McCann years was an interdisciplinary course between third year nursing students and first year medical students. The philosophy behind this interprofessional health education course was to foster understanding and respect between the two disciplines. A medical student and a nursing student were jointly assigned to a family, which they visited, and the students then reported back to the group. Two faculty tutors, one doctor and one nurse, worked with seminar groups. Although the program ran for only a few years, Ethel Warbinek described it as the only course at UBC that even tried to fulfil this vision of interprofessional education. The course was finally voted out at a Nursing faculty meeting.

CHANGES IN NURSING

Although this era was a short one, nursing and nursing education in British Columbia were on the threshold of many changes. This was a period of closure of many hospital schools and the establishment of new community college programs. For example, in 1972, the psychiatric nursing program at the Provincial Mental Hospital in Essondale, which began in 1931, graduated its last class. The registered psychiatric nursing program was not discontinued, but moved to the B.C. Institute of Technology and a second program opened at Douglas College in 1975. This development was contrary to trends in eastern Canada, where all psychiatric nursing programs were discontinued in the 1960s and mental health nursing care was provided by registered nurses. In the four western provinces, the provincial governments elected to continue to fund registered psychiatric nursing programs.

Another emerging trend during these years was the entry of men into nursing. It was during the Beth McCann years that the UBC nursing program admitted its first male student into the undergraduate program. Although a few male nurses had graduated from diploma programs in B.C., the first male generic student was Mike Lawerence (BSN 1973), who had previously been a registered psychiatric nurse. He later went on to take his master's degree in nursing. The first male student in the master's program was Walter Bredlow, who entered the program in 1970 and graduated in 1976.

ANOTHER REQUEST FOR FACULTY STATUS

The concept of a change from School to Faculty status was raised once again during the Beth McCann era. The idea had been raised before, in the late 1940s, when nursing's status in the University changed from Department to School. At that time, UBC had developed several new faculties, including Medicine, but a major stumbling block to faculty status for Nursing had been the lack of academically prepared nursing faculty. The suggestion that Nursing should be a Department or School under the Faculty of Medicine had roused the ire of nursing leaders, however, and the compromise decision was to let it remain in the Faculty of Applied Science, but with increased independence as a School.

However, the 1964 Report of the Royal Commission on Health Services had supported university education for nurses and recommended that 10 additional university programs be established across Canada. In line with the recommendations, UBC began plans for a master's degree in nursing. Several of the new nursing programs being planned in other universities would have faculty status, and established programs in other Canadian universities had achieved faculty status or were seeking it. Faculty members in the UBC program also wanted to achieve this mark of recognition and this led to the renewed requests to the University administration.

Evelyn Mallory prepared a *Brief Recommending the Establishment of a Faculty of Nursing* for submission to the Senate and Board of Governors on March 29, 1965.[24] In the brief, she emphasized the changes that had occurred since the 1919 decision that nursing should be located in Applied Science (rather than in Arts and Science or in Agriculture, the only other two faculties of the time). She noted that none of the courses taught in Applied Science (which had become increasingly synonymous with Engineering) were required or appropriate for Nursing students; most non-nursing courses were drawn from Arts or Science, although transfer to either of these faculties also was not appropriate. She noted in addition that new faculties of Medicine, Dentistry, and Pharmacy existed. As well, the building of the new Health Sciences Centre indicated development of a health sciences component on the campus, in which Nursing should have a major role. She noted that Nursing had played a large consultative role in the planning of the Health Sciences Centre, but that it was difficult for nursing students, and others, "to develop appropriate relationships unless nursing is in fact accorded co-ordinate status within the group and unless true colleague relationships are in fact demonstrated throughout the entire period of the students' experience."

Furthermore, Evelyn Mallory suggested, the search for her replacement when she retired would be greatly assisted if faculty status were to be achieved. The School needed to attract well-qualified and distinguished nursing leaders from the relatively small pool of potential candidates – and the status accorded to Nursing within the University would be seen either as a positive or as a negative factor. In other words, it would be easier to attract ambitious nurses for the position of dean of a faculty rather than director of a school.

No mention was made in the brief of the fact that the status of nurses within the University and within the health care community was closely tied to gender issues. Although this is well recognized in the 1990s, such a viewpoint was not acknowledged in the 1960s. UBC, like other universities across Canada, was male-dominated, and its administrative ranks even more so. The director of the School of Nursing frequently was the only female in senior academic meetings. On the other hand, her position as a director kept her from being seen as an equal to the deans of Medicine or Dentistry. Furthermore, the lack of academic qualifications of most Nursing faculty, which related directly to the lack of academic programs available in universities, meant female faculty members in other disciplines, most of whom had doctoral preparation, were not supportive of Nursing.

No progress had been made by Evelyn Mallory on this move for faculty status. Throughout her term as acting director, Beth McCann continued to press for recognition as a faculty, but was hampered by a new development. With the opening of the Health Sciences Centre and the plans for its further development, a Co-ordinating Committee of the Health Sciences was established, headed, as if it were a matter of course, by the dean of Medicine. Nursing was one player at the table but was hampered by traditional gender and hierarchical structures. As well, UBC's Board of Governors continued its traditional reluctance to increase, from 12, the number of faculties.[25] Nursing's important role was repeatedly downplayed and discounted.

To this end, Beth McCann and the faculty in the School prepared another brief to try to establish more equal footing. The brief from Nursing recommended to the Co-ordinating Committee that the Board of Governors create College status for all the health sciences disciplines.[26] These attempts also were not successful. Although the Co-ordinating Committee in general, and

John F. McCreary, dean of Medicine, in particular, assured everyone that Nursing's position was equal, in fact it continued to weaken. The Senate did not act on the recommendation for federated colleges.[27]

Support for the move to faculty status was contained in the *Report of The President's Temporary Committee, Administrative Structure for the Health Sciences Centre*, in October 1969. In this report, which made recommendations to President Walter Gage, the Committee strongly recommended that Nursing should have "equivalent status to Medicine, Dentistry and Pharmacy" and throughout the report referred to Nursing as a faculty "as it appears to this Committee that this is the most appropriate way of indicating equivalent status."[28]

In November 1969, the School of Nursing issued an unequivocal statement:

> After four years of intense study it appears that the dilemma of providing status for the School of Nursing as equivalent to that of Dentistry, Medicine and Pharmacy is soluble only through a change from the status of a School in Applied Science to that of a separate faculty.[29]

No action was taken.

STUDENTS OF THE PERIOD

Questionnaires and other information from students who graduated in the late 1960s provide some insights both into the program and into the ways that UBC may have affected their careers. Some of these students include Alison Rice (BSN 1967), B. Ann Hilton (BSN 1968), and Ada Butler (BAScN 1950, MSN 1971), all of whom later joined the faculty of the School and taught in its programs for many years. Alison Rice, who later took midwifery courses, was a proponent for midwifery care in B.C., which finally achieved government approval in 1993. While on faculty, Ada Butler developed a communications course for undergraduate students. Her major area of expertise in the School was the teaching of family nursing. Ann Hilton later took her master's degree at the University of Toronto and received her doctorate in nursing from the University of Texas at Austin. She initially taught in the undergraduate program, but based on her strong interests in quantitative research, has more recently taught in the graduate programs.

Bernadette Ratsoy (BSN 1968) became president of the Registered Nurses Association of B.C., chief nursing officer of St. Paul's Hospital, executive director of the Registered Nurses Association of Alberta, and director of the nursing program at the B.C. Institute of Technology. Heather Gesy (BSN 1968) eventually joined the staff of the Registered Nurses Association of B.C. as a member relations advisor.

Elizabeth Ann (Ann) Taylor (MSN 1970) was the only student of the six in the first MSN class who took the administration option rather than the teaching option. She recalled meeting, as "a lonely little petunia," every Monday afternoon for three hours with two senior professors, Margaret Street and Maude Dolphin. She also recalled studying statistics in the time before calculators were widely used and accepted. "That was torture. We would sit on the phone at night and compare our additions and divisions." She found the nursing faculty harder on the first class of students than probably was necessary or fair. "It was almost like, because it was women, because it was nursing, and because it was new, we had to be twice as good and go through twice as many hoops as almost any other graduate program on campus."[30] After graduation, she became executive assistant to Mary Richmond, director of nursing at the Vancouver General Hospital, and later was director of preventive programs for the Vancouver Health Department.

Wendy Jean Foster (later Trousdell) (BSN 1970) recalled driving a carpool of nursing students to the B.C. Penitentiary in New Westminster, instead of to the Oakalla minimum security unit, "and tapping politely on the door and asking about our tour."[31] She did not say what reception she received.

Graduates from 1969 who attended a coffee klatch in 1981 spent a great deal of time recalling extracurricular activities in which they had taken part during their student years. The Beth McCann years saw an initial interest in the feminist movement, which clashed with some of the traditional activities that nurses had participated in with the Engineers. Because Nursing was part of the Faculty of Applied Science, student events included combined Engineering/Nursing balls, "mixers" (informal dances), various other parties, and blood donor clinics. The Engineers frequently sponsored a nursing student as their candidate for Homecoming queen, and, in 1969, the nursing students cooperated fully in the "1st Leg Auction," a fundraising event ("We knees your money") for local charities. The students at the coffee klatch in 1981 noted that "times had changed," but were a bit nostalgic. "It's too bad that … [such events as the leg auction have] become so political, because it was fun and it was done with good intentions," said one.[32]

The Class of 1971, the last class under Beth McCann's directorship, designed the class ring, which is still in use.

CHANGES ON THE HORIZON

Beth McCann had always fully supported nursing student and faculty participation in extracurricular activities and campus events. She had a strong and supportive circle of friends among the university faculty outside as well as inside the School and she frequently travelled for ski weekends with one small, close-knit group. She and her long-time friend and colleague Basil Dunell, a professor in Chemistry, would attend the dances and events on

Figure 5.8   Beth McCann was a strong supporter of student events.
This picture of the faculty skit at an NUS banquet in 1981, depicts
Betty Cawston as "Afro" and Beth McCann as "Athena."

campus and they routinely attended the Engineering Balls and Nursing Grad Dances. During her tenure as acting director of the School she had maintained this active role, including a term as an elected member of the UBC Senate. However, the search committee finally managed to secure a successor, Muriel Uprichard, and Beth McCann was ready to step down.

She took a sabbatical leave in 1971-1972, when the new director took over. She needed surgery, but then spent six months in San Mateo, California, taking post-master's studies and visiting with her friend and former UBC nursing colleague Margaret Duncan Jensen. Following the sabbatical, she served the School of Nursing for another 10 years as a senior professor, frequently acting both as mentor to new faculty members and as advisor to the directors. Two of her main teaching areas included history of nursing and nursing administration. She taught at all levels of the program, from first-year to master's classes – and left an indelible impression on all nursing students who attended the School. Many of her students will remember that Beth loved purple and both wore and had many accents in this colour around her office, including a purple cow. The cow was one of a collection of more than 200 china and glass cows that she had received, mostly as gifts.

She served in a variety of senior teaching positions and for a time was coordinator of clinical placements, which involves liaison between the School and all of the many agencies in which students have clinical practice. A tireless worker, she was also active in University affairs and was well-known on campus. She was one of the founding members of the Faculty Club when it began its existence in temporary quarters in one of the campus "huts" and was on the executive of the UBC Faculty Club while the Club's building was being built on the Marine Drive site in 1959. She served on the Dean of Women's Committee for Women's Year in 1975, and was an elected member of the executive of the Faculty of Graduate Studies 1976-1977.

On her retirement in 1982, following 35 years on faculty, she said that her greatest commitments had been to patients and students. Working with students allowed opportunities to keep in touch with patients and ensure they received the good nursing care she considered essential. She was always concerned that the care given reflected the best nursing available at the time, but that her students would be aware, too, of changes in care that would be needed for the world of the future. "I am a nurse first, and a teacher as a close second," she said in an interview about her retirement. "I wouldn't do anything else if I had it to do over again."[33]

At the time of her retirement, the Nursing Division of the UBC Alumni established a fund in her honour, which became the Beth McCann Memorial Scholarship following her death. Two scholarships from this fund are given annually to undergraduate students who demonstrate a commitment to the nursing profession and a contribution to the University or the community. As well, a fund for the Beth McCann Chair for Nursing Research Fund was initiated by the Class of 1960 as a start to raising the necessary $1 million endowment needed to establish a Chair. Both these awards were started during her lifetime as a tribute to her many contributions. Her retirement dinner was held in the Faculty Club and was attended by 150 guests. Her gift from the School was a string of pearls.

Following retirement, she spent one year travelling (to New Zealand and Tahiti mainly), then returned to active involvement as a professor emerita with the School and to many activities with the professional nursing associations she had worked with over the years. As her sister Anna McCann said, "Nursing was Beth's whole life. There was not really anything that she wanted outside of it. Once she retired, she still continued on with all the different associations and groups and so forth connected with it."[34]

As one of her projects, she continued compiling information for a history of the UBC School of Nursing to be published for the School's 75th anniversary in 1994. Although she did little writing, she began to accumulate the records and documents that form the basis of this book. She sent questionnaires to students and collected an enormous amount of information, which now is a large part of the UBC School of Nursing Archival Collection.

At the time of her death, she was chair of the 75th Anniversary Celebrations Committee for the Registered Nurses Association of B.C.'s planned 1987 commemorations. She died January 13, 1986, of a heart attack while on

Figure 5.9 Beth McCann retired in 1982, after 35 years as a faculty member, as did her colleague and friend, Betty Cawston. The Nursing Division of the UBC Alumni Association established the Beth McCann Scholarship in recognition of her contribution to the School.

a brief holiday trip to Seattle with Betty Cawston. Her sister said that there had been no warning of a heart attack, except that, when she thought about it in retrospect, Beth had been slightly anxious about recently clearing snow around the home that they shared; this may have indicated that she had had some slight warning pains.

Among her many honours was the Registered Nurses Association of B.C.'s Award of Excellence in Nursing Education, given posthumously at the RNABC's annual meeting in 1986. Earlier, she had been named an Honorary Member of RNABC. She was also honoured in 1990 by inclusion in the CNA *In Memoriam* book at CNA House, Ottawa. Perhaps her greatest tributes come from the hundreds of students who responded to her appeals for information about their memories of the School. When asked who or what they remembered most about their time on campus, a majority of the respondents replied along the lines of: "You, of course."

CHAPTER SIX

The Muriel Uprichard Years
1971-1977

Figure 6.1

Muriel Uprichard, Director, 1971-1977, was not a nurse, but had for many years been associated with nursing both at the University of Toronto and the University of California in Los Angeles.

Muriel Uprichard, who took over as director of the UBC School of Nursing in 1971, was not a nurse, but had long been associated with nursing education, both in Canada and the United States. She came highly recommended because of her major research positions and her high-profile consultancies related to nursing education. She came with a commitment to a plan of nursing education based on use of a nursing model and a vision of an "educational ladder" that would streamline the approach to nursing preparation.

Born in Regina of Welsh decent on November 21, 1911, she was the second oldest in a family of six girls.[1] After elementary and high school education in Regina, she entered normal school to prepare for a teaching career. In 1930, just as the Great Depression began, she started teaching and for the next few years taught in rural, town, and city schools throughout Saskatchewan. Her annual salary in those early years was about $400, but because of the grim economic times she often did not receive any cash. Instead, she was "given script, and room and board with a local farmer, who in turn was given a credit on his taxes for looking after the teacher."[2] She sometimes taught up to 59 students in Grades 1 through 11, and no money would change hands, although, as with many other teachers, she would build up a credit with the Department of Education. When the Depression ended, the provincial government eventually paid her back wages.

When she received her money and paid all her debts, she found she had about $700 left and so decided to enrol at Queen's University in Kingston, Ontario, to complete work that she had started as an extramural student. She received her bachelor of arts degree, with honours in English and Philosophy, in 1943, graduating *magna cum laude*. An outstanding student, she received two scholarships and immediately went on to take her master of arts degree at Smith College, in Northampton, Massachusetts. She received further distinguished scholarships, including the Harvard School of Education Fellowship and, for three years, was a British Council Scholar: Canada to United Kingdom. This latter award went to only one student chosen annually from all Canadian university graduates. With this, she attended the University of London Institute of Education and graduated in 1947 with a doctorate in educational psychology, again *magna cum laude*.

Following her graduation, she spent a year as director of a study of the Florence Nightingale International Foundation, carried out for the International Council of Nurses. She and H.R. Hamley, professor of education, University of London, prepared a report[3] recommending ways that a fund of more than $250,000, raised from nurses around the world, could be effectively used. While carrying out research for the study, Muriel Uprichard travelled to 19 countries around the world. This study helped spark her lifelong interest in the history of nursing. Her experiences in London during the final years of World War II and its aftermath led her to become especially interested in the health of displaced children and, on her return in 1948 to Canada, she went to work for the Red Cross. She was hired first as deputy director, then as national director of the Canadian Junior Red Cross and editor of *Canadian Red Cross Junior*, where she continued her work for children displaced by the war. Among her treasured honours is a citation received in 1952 from the West German Red Cross for outstanding service to displaced children.

During the later years with the Red Cross, she began to work with the Canadian Nurses Association. In 1950-1951, she served as a consultant to review the CNA's administrative structure;[4] this probably was part of a larger study committee headed by external consultant Pauline Jewett.[5] She also was consultant to CNA during 1950 to 1955 on a five-year experiment in the improvement of patient care through an innovative program of nursing education.[6]

In 1955, she was invited to join the faculty of the University of Toronto School of Nursing and remained there for 10 years, first as assistant professor and then as associate professor. She taught history and philosophy of nursing, curriculum building, and theories of learning applied to nursing education, and chaired the curriculum committee. During this time, she also frequently served as a consultant to hospitals and agencies on innovative ways to improve delivery of nursing care. For example, in 1963-1964 she served as a consultant to the Toronto General Hospital on re-entry of older nurses who wished to return to nursing after a period away. This was the beginning of awareness about safety to practice and need for refresher courses, especially for nurses who were recruited back into the profession during critical nursing shortages. This also was a time when it became the trend for nurses to re-enter the work force after periods of childrearing, which necessitated this concern for refresher training. During her final sabbatical leave at the University of Toronto, Muriel Uprichard was a consultant to the Royal Commission on Health Services, chaired by Emmett Hall, and was responsible for the section of the report on more effective use of nursing personnel in improvement of patient care.

She was a member of the faculty at the University of California at Los Angeles (UCLA) School of Nursing from 1965 to 1971. There, she taught theories of learning, curriculum building, and teaching in schools of nursing, and continued to be an active consultant on administrative nursing problems and on other diverse innovative health care projects. For example, she was an evaluation consultant for the California Regional Medical Television Network on improvement of nursing care through use of closed circuit television.

Muriel Uprichard was considered a superb teacher by her students. Janet Gormick, who was one of her students at UCLA, described her as "exceedingly dynamic." She added that "there was a fair bit of fear in there as well – you stretched yourself to meet her expectations; one wouldn't consider going to her class without being fully prepared."[7]

A small woman, Muriel Uprichard had strong blue eyes, which could be piercing, and, when she came to UBC, her hair was white. She was a trendy dresser and liked bright colours. When she presented the Marion Woodward Lecture in 1971, she wore her academic regalia and had a striking presence when she appeared on the platform.

As well as being a dynamic speaker, she was a reasonably prolific author, having started her writing career in 1943 with a children's book, *Three Little Indians*, and in 1956 was editor for *The Canadian Speller*, a textbook for elementary school children published by W.J. Gage. After finishing as editor of the *Canadian Red Cross Junior*, she wrote numerous articles related to nursing and health. She noted in her curriculum vitae submitted when she came to UBC that she was working on a book, *The Making of Modern*

Nursing: A Study of Social Forces Influencing the Development of Professional Nursing; this had received some funding from the American Nurses Association and was to be published by Macmillan.[8]

On her arrival in B.C., she purchased a home in Vancouver. A sociable person, she would have large gatherings at her home to which she invited senior faculty from the School and from many of the other health science disciplines on campus. She frequently entertained deans and department heads as part of her effort to get to know key people on campus and was soon well known and involved in campus politics.

CURRICULUM CHANGES

Muriel Uprichard's appointment was finalized at UBC in the Spring of 1971. Although the appointment was not official until July 1, she immediately began looking for some recent University of California graduates with master's degrees in nursing to come with her to UBC. She arranged for the hiring of four junior faculty whom she knew and who knew her and her philosophies. This influx of new faculty had both positive and negative effects on the School and its existing faculty. On the one hand, the four young faculty members who came that summer were outgoing, enthusiastic young women who made sincere attempts to integrate with existing faculty; all proved popular colleagues, remaining on faculty for many years. On the other hand, the existing faculty felt threatened and resented the assumption that "new blood" was needed if change was to be effected.

The four new faculty immediately hired by Muriel Uprichard were Mary Cruise, Janet Gormick, Betsy LaSor, and Barbara Lee Herrick (later McGuire). Janet Gormick, still on faculty in the 75th anniversary year, said in an interview years later that Muriel Uprichard and the others exerted a major influence on the curriculum when they arrived.[9] Three of the four had taken curriculum development courses from Muriel Uprichard and, therefore, were familiar with the way curriculum change could be accomplished quickly within an existing program.

In the fall of 1971, soon after Muriel Uprichard's arrival, the UBC and Vancouver General Hospital schools of nursing set up a committee to explore the development of a new approach to education of nurses based on four two-year stages. After 14 meetings, the committee's proposals called for the two programs to merge.[10] The documents suggested that new programs in the community colleges were having an impact on nursing education and that students and others were beginning to question the three-year, hospital-based, service-oriented program at VGH. On the other hand, the committee was concerned that the UBC program was not graduating enough baccalaureate-prepared nurses to have a significant impact on nursing practice or on the nursing community. The committee's proposals called for four closely integrated, two-year programs to provide not only for vertical progression but also for lateral specialization at each two-year stage.

The first two years would prepare a "Nurse Technician" and would provide fundamental knowledge, skills, and attitudes for basic hospital-based practice of nursing and lead to the RN licensure. The next two years would prepare a "Nurse Clinician" with a baccalaureate degree in nursing from UBC and students could enter from community colleges as well as from VGH. Graduates would be prepared to work both in hospitals and in the community. According to the proposal, "Their professional practice will be distinguished from that of the nurse technician by the complexity of the problems they are able to meet, the depth of knowledge underlying their decision-making, and their skill in nursing interventions." The third level would be preparation of a "Clinical Nurse Specialist" with a master's degree in nursing in which the nurse would specialize in either hospital or community nursing, with some sub-specializations. The fourth level, which the committee envisioned as beginning almost immediately, would prepare a "Nurse Consultant" with a doctorate in nursing. The "lateral specialization" at the end of each two-year level would enable the nurse to develop expertise in a particular clinical area. The committee envisioned a full enrolment at UBC of about 1,000 students in the eight years of the program by 1984. This compared with an enrolment of approximately 400 in the undergraduate program and 36 in the master's program in 1973. In other words, within 10 years, the size of the UBC program was expected to more than double.

The committee's report stated that the program had received approval in principle by the minister of health, chair of the UBC Board of Governors, chair of the VGH Board of Governors, the UBC dean of Medicine, the VGH medical director, and the faculties of both programs. However, it appears that the plan never received funding because it was never fully implemented. The estimated funding proposals attached to the document indicated a projected operating cost of $1.75 million dollars annually when the eight-year program was fully operational. In addition, about $4 million was needed for capital expenses, and approximately another $500,000 for curriculum development and planning.

Although this UBC-VGH proposal did not proceed, a radically changed curriculum for the UBC program was developed based on this "ladder concept" and was accomplished in just one year. The proposal for changes went to the UBC Senate in the fall of 1972 and the program was approved in principle December 13, 1972. Muriel Uprichard told the Senate that even before she became director it had been made quite clear to her by faculty members of the School, others at UBC, the Registered Nurses Association of B.C., and students that the curriculum "needed a tremendous overhaul."[11]

And this is exactly what we've done.... We set up a small committee which devised a behavioral systems model, and on the basis of this conceptual framework we have looked into what nursing is and what nursing should be doing. We have had people on our staff examining the directions in which the health-care systems are moving in this province and in this country.... The emphasis in nursing in the future is going to be on community nursing and not on hospital nursing. This does not mean that nursing will not continue to support medicine in its efforts to cure illness and disease but that this will not be its sole occupation, and its chief occupation, indeed, will be quite different. This program reflects this kind of thinking.[12]

The new four-year curriculum, which started in the 1973-1974 academic year, deleted the pre-nursing arts and science year that had previously been required; qualified high school students were admitted directly into the program. The science courses from that preadmission year were replaced with two new "integrated" science courses, one in human life sciences and the other in the social sciences. As well, the elective courses were expanded to "provide for the breadth and balance characteristic of a liberal education, for the pursuit of individual interests, and for an expression of creativity."[13]

In 1973, the School also discontinued the one-year diploma program in community health nursing, which dated back to 1920. The School had been recommending the closure for several years. Changing trends in public health and increasing complexity of family and community needs had led to the realization by employers that public health nurses needed a baccalaureate education; the demand for diploma-prepared graduates was decreasing.[14]

At one point in the development of the curriculum for the new program, the School considered integrating courses at junior levels for students in health science disciplines, as had been planned in the Mallory and McCann years. For example, Muriel Uprichard approached David Bates, dean of Medicine, in September 1972 to discuss an interdisciplinary physiology course.[15] Unfortunately, such a course did not materialize, although courses in human biology and microbiology were developed by Science faculty specifically for nursing students. These replaced courses such as chemistry 230, microbiology 201, and zoology 303 given in the old programs, but led to philosophical debate over whether courses designed exclusively for one discipline are equivalent to those offered for all students.

The nursing curriculum was also markedly changed to reflect the move to a theoretical framework that included the new UBC Model for Nursing. The new program also incorporated into the four years the concepts of teaching and leadership that were considered essential to the general practice of nursing. However, the emphasis on teaching and administration, which had for so long been components of the final year of the program, were no longer considered appropriate in undergraduate preparation; instead it was decided that these were advanced concepts that should be taught at the graduate level.

Even though the UBC-VGH proposal had not gone forward, the two-year college programs were producing some graduates who wished to articulate into the degree program. The School planned to increase the numbers of degree graduates and to provide a pool of nurses who could progress into the MSN program. Registered nurses from diploma programs therefore could enter at the third-year level after passing an entrance examination.

The new basic program required UBC students to take three-month summer sessions at the end of the first and second years. These were considered necessary to ensure clinical competency by the end of the second year. These changes led to a submission to the Registered Nurses Association of B.C. in July 1974 for approval for students to apply for registration at the end of the first two years of the program. The new curriculum provided an option for UBC students to be able to write the registered nurse examinations at the end of the second year and, if they wished, to begin working. As the Report to the Registered Nurses Association of B.C. stated:

It is logical to assume that the first two years of the four-year curriculum constitute a programme preparing for nurse registration. All students who enter at the first year level will be given the option of writing the registered nurse examination at the end of the second year. It is hoped that they will continue in the programme; the status of registered nurse should make it easier for the financially disadvantaged to continue into the third and fourth year.

In the design of the four-year curriculum, the ladder concept has been utilized, implying differences in preparation between the student who completes the first two years and the graduate of the four-year baccalaureate program.[16]

The Registered Nurses Association of B.C., as part of its mandate as a regulatory body, must approve all courses leading to nurse registration. In September 1974, the Association granted the curriculum initial approval for two years, with a proviso that its Committee on Approval of Schools of Nursing would review the program and make recommendations to the University.[17] This meant that the first two classes could write the registration examinations at the end of second year.

However, the RNABC expressed some concerns about the curriculum.[18] It noted that only about one-third of the students chose to write at the end of second year and the other two-thirds remained in the four-year program without seeking registration status. In a letter, the RNABC noted that not all members of the UBC faculty seemed committed to the exit point at the end of second year. The RNABC said that a brochure released by the School promoted the four-year program and seemed to imply that students choosing the UBC program should remain for all four years.

This was, in fact, true, and students entering the UBC program were committed to the four years. In the first three years of the new program, although students had the option of leaving at the end of the second year, only 26 students out of approximately 300 did so, and of this number eight returned within the next two years and four others indicated an intention to do so as soon as possible.[19]

Another thing that the RNABC Committee found "contradictory" about the principles of the ladder concept was the requirement that registered nurses coming from other programs to enter the third year at UBC were required to take a "transition course" called Nursing 225. The Committee's report suggested that, if the program truly was a "ladder," graduates from college programs should be able to transfer directly into third year.[20]

The real problems arose because the UBC curriculum was based on the new UBC Model for Nursing, which emphasizes an understanding of "wellness" throughout the developmental life stages. The curriculum for the first year therefore bore little resemblance to the traditional "illness" approach focussing on hospital clinical experiences.

THE UBC MODEL FOR NURSING

Faculty members at the UBC School of Nursing had been working for several years on a "Model for Nursing" when Muriel Uprichard arrived.[21] The development of theoretical models for nursing practice and nursing education was a major advance in nursing beginning in the 1950s. Models are based on scientific nursing theories or on nursing practice, or on both together, and state beliefs and goals. They vary considerably. For example, one of the earliest, although it was not called a model, was developed by Virginia Henderson in 1952; it viewed humans as having 14 fundamental needs, which formed the basis for all nursing practice. Another model, developed in the 1970s by Calista Roy, used four modes of adaptation on which nursing practice was based. Dorothy Johnson used eight behavioral systems as the basis for her model. Yet another model, by Dorothea Orem, took six universal self-care requisites as its base and it was adopted in the late 1980s by the nurses in the Vancouver Health Department.

Nursing faculty at UBC began work in the late 1960s on a theoretical framework for curriculum development and on investigation of a model that could guide nurses in their practice, whether in institutions, communities, or homes. However, when Muriel Uprichard arrived and announced that the new curriculum would be based on a nursing model, this work suddenly became more urgent. A committee was struck, chaired by Margaret Campbell, who had recently returned to UBC from doctoral studies. The committee developed a model based on a behavioral systems model, similar to that developed by Dorothy Johnson. The UBC Model focussed on "well"

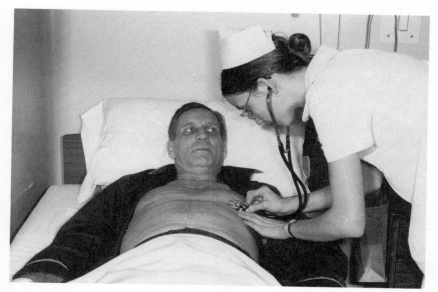

Figure 6.2   The emergence of nurse practitioners in the early 1970s together
with the introduction of the UBC Model for Nursing meant that UBC students
had to develop physical assessment skills.

individuals who may face crises during their life cycles and may require
nursing interventions. These crises may be unpredictable events, such as
illnesses, or maturational events. The nurse, as nurturer, assists individuals to
develop suitable coping behaviours in pursuit of the optimal goal of "health."

The model, which almost immediately became known as the UBC Model
for Nursing, required intensive work by a small, dedicated committee of faculty
during 1972 and 1973. Nursing assessment tools and other data bases had to be
developed as well. For example, the "loss framework," which focusses on the
"loss of wellness," became the pivotal point for the second year, during which
students became involved with ill individuals who required hospital-based
nursing care. In the third year, students focussed both on the individual and on
the family. In the fourth year, students continued their focus on individual and
family, but expanded their practice to include the complexities of communities. So that the Model would be ready for the start of the new program in
1973, the five-member "Model Committee" (Margaret Campbell, Helen
Shore, Janet Gormick, Rose Murakami, and Mary Cruise) worked evenings,
weekends, and statutory holidays.

In 1976, *Nursing Papers* (later called the *Canadian Journal of Nursing
Research*) devoted an entire issue to articles written by several UBC faculty
members about the UBC Model and its implementation.[22] As well as
depicting the model, the articles also described some of the independent

study modules that were developed in these years, the tools for clinical evaluation, and an on-going research project designed to assess student satisfaction with the new program. These innovative projects were considerably in advance of their time.

The UBC Model has continued to be refined, but has changed only slightly from its original innovative base. Its theoretical underpinnings have been tested and it has been adopted successfully in a variety of practice settings throughout the province. The first agency to use the UBC Model was the Psychiatric Unit of the UBC Health Sciences Centre Hospital under Nursing Director Helen Gemeroy. When the new 300-bed Extended Care Unit (the Purdy Pavilion) of the Health Sciences Centre Hospital opened in 1977, Mary Cruise, who had been a member of the Model committee, became the nursing director and selected the UBC Model as the basis for practice. The G.F. Strong Rehabilitation Centre adopted the UBC Model as the basis for its care in the mid-1980s. Students who have learned how to use the Model find it a valuable tool throughout their careers as a guide for collection and analysis of information.

CHANGES IN THE MASTER'S PROGRAM

As well as the changes in the undergraduate program, several major revisions were made in the MSN program starting in the 1973-1974 calendar year. The adoption of the UBC Model for Nursing was a prime factor; the Model directed the focus of the undergraduate program, but it also became a driving force in the master's program. Another prominent change was the decision to allow students the option either of doing a thesis or of completing a major paper and a comprehensive examination. Students also "required fewer units" and were "offered a greater choice of clinical courses leading to specialization."[23]

These areas of special study allowed students to pursue their interests in education, administration, or a new, third area titled consultation in nursing practice. This latter course, basically, was to prepare nurse consultants, the forerunner of clinical nursing specialists of the 1980s and 1990s. Sheila Creeggan Stanton, who was acting director for part of the period, noted that the clinical specialization was unique in Canadian university nursing programs of the time. "The clinical component was not so much hands-on, but at least there was a belief that there needed to be a clinical component; it was not all teaching and administration."[24]

The master's program in these years was seen to represent "the third rung on the ladder," as Margaret Campbell described it in a presentation to a national conference in Ottawa.[25] The enthusiasm that had created the ladder concept in the undergraduate program also influenced the graduate program.

The MSN program at UBC received its share of criticism during this time, especially when compared to older, more established graduate programs on campus. For one thing, there was a shortage of doctorally prepared faculty to teach in the program, carry out research, and supervise theses; this problem was closely tied to the shortage of doctoral programs in nursing to prepare such leaders. Sheila Stanton, who later did a major evaluation of the MSN program, noted: "For the time and the preparation of nursing faculty, it was as good as you could expect. It was producing and giving leaders for faculty positions.... It attracted good people."[26]

Between 1974 and 1976, the number of graduate students increased rapidly, growing from 36 in 1974 to 49 in 1976. Faculty and support staff also increased significantly with full-time faculty going from 34 to 69 and support staff from 6 to 14 in the same period.

CRISIS OVER THE LADDER

In 1975 and 1976, matters between the Registered Nurses Association of B.C. and the UBC School of Nursing reached a crisis point. Although the Association had given the two-year RN portion of the program provisional approval, it continued to criticize the content of the first two years. Then, in 1976, it suddenly announced that it was withdrawing approval for registration examinations at the end of second year. The announcement came too late in the academic year for faculty to change the major second year course, Nursing 210, the teaching of which was already well underway.

Students in the program and second-year faculty were extremely upset. The latter had previously voiced the concern that, because first year was devoted to the "well" individual, the second year was too short in which to teach all the clinical content required by RNABC. However, this concern had not been addressed. Faced with the withdrawal of approval, the School developed a contingency plan. The summer course, Nursing 215, was increased to 15 weeks from 12 weeks, and clinical time each week increased to 32 hours from 24 hours. The School also instituted "performance testing" to ensure that students had the required clinical skills before they began their final experience in second year. These revisions were acceptable to the RNABC and approval was reinstated. These students were allowed to write the exams.

A great deal of credit must go to the students in the second year in 1976-1977; they made a supreme effort to do extraordinarily well in the course, performance testing, and exams just to "prove" they were, in fact, competent to practice. Second-year faculty under coordinator Anne Wyness also worked diligently to ensure that RNABC's criteria were met, given the short notice that second year needed changing. As well, second-year faculty members strongly supported the students and their efforts. It may be that the students who completed this "mammoth" second year were among the most clinically competent the School ever produced.

Once the crisis was over, the School made changes in both years of the program and received final approval from RNABC. However, despite the changes necessary to achieve RNABC approval and regain the respect of the nursing community, many UBC faculty members never completely resolved their concerns over the focus of the first two years. This led to a "philosophical split" among faculty members. Those faculty members who supported the concept of beginning the program with "wellness" misinterpreted the intent of the second-year faculty, who were driven by the reality that students had to be clinically prepared to practise as registered nurses at the hospital bedside at the end of second year. This philosophical rift continued until the ladder program was discontinued after Muriel Uprichard left.

The ladder concept did make it easier for students from college programs to enter the program, although the "bridging course" continued to be required. However, the School did make some attempts to coordinate with colleges in the 1970s. For example, in 1972 UBC faculty offered credit courses designed for registered nurses at Douglas College in New Westminster.

In essence, the UBC ladder of the 1970s was a precursor to the college collaborative programs of the 1990s. College programs that intend to have a well-rounded, four-year, generic baccalaureate degree also face the same dilemma faced by UBC in the 1970s. In any program that allows diploma exit at the end of two years, faculty must prepare students for safe practice. This emphasis on clinical preparation in the first two years may conflict with the need to prepare professional nurses with a broad, basic, liberal education on which they can build after graduation. What is different in the 1990s is the cooperation between university and college program planners.

INNOVATIONS IN TEACHING METHODS

During the early 1970s, the UBC nursing faculty also began to recognize the need for a program that could reach registered nurses outside the Lower Mainland area. However, energies were committed to implementation of the new curriculum and faculty were unable to devote much time and effort to development of "correspondence courses." Pressures for more programs for registered nurses continued, however; according to a report by Muriel Uprichard, in 1973 only 5 per cent of registered nurses in B.C. had baccalaureate degrees and 0.12 per cent had master's preparation.[27] In 1976, the University of Victoria opened its School of Nursing, which was limited to a degree completion program for nurses with diploma preparation. This was part of a government policy to address the shortage of university-prepared nurses in B.C.

Figure 6.3   N.110 teaching team, taken outside the Task Force building
in 1973. L-R: Peggy Saunders, Noreen O'Brien, Robin Anderson, Helen Shore
(first year coordinator), Ray Thompson, Janet Gormick, Ada Butler, Margery
Furnell. The "ladder" program was introduced in 1973. Student and faculty
members tripled. Faculty offices were located in nine different areas on campus.

The UBC program also was increasing its numbers. Because of the shorter
program, the 1973-1974 UBC class included both students directly from high
school and those with first year arts and science. The numbers were nearly
triple those of the previous year – 152 from 59. Despite the influx of new
faculty members, this placed a tremendous load on the first year team, led by
Helen Shore. The transition or "bridging" course (N225), which allowed
registered nurses to enter the third year of the program, began in May 1975
with 54 students, which also increased faculty workloads. Team teaching was
introduced at this time because of the large numbers of students, but
introduction of teams, which could involve up to 18 individuals, involved
many planning meetings.

Another new and time-consuming activity for faculty during this period
was development of "independent study materials" to encourage students to
progress through course work at their own pace. This non-traditional teaching method involved use of slides, audiotapes, videotapes, various printed
materials, and computerized lessons and tests used by students working on
their own. Such independent study was being widely adopted in Canadian
nursing education and the UBC School was one of the first to develop its
own programs. UBC's Department of Continuing Education in the Health
Sciences bought and outfitted a bus and converted it into an audiovisual

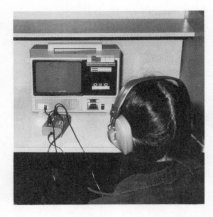

Figure 6.4

The first independent study modules were developed in 1973. Carrels were set up in Wesbrook where students could view audiovisual programs.

library and classroom to travel throughout the province. The Registered Nurses Association of B.C. donated $13,000 for the bus program toward the purchase, production, and development of audiovisual materials and instructional packages. Several packages were produced by UBC Nursing faculty under Sue Rothwell, who was coordinator for continuing nursing education. Nurses throughout the province used this travelling centre more than the other health disciplines.[28]

Another innovation tried at this time was introduction of a proposal that one faculty member should be assigned to a group of students and teach them throughout all years of the program. This idea proved extremely difficult to implement, although Ada Butler was one faculty member who did progress through all rotations with a group of students for their first three years.

Starting in June 1973, because of the increase in the numbers of nursing students, the Board of Governors regularly had to allot additional money for new nursing faculty and extra space for the School. Although the Director, her secretary, and a few other faculty had moved into offices in the new Instructional Resources Centre (IRC) when it opened in 1972, faculty offices and classrooms remained scattered over the campus: in Annex #4, which previously housed one of the campus fraternities; the Task Force Building, an old, frame, storage building that had been taken over by architects and planners during construction of IRC; and three old huts, which had been abandoned by the Faculty of Law. Some classrooms and seminar rooms were available in IRC, especially for larger classes. One hut was converted into "a simulated hospital-cum-community health centre."[29] As well, one room in the Wesbrook Building was made into an independent study laboratory with audiovisual equipment, a forerunner of the modern Learning Resource Centre developed in the 1980s.

The need for a new School of Nursing building was urgent. Several options were discussed at faculty meetings, and it was generally considered that Nursing was high on the list for a new facility. However, when planning for the new Acute Care Hospital began, University administration recommended that the third floor of the new building should be shared by the School of Nursing and the School of Rehabilitation Medicine.

OUTSIDE FUNDS AVAILABLE

In the 1973-1974 academic year, the UBC School of Nursing was awarded a grant, totalling $330,046 over four years (September 1973 to August 1977), from the W.K. Kellogg Foundation. The grant was "to develop a new pattern of nursing education involving four sequential two-year levels from basic preparation through doctoral study."[30] Muriel Uprichard, who had approached the Kellogg Foundation for the money, reported that the grant was "a recognition of this new approach to nursing education, especially the articulation of the two-year nursing program in the community colleges and the new four-year bachelor's program now offered at the university."[31] She also said that the grant would allow the School to begin to plan for the doctoral program.

That same year, the School also received a $16,000 grant from the Mr. and Mrs. P.A. Woodward Foundation to purchase "independent learning materials."[32] As well, the School received special bursaries from the B.C. Hospital Insurance Service in recognition of the new program. Dennis Cocke, provincial minister of health, approved a series of bursaries of $150 a month for undergraduate and $200 a month for master's students to help them cover costs of their nursing education. The arrangement for the master's students continued until 1980.[33]

Muriel Uprichard was extraordinarily successful in attracting grant money for the School. Another grant from the provincial government was received in July 1974, this one of $284,249, as well as other small government grants for self-learning materials. As the director noted in a report, "we were able to have the faculty, support staff and materials we required. As this was the first time in the history of the School that this happy state of affairs had pertained, the morale of the faculty was good."[34]

Some of the money was used to purchase portable video equipment that could be used to tape clinical practice sessions and special interviews so that these could be played back later and analyzed. One students recalled taping a session with a patient, which was an interesting new experience. "The patient behaved just as though he was on TV. I'll never forget. He was so proud, sitting up straight in bed and enunciating clearly, and saying the right things."[35]

The extra grant money may have been a mixed blessing. A fiscal problem that haunted the School for some years following Muriel Uprichard's retirement concerned allocation of money for community health field guides. The health units began receiving yearly grants from the School if students were placed there, a practice that was gaining popularity at this time. Muriel Uprichard believed staff from community health agencies should be paid out of education budgets rather than health care budgets for time devoted to education of students, so she instituted this plan at UBC. That meant a portion of the School's budget, around $130,000 a year, went to community health agencies.[36] Unfortunately, the School then lost control of the money. However, once the practice was instituted, it was difficult to discontinue and went on well into the 1980s.

Some senior faculty during this period were Margaret Campbell, Betty Cawston, Beth McCann, and Helen Shore. Faculty who retired during these years were Polly Capelle, Helen Gemeroy, and Margaret Street. Those who left to go on to other positions included Alice Baumgart, Maude Dolphin (later Anderson), Floris King, and Margaret Neylan. Those who were there before and after the Uprichard years included: Sylvia Holmes, Rose Murakami, Kirsten Weber Hyde, and Ethel Warbinek.

Margaret Campbell (BASc(N) 1948) was the most senior faculty member throughout the Uprichard years. She began her sabbatical and study leave at the beginning of the 1967-1968 year, just as Evelyn Mallory retired, and she was the first UBC graduate on the faculty to obtain a doctorate. She received the degree in 1970, and began the trend for existing faculty to take doctoral studies. On her return to the School, during the Beth McCann era, she joined those teaching in the master's program but at first continued to teach in the undergraduate program as well. During the Muriel Uprichard years, she became one of two assistant directors, and she chaired the curriculum committee. From then until her retirement in 1988, she taught almost exclusively in the master's program. She had another study leave in 1981-1982, during which she continued to perfect her work on the UBC Model. She completed the official document, *The UBC Model for Nursing: Directions for Practice*, commonly referred to as "the blue book," in 1987.

Although Margaret Campbell seemed a shy, retiring personality, she was always active in provincial and national nurses' associations. She served on many education committees and was a long-time member of the CNA Testing Service committees, which prepared registration examinations throughout the 1970s. An extremely conscientious teacher and attentive to detail, she became a much-admired and respected advisor for many master's students. Anyone who took her courses became expert at formulating objectives. From 1978 to 1986, when Marilyn Willman was director, she was coordinator of the MSN program and the graduate advisor. In 1987, she received the RNABC's Award of Excellence in Nursing Education. She was also honoured by the UBC Alumni Nursing Division on her retirement from

Figure 6.5

Margaret Campbell (BASc(N) 1948) joined the faculty in 1955 and remained until retirement in 1988. During the last part of her career at UBC, she taught in the MSN program. In 1987, she wrote *The UBC Model for Nursing: Directions for Practice.*

Figure 6.6   In 1990, Alice Baumgart (L) and Margaret Campbell (R) were recipients of the UBC Alumni Association's 75th Anniversary Awards of Merit in recognition of their contributions as UBC graduates.

UBC in 1988. In 1990, she, along with Alice Baumgart, received one of the 75 UBC Alumni Association 75th Anniversary Award Certificates of Merit "for distinction to the University throughout her professional career and professional dedication and exceptional contribution to the community."[37] Six months following her retirement, she was diagnosed with lung cancer and, despite an aggressive treatment regime, died of the disease in January 1992.

Another faculty leader during this period was Helen Shore, who filled the challenging job of first year coordinator during implementation of the new curriculum. She had graduated from the Vancouver General Hospital program and worked as a staff nurse first at VGH, then for a year in Bermuda. After taking a certificate in teaching and supervision in 1951, she taught for eight years at the Royal Columbian Hospital School of Nursing in New Westminster. She returned to UBC to obtain her baccalaureate degree in nursing in 1961 and next worked as a public health nurse for the Vancouver Health Department for four years. Evelyn Mallory then recruited her to teach in the UBC program, and encouraged her to pursue graduate studies; she obtained her master's degree specializing in adult education in 1971.

Helen Shore said that the challenge of developing a nursing model and a new curriculum based on it was one of the most memorable experiences in her career. Undoubtedly, her strong leadership skills and her ability to motivate faculty members to face innumerable details with so little lead time contributed largely to successful implementation of the new curriculum.

> I remember many days we would have a team meeting. We would decide what we were going to teach that week. We would get the materials together. We would staple them together and run over to class with the materials. It was hectic.[38]

Later she taught mainly public health content in the fourth year of the program and supervised students in their community health field work. She retired from UBC in 1990. Throughout her career she had been active in the RNABC's Vancouver chapter and on its committees. She received an RNABC Recognition Award from the Vancouver chapter, an honorary membership and Recognition Award from the RNABC, and the UBC Nursing Alumni Award of Distinction. Following her retirement, she began to pursue an interest in nursing and B.C. history and to write extensively on pioneer B.C. nurses. She served as president of the History of Nursing Professional Practice Group of the RNABC as well as being an active member of the B.C. History Association and other community organizations.

Margaret Street, who retired in 1972, was honoured several times during the Uprichard years. When her book on the life of Ethel Johns was published, the School honoured her at a reception at the Faculty Club. Her book received the Walter Stewart Baird Medal for the best historical book on health sciences published in 1973. During this part of her retirement,

Figure 6.7

Helen Shore (BSN 1961) faculty
member from 1964 to 1990 was
coordinator of first year during the
turbulent Uprichard years. During the
1980s, she taught community health
nursing. She retired in 1990 and is a
well-known nurse historian.

Figure 6.8   Reception in 1973 honouring the launching of Margaret Street's
book *Watch-fires on the Mountains: The Life and Writings of Ethel Johns.*
L-R: Muriel Uprichard, Margaret Street, and Patricia Catton (BSN 1970),
president Nursing Division UBC Alumni Association.

Margaret Street also compiled and indexed the Ethel Johns and Mabel Gray papers for presentation to the UBC Library Special Collections Division. For her many contributions to nursing as well as for the excellence of her book on Ethel Johns, Margaret Street was awarded the Order of Canada.

The faculty grew dramatically during the Uprichard years, a growth that was related to expansion of the new program and tremendous growth in student population. For example, in 1974, the second year faculty jumped from six to 18. Among UBC graduates who joined the faculty in the Uprichard years were Joan Anderson (MSN 1973), Ada Butler (BASc(N) 1959, MSN 1971), Ann Hilton (BSN 1968), Gloria Joachim (MSN 1976), Linda Leonard (BSN 1966, MSN 1975), Jo-Ann Perry (MSN 1976), Alison Rice (BSN 1967), Shelagh Wheeler Smith (BASc(N) 1950, MSN 1982), Pat Valentine (BSN 1962), and Anne Wyness (BSN 1965).

Several others from the University of California also followed the movement to UBC during this period, including Betty Johnson, Clarissa Green Rogers, and Sue Rothwell. Ray Thompson, a Maritimer who took his master's degree at Western Ontario, also was hired during this period and was the first male faculty member. Others who joined the faculty and remained included Elaine Carty, Sharon Ogden, Olive Simpson, and Sheila Creeggan (later Stanton). Sheila Creeggan was appointed in 1975 after having served on the faculty at the University of Western Ontario and came as an assistant director (general administration).

As part of the reorganization that year, Muriel Uprichard had obtained permission from Dean W. D. (Liam) Finn to appoint two assistant directors.[39] The heavy workloads were beginning to take a toll on Muriel Uprichard's health and on her abilities to cope with the many details of running the School. Margaret Campbell was put in charge of curriculum and Sheila Creeggan in charge of administration. As well, Kirsten Weber was appointed as her executive assistant to take care of day-to-day office management and coordination; this position was necessary because faculty and clerical support staff were still scattered in nine different locations on the campus.

Another well-known Canadian nurse who taught at UBC during this period was M. Andrea Baumann, in the 1990s co-director of the Quality of Nursing Worklife Unit, McMaster University. Ruth Elliott, an Albertan who joined the faculty during this period, collaborated with Betsy LaSor on the writing of a textbook, *Issues in Canadian Nursing*, the first Canadian text examining national trends and issues.

TRENDS OF THE 1970S

The chaotic social, cultural, economic, and political happenings of the mid-1970s had profound effects on the School of Nursing during the Uprichard years. The population of the province had reached more than two million and was beginning to reflect more cultural diversity with small, but significant, shifts in the countries of origin of immigrants. As well, the demographics reflected change in numbers of elderly, a trend that became even more marked in the 1980s and 1990s. British Columbians had begun to include increasing numbers of retired individuals from other parts of Canada and to show increased longevity. In the early 1970s, about half of adult Canadian women in B.C. and elsewhere were in the work force, although on average a woman's salary was only 64 per cent of a man's.

The 1972 election saw installation of a New Democratic Party provincial government under Premier David Barrett just as the larger world economy was entering a period of severe recession. The NDP proposed a large number of major changes in health care as part of its mandate. A massive report on health care in B.C., *Health Security for British Columbians*, had been prepared by Richard Foulkes and recommended that community human resource and health centres should be the local delivery points for a total health system in the province. The government attempted to implement some of its findings, one of which was establishment of a B.C. Medical Centre. Recommendations that were adopted included financial stipends for all nursing students and more financial aid for graduate nursing education. The government also recommended nurse representation on hospital boards and other health policy-making groups.

A major part of the government's plan was a provincial medical centre, to be administered from a Vancouver site, with greater decentralization of services and more regional control through five regional health centres. The five centres, which would cost up to $2 million for the first year, would be staffed by clinical nurses and public health nurses would be available for services such as home visits.[40] However, the NDP government remained in power only three years and, with the return of the Social Credit party to power under William Bennett, son of the previous Social Credit leader, most of the major health care changes, including the B.C. Medical Centre, were scrapped as being too expensive during recessionary years.[41] During the mid-1990s, another NDP government introduced *New Directions for Health*, a similar plan for decentralization and regional boards; as well, emphasis on health and wellness centres resurfaced.

One change in the 1970s, however, was introduction of more home care nursing services under the provincial health department rather than through such private agencies as the Victorian Order of Nurses. A pilot project in New Westminster had shown that increased home care services could reduce hospital stays and result in considerable savings. Home care coordinators were hired to set up programs in various parts of the province as the "Hospital Days Replacement Program" and by the mid-1970s home care service was available in all large and medium-size communities and was reaching 80 per cent of the population.[42]

As well, public health nurses began to be concerned with care of the elderly, which mainly had been delivered in small, privately run "nursing homes" or "rest homes." Inspection and licensure of private hospitals became a government priority. Provincial authorities recognized the need for "extended care facilities," particularly for the elderly and those with long term disabilities; this started the trend to separate institutions for various levels of care. A result was that acuity of patients increased in what came to be known as acute care hospitals.

Lions Gate Hospital in North Vancouver opened B.C.'s first diabetic day care centre in the early 1970s. In 1971, St. Paul's Hospital in Vancouver initiated family-centred maternity care, which allowed both mother and father to have a greater responsibility for decisions related to delivery and early parenting. UBC graduate Bernadet Ratsoy (BSN 1968) wrote an article about this new care for *The Canadian Nurse*.[43] Crisis clinics, self-help clinics for women, and "store-front nursing offices" were being evaluated. Science and technology were advancing quickly. For example, genetic manipulation was being explored and the first "test-tube baby" was conceived. Computerized and portable cardiac care monitors were introduced as was laser photocoagulation for retinal vascular disease. Invasive diagnostic procedures, such as heart catheterization, and total parenteral nutrition rapidly became common.

In 1974, the federal Department of Health and Welfare released *A New Perspective on the Health of Canadians* (Lalonde, 1974a), which signalled a change in the focus for the funding of health care. Health Minister Marc Lalonde proposed that priority be given to health promotion and recommended programs that would foster safer environments and lifestyles conducive to good health. In an editorial, he challenged nurses to re-evaluate their roles and help bring the changes about.[44] This change of emphasis from curing illness to promoting health reflected curriculums that had been offered for years in university nursing programs, including the UBC School. However, the report rapidly caught the attention and imagination of all Canadians, especially nurses, and marked a turning point in federal health care policy.

The Canadian Nurses Association became more politically active during the 1970s and began to issue major policy statements on nursing issues, such as a statement on "specialization in nursing" prepared for CNA by Alice Baumgart, who was on study leave from the UBC faculty. As well, CNA also prepared a major position statement on functions and qualifications for nurse-midwives.[45] The CNA Testing Service (CNATS) had taken over preparation of examinations for licensure and UBC students, like all other Canadian nursing students at the time, wrote CNATS exams. One major issue on which CNA had taken a firm stand was the introduction of "physician assistants," which was increasingly common in the United States but opposed by CNA. Instead, CNA recommended that professional nurses were best qualified to assume an expanded role, noting that many of the suggested functions and responsibilities of the physician assistant already were a part of nursing practice in Canada.[46]

Increasing emphasis was given to research in nursing as shown in 1971 when Dorothy Kergin (BSN 1952) was the first nurse appointed to Canada's Medical Research Council. The Social Sciences and Humanities Research Council of Canada began operation in 1977 to further Canada's university-based research. However, in its early years it rarely provided funds to nurses or nursing studies, saying these should come under the Medical Research Council. Once again, nursing fell between the cracks, because the Medical Research Council directed most of its funds into medical and drug research.

More and more UBC nursing faculty began to pursue research interests and to seek funding during this period despite the heavy faculty workload. Helen Elfert was one of the first to receive a National Health Research and Development Grant and Olive Simpson also received one of the early grants.

Economic issues for nursing became increasingly important during the 1970s and in 1977 the Registered Nurses Association of B.C. formed a separate Labour Relations Division to bargain collectively for members. Public representation was another issue of the 1970s and, in 1973, RNABC began appointing lay members to its board of directors to ensure that the public interest would be taken into account when decisions were made.

The Uprichard years also saw nurses increasingly interested in feminism and "women's liberation." American authors Betty Friedan, Gloria Steinem, and Germaine Greer had focussed attention in the 1960s on stereotypes that had led to passive roles for women and spearheaded the contemporary women's movement, but courses in women's studies only began to be offered at UBC in 1972. Increasing awareness of inequality also began to be recognized by the women on faculty at UBC. In 1974, the University decided to participate in plans for International Women's Year in 1975 and launched a series of more than 30 activities "to increase awareness on the campus and in the community towards the inequitable status of women"; a special committee "developed and promoted programs to demonstrate women's new and changing roles."[47] At the time, only 16 per cent of full-time faculty members at UBC were women, and these figures included Nursing and Home Economics, which were almost exclusively female.[48] Margaret Fulton, dean of women, was the only female dean and was appointed to chair an Ad Hoc Committee on International Women's Year. Beth McCann of the School of Nursing was appointed to this committee and subsequently was named to head a President's Task Force on Women and recommend ways to achieve equal opportunities for women on campus. The UBC Academic Women's Association was formed in 1976.

Other controversial social issues of the day concerned reform of abortion laws and opening of birth control clinics. The latter were controversial because women could get information on "the Pill," new IntraUterine Devices (IUDs), and the relatively new and simple laparoscopy for tubal ligation for female sterilization. The Vancouver Women's Health Collective was formed in 1972 to offer alternatives to traditional methods of seeking health care; among its activities were self-help groups, which were a new way of educating women on health issues. Helen Elfert of the UBC School worked closely with the Collective and received a National Health Research and Development Grant of $20,800 to set up a demonstration project.[49]

Students in Education organized a series of classes on sexuality and asked George Szasz, professor of psychiatry and an expert in sexual medicine, to give the classes. A nursing student later recalled, "They thought they could get out 70 students if he said he would come. He came and there were 900 who turned out."[50] He drafted nursing students to serve as small group leaders for discussion sessions following his Monday evening lectures. This popular non-credit course later became a credit course.

During the Uprichard years, several major changes occurred at UBC. First, a new Universities Act was passed that required all three universities in the province to be financed through a single University Council. Muriel Uprichard was one UBC member named to the first University Council Finance Committee, which allocated budgets for the three universities. Second, Douglas Kenny succeeded Walter Gage as president of UBC. Finally, the new student residences, including the Gage Tower, a co-educational residence, opened.

STUDENTS OF THE PERIOD

More than 500 BSN students graduated during this period and almost all joined the work force, most of them as bedside nurses in hospitals. The growing numbers of baccalaureate nurses meant that fewer new graduates automatically took senior positions or automatically went into community health nursing. Most graduates of these years who replied to questionnaires about the program rated it fairly positively, although many indicated that they did not feel confident about their clinical roles at the beginning of their practice.

Melodie Funk (later Herbert) (BSN 1975) said that some faculty and students tended to value psychosocial and community based nursing practice and downgrade clinical and pathophysiological skills, which she felt was "a serious short-coming."[51] However, the fact that many worked during the summer periods following second year increased their confidence, she said. The Vancouver General Hospital during this period hired university nursing students from across Canada; this was partly to relieve a serious shortage of nurses during the mid-1970s. Melodie Herbert worked as a staff nurse at St. Paul's Hospital in Vancouver on graduation, and later became a critical care instructor at Vancouver Community College before going into Medicine at UBC.

Figure 6.9　Some traditions continued throughout the Uprichard years, such as the annual Teacup game against Home Economics. This picture shows Teacup 1974; Nursing won that year.

She and several other graduates of this period said that those outside the School rated it poorly, because graduates lacked clinical skills necessary for hospital care. On the other hand, Joanne Ricci (BSN 1975, MSN 1977) said she felt quite competent and that most students found clinical skills could be acquired rapidly once they were working in a clinical setting. Some comments indicated that, although the School tried to offer sound clinical experiences, hospital-based role models often left much to be desired. Julie Glanville (later Waller) (BSN 1973) recalled that one head nurse "insisted that A.M. care consisted of emptying the garbage can, removing last P.M.'s *Sun*, and ensuring the blinds were at the same height on the windows."[52]

Several students also recalled their public health experience as excellent, but two especially remembered having to travel by bus across town carrying baby scales. Fewer students from this period mention campus activities or events, perhaps an indication of change to a shorter program that focussed more specifically on nursing content. Many students recalled, however, the "huge cinnamon buns," a specialty of the campus food services and a UBC tradition.

This era marked a time when informality became the order of the day. For example, during the 1970s, it became accepted practice for students to call faculty members by their first names. Although individual faculty had previously encouraged this practice on campus, formality had still been expected in health care settings. As well, student dress and behaviour in class became much more relaxed and informal. Some students even brought babies

Figure 6.10   Students in the class of 1975 at the Vancouver General Hospital during their second year. L-R: Val Cartmel, Janet Henderson, Debra Harrison, Suzanne Faddegan. Note the uniform with UBC embroidered on the pocket. This replaced the pink uniform introduced in 1958.

Figure 6.11

With introduction of the new curriculum in 1973, students no longer wore distinctive UBC uniforms. This picture shows a UBC student and patient. The cap is still being worn and a crest was placed on the uniform so that students could be identified as UBC students.

and/or dogs to classes. Some faculty members accepted this informality as they, too, could relax their dress standards and bring pets to work.

Just around this time, the student uniform changed from the pink-and-white striped dress introduced when clinical experiences moved to St. Paul's Hospital. Now that students had experiences in a variety of agencies, a new uniform was developed and made by a local manufacturer for the School. This new uniform needed to be easy to care for because students no longer had access to hospital laundry facilities. Female students wore a plain white dress with the letters UBC embroidered in pink on the left bodice. Male students wore a white two-piece uniform typical of that used by other male health professionals. Starting in 1973, when the new curriculum was implemented, a new uniform policy was instituted; students could purchase uniforms, within some general guidelines. Distinctive UBC uniforms were no more. As well, about this time, wearing a cap became optional and was soon discontinued.

Approximate costs for each academic year in the mid-1970s were between $650 and $700 exclusive of board and lodging, which were estimated in a School report as about $1,000 for the academic year (not including the summer terms). Extra expenses included transportation costs, other miscellaneous costs, and graduation expenses of about $100 in the final year.[53]

A new "RN pin" was designed at this time for students who left at the end of second year. A crest was also developed, and had the same motif of two clasped hands, to indicate caring and support, over a blue and white background. Helen Shore recalled that the project had been turned over to the students and that the design had been done by a first year student, although she could not recall his name. A Nursing Undergraduate Society report of the time noted that the pin was to be slightly less than an inch in diameter and would cost approximately $15. The pin was produced for only a few years, until the second-year exit option was discontinued, but the crest was used throughout the 1970s and 1980s.

Figure 6.12

A UBC crest was introduced during the 1970s and shows two clasped hands, indicating caring and nurturing. The blue and white crest was worn on the uniform until 1990, when it was replaced by a more traditional one.

Figure 6.13

UBC crest which replaced the
"clasped hands." This crest was still
worn in 1994 and is based on the UBC
pin designed in 1958.

Nursing students during this period came to have more say in decision
making about their courses and University policies. For example, when
faculty recommended that students not write their registration examinations
at the January sittings, the students objected strongly. After the Nursing
Undergraduate Society circulated a petition and gathered 90 signatures and
submitted these, with their reasons for objecting, faculty rescinded the
decision. As well, when students in fourth year wanted a course in which they
would learn to do physical assessments, faculty arranged for weekend sessions, although students had to attend on their own time. One graduate
recalled that students were pleased that the faculty had acted on the request
and that students were considered "important, and not just there."[54]

Deborah Taylor, who was president of the Nursing Undergraduate
Society, recalled forming a work party to paint the Common Room in the
Wesbrook Building while she was a student. The class considered the room to
be in a "shocking state" and had painted the walls and tried to get donations
of carpets and paintings.[55]

Among BSN graduates of this era who have become well-known in
nursing are Lynette Best (BSN 1972, MSN 1982), a nursing administrator at
the UBC Hospital and more recently at Lions Gate Hospital; Joanne Kon-
nert (BSN 1971, MSN 1977), nursing administrator at the Royal Columbian
Hospital in New Westminster; and Dale Walker (BSN 1972), chief nursing
officer for the Vancouver Health Department. Nora Whyte (BSN 1973,
MSN 1988) was instrumental in development of the "New Directions for
Health Care" program of RNABC in the early 1990s and has acted as a
consultant to the provincial government on health care policy matters.

During the Muriel Uprichard years, 58 MSN students graduated. Joanne
Ricci (BSN 1975, MSN 1977), who joined the UBC nursing faculty, went
directly into the MSN program following BSN graduation. Among others who
graduated from the MSN program are Mary Adlersberg (MSN 1977), who

Figure 6.14   Graduation procession in the mid-1970s. Convocation was held in
the War Memorial Gymnasium, where it is still held in 1994. In 1976, the School
limited admission to first and third year because of budgetary problems.

joined the staff of the Registered Nurses Association of B.C.; Matilda ("Tilly")
Burk (later Bara) (MSN 1974), a senior administrator with Vancouver General
Hospital; and Mary Fewster (MSN 1975), director of the Douglas College
School of Nursing program and on the Canadian Nurses Association Testing
Service for several years. Chinnama Baines (MSN 1974) later became director of
the nursing program at Cariboo College and was instrumental in working on
the collaborative program between the University of Victoria School of Nursing
and five B.C. college diploma programs. Under her direction, in 1991, the
University College of the Cariboo graduated the first students from its four-year
nursing program, which is similar to UBC's original "ladder concept."

Carol Jillings (MSN 1977) and Joan Anderson (MSN 1973) are among
graduates of this period who went on to take doctoral studies in nursing.
Both joined the faculty of the UBC School and have become well-known
nursing scholars. Joan Anderson has become a recognized researcher in
multicultural nursing and has attracted considerable research funding. Carol
Jillings was appointed acting director of the School for a six-month period at
the beginning of 1994.

END OF THE UPRICHARD YEARS

Toward the end of Muriel Uprichard's directorship, the School began to
experience severe financial difficulties and Liam Finn, dean of Applied

Science, often was forced to find additional funds for commitments made by the director. When Muriel Uprichard retired, the new director came knowing that sound fiscal management would be needed and that the School's spending had to be brought under control.

Soon after her arrival, Muriel Uprichard set up a new committee structure in the School, which included an "Executive Committee" that served in an advisory capacity to the director. Each of the six committees was kept small, with approximately five members. However, some faculty members soon were asking for a greater say in planning. For example, there was no faculty committee for appointment, reappointment, promotion, and tenure; although the director might approach tenured faculty for advice, there was no formal structure. As numbers of faculty increased, this became more and more of a problem.

Toward the end of the Kellogg grant, the School had to put a quota on undergraduate admissions. Dean Liam Finn, who supported the School of Nursing strongly during his tenure, attended a faculty meeting to explain that all faculties, including Applied Science, had been asked to cut their budgets by five per cent for the fiscal year 1976-1977. Although he was prepared to assume a greater portion of these cuts in Engineering, he said that "some of necessity will be felt in Nursing."[56] He noted that the School was expensive to run. For example, summer sessions for clinical experience for undergraduate students and bridging sessions for registered nurses entering third year were costly. Because faculty in other departments worked an academic year of eight months, faculty in Nursing were paid a stipend of $240 a week, usually for 12 weeks, to teach in the summer programs[57] and this added to the costs.

The budget for the School for 1975-1976 had been $1,770,321. Muriel Uprichard noted then that, although the University had experienced a severe cut in its budget, the administration had not cut the School of Nursing's budget at all and, in fact, had given money for two additional salaries.[58]

In April 1976, however, the faculty was told that the Senate had decided to set a quota of 113 students for first year nursing and would limit total enrolment for the School to approximately 500 students; this limit was to remain in effect for five years. A quota for registered nurses entering the program in third year also came into effect; the quota was 50 per year, but this was later increased to 72.

Faculty discontent continued to escalate, with some faculty achieving favoured status with the director as an "in-group" of advisors and confidants, and others feeling they were "scapegoats." Workloads remained extremely heavy, with little time for research and other scholarly activities because the program was always in a state of flux. Faculty began to feel extremely pressured.

Not only faculty members felt pressured. Muriel Uprichard herself became ill, which increasingly kept her away from the School. After a time, Sheila

Creeggan Stanton was appointed acting director, at first for a period of four months. Muriel Uprichard then was well enough to come back for six months or so, but became ill once more, this time with high blood pressure, back and leg pain, and depression that required hospitalization.[59] In January 1977, Dean Liam Finn announced that Muriel Uprichard's leave of absence for disability had been extended to June 1977, which was her retirement date. The search for a new director began.[60]

In June 1977, a retirement dinner was held by the School for Muriel Uprichard at the Airport Inn in Richmond. She was presented with a watch.[61] She originally planned to remain at her home in Richmond and write; she had begun work on a history of nursing and told a reporter covering her retirement that she had a novel about half finished.[62] Later she moved to Montreal, where she was hired by Concordia University to plan a baccalaureate program for registered nurses, although this never received funding from the Quebec government.[63] She also continued to consult with schools of nursing in various parts of Canada and eventually settled in Kingston, Ontario.

During one of her guest presentations for master's students at McGill in 1979, she recalled some of the changes she had made at UBC. In retrospect, she said that perhaps elimination of the pre-nursing year at UBC "was not entirely a good idea."[64] She went on to say that, although the decision at UBC was appropriate for the time, largely because of the shortage of university-prepared nurses, the shorter program had weaknesses because "hard sciences," such as chemistry, physics, and basic anatomy, had to be adapted and fitted into the shorter program.

> It has its weaknesses. There is much to be said for staying with the older method of insisting upon a year of science and then admission to the school of nursing. You have to weigh the balance: For this particular society at this moment in time, which is more important.[65]

Helen Shore summed up the Uprichard years as both an "exhilarating and frustrating time." Although Muriel Uprichard's illness coloured her contributions to the School, she was a woman of vision and a great conceptualizer and innovator. Her "ladder concept" was a novel idea that may have been ahead of its time, given contemporary socioeconomic, professional, and political pressures. But her support for a nursing model, in general, and for development of the UBC Model for Nursing, in particular, has proven an significant legacy in the history of the School.

CHAPTER SEVEN

The Marilyn Willman Years
1977-1993

Figure 7.1

Marilyn Willman,
Director, 1977-1993.

Opportunities to expand the master's program and to develop new continuing education programs for nurses were two prospects that attracted Marilyn Willman to the University of B.C. School of Nursing as its new director in July 1977. She had been President of the System School of Nursing in Texas, an organization of six schools of nursing across the state, but the structure was being revamped and her position eliminated. She had been offered administrative positions in nursing programs at a number of universities, but decided she wanted an entirely new and different challenge. When she received a letter asking if she would be interested in applying at UBC, she decided to visit the School for an interview.

Actually I knew nothing about the Northwest. I had been to Seattle on one occasion, but I didn't know anything about the Northwest and I certainly

didn't know anything about Vancouver or British Columbia. But I decided
that, since I was looking, I might as well have a look. So I came.[1]

From the interview, she learned that many interesting developments were
taking place in nursing in Canada. Having had experience in Texas with
innovative ways of delivering nursing education, she perceived a "potential
for some interesting kinds of programs to develop.... The possibilities were
there for extending the influence of the University and its nursing programs
out into the province to meet the needs of the people there."[2]

Marilyn Willman was born in Hancock, Michigan, on December 31, 1928.
Her father was an engineer and the family lived in a number of places in
Michigan as he moved from job to job. She received her high school
education in Cadillac, Michigan, and then took her baccalaureate in nursing
at the University of Michigan, Ann Arbor, graduating in 1952. She worked as
a staff nurse in Madison, Wisconsin, and also taught in a diploma program at
the Madison General Hospital School of Nursing. In 1957, she decided to
obtain a master's degree and went to the University of Texas in Austin and
Galveston, where she obtained a master's degree in nursing in 1959. Her field
of specialization was in administration in nursing education and her thesis
on prediction of academic achievement in nursing.

She had chosen the University of Texas because it offered both the
opportunity for specializing in educational administration and federal
"traineeships," which provided a monthly stipend and tuition. The trainee-
ship program had been introduced in an effort to recruit more nurses
into graduate nursing studies and, as she said, "The University of Texas
offered me one – so I went to Texas."[3] While in the master's program she
worked with a professor who taught educational psychology and human
development and became interested in that area. She then pursued doctoral
studies, supported by a federal doctoral fellowship and received the doctorate in 1961.

She immediately joined the faculty at the University of Texas School of
Nursing and, after a year, took on the position of assistant dean and director
of graduate programs. She remained at University of Texas, moving up the
administrative ladder, first as dean, then as president of the University of
Texas System School of Nursing.

As president of the System School of Nursing, she initiated and coordinated development of four new programs throughout the state. These were
added to two programs already in existence to form a six-campus University of Texas System School of Nursing. There was no other similar
organization for nursing education in the U.S. at the time, and development of the System School was an exciting challenge for all those involved.
In her last year in Texas, she also served as a consultant in graduate
education in nursing to the Brazilian government.

I thought, in some respects, that B.C. was similar to Texas in that it had large areas in which there were no educational programs and in which there were needs for educational programs for nurses. Certainly that was the case in Texas and I had some experience with continuing education and distance master's programs, and so on, and I thought I could see similar opportunities here.[4]

During her tenure at Texas, Marilyn Willman was actively involved in a variety of organizations and activities. In 1973, she became a charter Fellow in the American Academy of Nursing, which recognizes substantial achievements and contributions to nursing.

This move to a new country proved to be exciting and stimulating, and Marilyn Willman came to love the area. However, the position did provide some unexpected challenges – "more after I got here, I discovered, than I had realized when I took the position."[5] Although she had recognized from the interviews and visits that the School was going through some difficult times, she said that she had been willing to tackle these. However, she found on arrival that "the problems were more profound than I was led to believe."[6] The "most urgent problem" she faced on arrival related to the heavy workload for both students and faculty in the undergraduate curriculum.

There were very serious problems with the undergraduate program. It was the 'two-plus-two program' and there was an exit point after the second year. There had been quite serious problems with the RNABC in terms of approval. In fact, at the time I came, it was 'under the gun' and something had to be done. So, certainly that was *the* most urgent problem. I suppose that the other side of the coin was that faculty were concerned, obviously quite concerned, about the problem and, as a result, were ready to see some changes – and that I see as a strength. They were really ready for change.[7]

ADDRESSING UNEXPECTED CHALLENGES

Although the previous director also came from the United States, Muriel Uprichard was a Canadian and had taught in Canadian nursing programs – although some criticism was directed at the fact that she was not a nurse. Similarly, the hiring of the first American director prompted some nationalistic feelings. However, at the time, few Canadian nurses had doctoral preparation and even fewer had nursing doctorates. So, although she was not the first American to be on faculty and although Marilyn Willman later said that she did not sense any resentment, appointment of an American director raised concerns in the nursing community and among faculty, some of whom had urged a less qualified Canadian candidate.

A full faculty meeting was held almost immediately after Marilyn Willman came and minutes of this early meeting indicate that she was prepared to meet some of the concerns that she had inherited. At this meeting, she identified some of the concerns as she saw them, including the question of whether or not the curriculum needed a major overhaul. Nothing could be done for two years – "the School has a responsibility both to the September 1977 students for two more years, and also to the RNABC"[8] – so there was little room for immediate change. For two years the faculty would have to support the ladder concept and work out how to do this effectively. However, planning could and should start on what to do after that.

The minutes report that she was concerned that the heavy program, including the summer courses Nursing 115 and Nursing 215, "had resulted in tired faculty and tired students due to attempts to teach too much too quickly, with insufficient time for consolidation."[9] In the discussions at this meeting, faculty raised the matter of "division between first and second year, the differing philosophies in each year, and the lack of opportunities for naturally occurring exchange between the two years."[10] Faculty stressed the fact that there was little coordination between the years and wanted a "curriculum committee" that would address these concerns.

Marilyn Willman acted quickly on this recommendation. A practical woman and a proponent of decentralization, she appointed a faculty committee to develop a plan for decision making within the School. The plan that was finally approved called for a full caucus of all faculty; this caucus would have the ultimate say in academic decisions in the School. As well, there would be a number of faculty committees that would deal with issues and bring recommendations to caucus. A curriculum committee was formed in September 1977 as part of a complete restructuring of all committees in the School. There were 11 standing committees, which allowed for much greater input from faculty. In other words, the new structure, approved by a full faculty caucus, allowed for faculty involvement and its by-laws stated clearly that "Faculty Caucus is the policy and decision-making body of the School of Nursing."[11]

Student representation was also ensured through Nursing Undergraduate Society appointments of one student to each standing committee related to the undergraduate program. These students also were to be voting members at faculty caucus meetings, although this opportunity was not used as effectively as it might have been. Graduate students also had representation on the committees concerned with graduate affairs.

In addition, Marilyn Willman deleted the two assistant director positions, which had been held by Margaret Campbell and Sheila Stanton. In other words, she advocated a decentralized administrative model, with a "flatter" hierarchical structure; she would be the chief administrator, but faculty would have more decision-making power through the committees and faculty caucus. Most of the committees identified in the original structure continued throughout Marilyn Willman's directorship. The decision-making process was reviewed and fine-tuned several times, but remained essentially the same.

One of the most urgent problems facing the new director was the School's overextended budget. Almost immediately, she had to address serious cuts in finances proposed by the University administration. As noted in the previous chapter, rapid expansion had been necessary to meet the demands of rapidly increasing student numbers. This was combined with the introduction of a completely new and different curriculum that affected all six years of study at both the undergraduate and graduate levels. Although Muriel Uprichard had attracted a number of large grants to support some of the changes, the School's budget had been under constant pressure. Near the end of her directorship, the University administration established a quota to check growth of the program, but her illness meant, in effect, that Acting Director Sheila Stanton was simply keeping a watching brief on the budget.

Among Marilyn Willman's immediate actions were meetings with Liam Finn, dean of Applied Science, to try to bring the School's budget into some kind of order and plans were initiated for faculty and administrative cuts. Removal of the summer program saved some money. One budget concern related to payments being made by the School to community health agencies for student experiences, a practice begun in the Uprichard years. Annual costs for community health placements for students were more than $100,000. A School committee of Sylvia Holmes, Ray Thompson, and Kirsten Weber was appointed to look into this practice; it surveyed 21 university schools in Canada only to discover that UBC was the only one paying health agencies for such placements.[12] The committee submitted an extensive report and after considerable discussion with the agencies, which of course were loath to give up the payments, the practice was discontinued in the early 1980s.

Thus the challenges facing the new director were many and intense.

CURRICULUM CHANGES NEEDED

At a meeting in June 1977, just before Marilyn Willman arrived, the entire faculty had decided to clarify the issues they wished to raise with the new director. The core issue identified at this meeting was the "ladder concept." Faculty remained divided over the philosophy of an exit point at the end of second year, but all seemed united in their concern that the first two years of the program were exceptionally heavy for both students and faculty. The faculty division over the ladder concept should be seen within the context of the mid-1970s. At that time, provincial and national nurses' associations strongly supported two-year programs for preparation of diploma-level nurses. Hospital-based schools of nursing were phasing out and two-year college-based programs were considered the norm. It was not until the early 1980s that the Canadian Nurses Association began to promote a baccalaureate nursing degree as the basis for entry into nursing practice. In 1982, both the Canadian Nurses Association and the Registered Nurses

Association of B.C. formally advocated the year 2000 as the target date after which all new graduates would need a baccalaureate nursing degree for initial entry.

This move from two-year diploma programs to four-year (or more) university-level basic preparation was tied to social trends. Not only were there many advances in science and technology related to health care and medical treatment, but nursing theory and knowledge were expanding as nurses took larger, more significant roles in health education, health promotion, and health counselling. In keeping with the changes, the nurse had become more and more a partner in care of the patient during acute illness, and the nursing role involved many new aspects entirely independent of the roles of other health care professionals.

An important change in nursing in Canada during the late 1970s involved the role, not new but with a new facet, of "the nurse as patient advocate." With the rapid advances in treatment modalities, the health care team suddenly expanded from the tradition of one family doctor and one small group of nurses. Instead, there was likely to be a large number of medical specialists involved, plus an expanded team of health professionals that included laboratory specialists, X-ray technicians, respiratory technologists, social workers, dietitians/nutritionists, pharmacists, and, often, a team of expert technicians to deliver specialized treatment such as radiation therapy. Furthermore, patients were being cared for in a variety of locations throughout their illnesses, including intensive care units, general care units, rehabilitation units, ambulatory care units, and, increasingly, their homes. Nurses had much more responsibility for ensuring that patients understood what was happening. Without nursing coordination and patient teaching, patient care was fragmented and disordered. To meet these expanding patient needs, nursing science needed to incorporate more and more knowledge and skills from psychology, education, sociology, and other behavioral sciences as well as from the traditional sciences of chemistry, biology, bacteriology, anatomy, and physiology.

There also were significant changes in education generally; a new generation of Canadians was demanding more and better postsecondary education, although Canada still ranked behind many other developed nations in percentages of university graduates. This meant the new generations of patients were more and better educated; health care teaching needed to be at more advanced levels. The idea that lifestyle played an important role in health and prevention of illness had just been put forward in the Lalonde Report (1974a). Nurses were being asked to fill new roles in lifestyle teaching and health promotion. The idea that individuals needed to take more responsibility for their own health and treatment, as advocated in the Epp Report (1986), was still almost a decade away. Patients had been used to leaving all decisions up to their caregivers and, until the 1970s, the public's level of knowledge about medical treatment and health care was generally low. In the late 1970s, however, the public media, especially magazines, newspapers, and television, assumed a larger role in informing Canadians about various illnesses and making them aware of health care options.

All these social changes were fuelling the increasing recognition that two years was not enough time to prepare nurses for their expanded roles. Irmajean Bajnok, an expert on development of nursing education in Canada, noted that in the early 1980s there was "general agreement within the profession that education must reflect the more complex nature of clinical nursing judgments and interventions and that nurses need to understand and be more involved in health care decision making."[13] This supported the long-standing awareness of nursing educators at universities that *all* nurses needed a broad based, liberal education, as well as a sound grounding in the sciences, to prepare them for a rapidly changing world.

Unfortunately, just at this time, enrolments in nursing programs across Canada were declining. The decline was related to the wider educational opportunities and career choices available to women; nursing, home economics, and teaching were no longer the only options. Nursing educators everywhere began to question traditional approaches to nurse preparation and to recognize the need for more nursing theory, nursing models, and nursing research. UBC nursing faculty members, who had already integrated these into the program, were questioning whether it was the best use of time and resources to continue to prepare two-year graduates at the University, particularly as two-year college programs were rapidly increasing. As well, some were disillusioned by the two-plus-two experiment and wanted to return to a focus on baccalaureate education.

CHANGES IN THE CURRICULUM

Planning was soon underway for development of a new curriculum in which the two-plus-two undergraduate program would be discontinued. In the 1979-1980 academic year, a new program was implemented and introduced year by year until all four years were in place in 1983. Students enrolled before September 1979, even those taking the program on a part-time basis, could write the registration examinations at the end of their first two years. Anyone enrolled after September 1979 would be unable to write the licensing examination until the end of fourth year.

This curriculum change allowed termination of the heavy summer teaching programs and released faculty time and energy for research and other scholarly pursuits. The change also made it easier for registered nurses to enter the baccalaureate program, which was a significant response to growing numbers of diploma nurses in B.C. who wished to take the degree program. These registered nurses, who sometimes referred to themselves as "retreads," had been critical of the entry requirements for the UBC ladder program. They objected to its length, which involved a full summer of course work before they could enter at the third-year level in the fall. In the new curriculum, the material from this summer "bridging course" was incorporated into the first term of third year.

The four-year undergraduate program at this time became generally known as the "generic" or "basic" program and the two-year program for registered nurses was called the "post-RN" or "post-basic" program. Although the term generic program had been used previously, these terms were needed much more frequently as the demand for post-basic education grew. Nursing at UBC had to cope with increasing numbers of diploma-prepared students who recognized they needed more education and the broad base that university nursing schools had always advocated.

The new curriculum made better use of courses already offered by other departments at UBC, such as the introductory nutrition course offered by the School of Home Economics and the epidemiology course offered by the Department of Health Care and Epidemiology. As well, other departments were asked to develop and offer courses with content specific for nursing and open only to nursing students, such as pharmacology for nurses offered by the Faculty of Pharmaceutical Sciences.

The most notorious course offered by other departments was physical education (PE) for nurses, which involved three levels of physical conditioning and had to be taken by all nursing students. Basic students took one PE course a year, but post-basic students had to fit all three PE courses into two campus years. Some students were not exactly physically fit – and all definitely were not enamoured of the course, which was given by the School of Physical Education and Recreation. This course, according to Ethel Warbinek, who chaired the undergraduate curriculum committee during this time, "generated more complaints and petitions than any other course in the history of the School."[14] It was eventually dropped from the curriculum in 1987.

The faculty remained committed to the use of the UBC Model and to the idea of introducing the first year student to the concept of "wellness" as a basis of nursing practice. Thus, first year continued to focus on "the well adult," and content related to maternal/child care was moved to third year. Second year focussed on care of the acutely ill adult and experiences were provided in medical, surgical, and psychiatric settings. Third year focussed on the family, and clinical experiences in obstetrics and pediatrics were included. In fourth year, courses brought in content related to individuals and family facing both acute and long term illnesses and included care in

Figure 7.2   Faculty member Donelda Ellis (MSN 1976), far left,
with a group of third year students in their maternal-child rotation at
Grace Hospital in 1985.

acute settings, long term care settings, and the community. As well, management skills and a clinical nursing elective (for in-depth study in a selected clinical area) were included in fourth year. Students also were given opportunities to include 300-and 400-level electives; later, all electives in third and fourth year had to be at the 300 and 400 level and a greater variety of non-nursing upper level courses were available.

SOCIETAL TRENDS

Some of the changes affecting the School and its new curriculum were influenced – as always – by the social, political, economic, cultural, educational, scientific, and technological trends. For example, an international meeting sponsored by the World Health Organization (WHO) in Alma Ata in the Soviet Union in 1978 had brought together representatives of 127 nations and 72 international organizations. The result was a declaration of the World Health Organization's goal of "health for all by the year 2000." The concept was that primary health care was the best means of attaining equitable distribution of resources so all people could have a level of health that would enable them to lead socially and economically productive lives. Primary nursing care was seen as an important means of reaching this goal.

As well, in the 1970s, growth in the health care system was still the norm. The 1979 Mission Statement of the University of B.C. reflected this in the first of its goals for the coming decade. Part of this goal called for expansion of programs in the health sciences to increase the number of health care professionals and to foster affiliation with teaching hospitals.[15] Nevertheless, by the end of the 1970s, Canada's federal and provincial governments were beginning to feel the effects of the massive growth of health care systems. Health care budgets were taking increasingly larger percentages of tax dollars.

Governments began taking an increased interest in health care and, as part of their scrutiny, in nursing and nursing education. One major study on nursing education was carried out in B.C. by the provincial Ministry of Education, Science, and Technology. The "Nursing Education Study Report," prepared by Claire Kermacks of North Vancouver, an independent nursing consultant, was released in April 1979.[16] Among the 43 recommendations in the Kermacks Report were controversial calls for a government-directed "classification system" for five functional levels of nursing care workers and for psychiatric nursing educational programs to be eliminated and the Registered Psychiatric Nurse Act repealed. As well, the report recommended that B.C.'s four remaining hospital diploma schools should be phased out by 1980. Several less controversial recommendations touched on concerns related to university nursing education: the need for more funding for nurses taking study leaves; strengthening of the curriculum for bac-calaureate students in skills related to administration and management; more programs to be offered outside the Lower Mainland; more post-basic clinical specialty courses, including one in occupational health nursing; increases in enrolments at both UBC and the University of Victoria; and establishment of a master's program in nursing at the University of Victoria.

The recommendations were examined by a special task committee appointed by the Registered Nurses Association of B.C.; this four-member committee included UBC faculty members Margaret Campbell and Helen Elfert as well as Helen Gemeroy, who formerly had held a joint appointment at UBC. The RNABC endorsed many of Kermacks' recommendations, especially several that called for more funding for post-basic clinical educa-tion. The UBC School, which had been exploring some of these options anyway, was able to take action on several recommendations, such as development of a post-basic critical care course, because the report led to increased government funding. The recommendation to discontinue prepara-tion for registered psychiatric nurses was not accepted by the B.C. govern-ment. Although eastern Canada, had discontinued such programs, the four western provinces continued to offer them. However, the B.C. government did begin a major campaign to close beds in its large psychiatric hospitals and to introduce community-based mental health care.

Throughout the 1980s, several provincial and national commissions were set up to look at control of costs and to decide on directions health care should take.[17] In 1984, after much study, the Canada Health Act was revised. The Canadian Nurses Association had been active in lobbying for changes so that services of nurses and other health care professionals (not just those of physicians and dentists) could be covered by health insurance. This small but fundamental change would mean that physicians were not the only entry point into the health care system. The Act also changed the funding formulas and limited (capped) the amounts of money that would be provided by the federal government for health care.

Many other political changes that would affect nursing happened during this decade. One local "crisis" indicates some of the growing political discontent among nurses with what often could be an oppressive health care system. Nursing leaders were well educated and competent, but they were seeking to maintain control of nursing while increasing numbers of hospital administrators seemed determined to apply assembly-line techniques to care of patients. In many hospitals across Canada, chief nursing officers were being shuffled out of top levels of the administrative hierarchy and replaced by new, business-oriented, non-nurse managers. The 1978 controversy at the Vancouver General Hospital over the place of nursing in the administrative hierarchy became "the most widely-publicized nursing issue in all Canada."[18] The controversy eventually led to formation of a Committee of Concerned Nurses representing some 800 nursing staff at VGH. It spread to involve the Registered Nurses Association of B.C., the media, the provincial government, and the general public. Finally, after almost a year of highly public political action by VGH nurses, Health Minister Bob McClelland appointed a public administrator to replace the Hospital's Board of Trustees and its President.

During the 1980s and early 1990s, restructuring of administrative hierarchies in hospitals and other health care agencies has continued, with levels of nursing administration being sharply reduced. Nursing has had to fight to maintain its power base so that nursing care of patients is not jeopardized. Decentralization has continued, and shared governance has become one of the new trends in organizational planning. Often, however, decisions are made and new structures implemented without valid evidence based on research into the effects on nursing care and patient outcomes.

Canada's prime ministers during this final period leading up to the 75th anniversary of the UBC Nursing program included Conservative Joe Clark (1979-1980), Liberals Pierre Elliott Trudeau (re-elected 1980-1984) and John Turner (June-September 1984), and Conservatives Brian Mulroney (1984-1993) and Kim Campbell (June-November 1993). In B.C., the Social Credit party had returned to power in 1975 under William (Bill) Bennett, who was followed as Premier by William Vander Zalm (1986-1991) and Rita Johnston (1991). Despite some bitter opposition from labour unions, the Social Credit party remained in power until November 1991 when the New Democratic Party under Michael (Mike) Harcourt was elected.

Throughout most of this period, all governments were plagued by economic downturns and a sluggish economy that continually kept pressure on social services, including health care. The mid-to-late 1980s saw a brief period of recovery during which some gains were made in wage settlements; during this period more than 8,300 members of the B.C. Nurses Union went on strike for 17 days for increased salaries, weekend premiums, and a greater say in workplace issues.[19]

Economic pressures on government were increased by the growing power of various unions, including the nurses' unions; the latter gradually improved financial and working conditions for nurses. The Registered Nurses Association of B.C., which had long been in the forefront of collective bargaining for nurses in Canada, formed a special labour relations division in 1977. However, legal challenges in Saskatchewan had shown the need for the bargaining arm to be further removed from the professional organization and in 1981 the RNABC's collective bargaining unit separated completely and became the autonomous British Columbia Nurses' Union (BCNU).

In 1985, the Registered Nurses Association of B.C. began to seek mandatory registration, which would mean that all those who practised nursing in B.C. would have to be registered and meet provincial standards. Mandatory registration finally was approved by the provincial government in 1988. As well, RNABC increased its role in policy development affecting nursing and health care and launched a number of projects under the banner of "New Directions in Health Care." These projects, which were coordinated by Nora Whyte (BSN 1973, MSN 1988), helped demonstrate the effectiveness of nurses in new roles. Unfortunately, in the early 1990s, the B.C. Nurses' Union began to challenge RNABC's policy-making role – including its support for a baccalaureate nursing degree as the basis for entry to practice. Late in 1993, RNABC altered its stance on the year 2000 as the target date, although it maintained support for the need for the baccalaureate as the basis for entry.

In 1990, the B.C. government appointed a Royal Commission on Health Care and Costs under Justice Peter Seaton, which released its report, *Closer to Home*, in November 1991. Although the Report was commissioned and received by the Social Credit government, the New Democratic Party government acted on many of its recommendations, some of which paralleled recommendations of the Foulkes Report of more than 20 years previously. One major recommendation called for establishment of regional health councils and boards to oversee regional health care budgets; for example, these councils decide on proportions of revenues going to hospitals and to other health care agencies in the community. The government's "New Directions" policies call for more care to be delivered in the community and encourage better coordination of care between the various levels of hospitals, other agencies, and community/home nursing.

Governmental decisions were influenced by on-going escalation of costs. Although acute care hospitals continued to expand and new technologies continued to be introduced, nursing was definitely affected: staff allotments were reduced; more emphasis was placed on care at home, leading to greater acuity in hospitals; and nurses in the community took on new roles in care as well as increased workloads.

Other economic and social trends that influenced the UBC Nursing program during the 1980s and early 1990s – and which will continue to have effects in the future – include the greater awareness of women's issues, including pay equity issues, sexual harassment and violence against women, and safety issues for women and nurses in the workplace. Environmental concerns, including safe disposal of hospital refuse, is another contemporary issue.

Scientific and technological advances proliferated during the 17 years of Marilyn Willman's leadership, and these, too, had an impact on nursing curriculums. Funding for medical and health care research continued to be provided through many government agencies and some of the research funding was beginning, during this period, to go to nurse researchers. In 1977, the Social Sciences and Humanities Research Council of Canada was created by an act of parliament, and this new agency offered some funds to nurse researchers. However, nursing continued to receive only token amounts from the Medical Research Council; for example, in 1990-1991, nursing research projects received only $322,000 (0.14 per cent) of the $230 million awarded by the Council.[20]

Major scientific advances affecting nursing occurred in many areas, such as in treatment and care of diabetes and in better control of most cancers. For example, in 1983, the UBC Faculty of Medicine initiated an in vitro fertilization program for women whose fallopian tubes were blocked. Further genetic engineering, organ transplantation, and life-preserving technologies undreamed of a generation ago became routine in the 1980s, but brought new nursing education challenges, including a greater need to help nurses deal with legal and ethical issues. New diseases, such as Acquired Immune Deficiency Syndrome (AIDS), virtually unknown in the 1970s, and resistant strains of sexually transmitted diseases (STDs) and tuberculosis have led to new threats to health. They have also reinforced and re-emphasized the need for nurses to develop advanced knowledge in the scientific principles of infection control for protection of patients, the public, and health care professionals themselves.

The rapid growth of multicultural groups in B.C., especially in Greater Vancouver in the 1980s, changed the face of community life and affected education, health, health care research, and nursing education. Nursing, whether in sickness or health, is often intricately tied to cultural heritage and background. Because of this, the challenge for nursing educators was to assist nursing students to acquire knowledge about many cultures and put it into a health care context. These multicultural challenges in the 1990s may be more complex in Canada than in any other country.

In response to these many changes and challenges, nursing education at UBC changed markedly during the Marilyn Willman years. One of the most important changes concerned the need to find new ways to reach nursing students who, for a variety of reasons, could not attend classes on campus.

EXPANSION OF CONTINUING NURSING EDUCATION AT UBC

Continuing nursing education had been offered at UBC since the Ethel Johns era. However, by the late 1970s, nurses had more leisure and more disposable income to devote to education, and "continuing education" became the new catch phrase. The First National Conference on Continuing Education in Nursing was held in April 1979. Among its chief organizers were Helen Niskala, who had been on the faculty of the UBC School of Nursing, and Ruth Burstahler (MSN 1973), who was a consultant on continuing education at the Registered Nurses Association of B.C.

The UBC Nursing program tried to deal with the increased demand for continuing education despite increasing restrictions on its budget. During the Muriel Uprichard years, the School of Nursing had focussed on development of the ladder program as its major response. Unfortunately, this response did not meet the needs of the many hundreds of nurses outside the Vancouver area. In the mid-1970s, Sharon Turnbull, who had been teaching in the School, took over the continuing education program developed by Margaret Neylan in the Evelyn Mallory years and continued by Sue Rothwell. The Nursing courses had become part of a larger program of Continuing Education in the Health Sciences; this had been developed cooperatively with the other health professions at UBC and was intended to be self-supporting. Sharon Turnbull stayed only a couple of years and left just as Marilyn Willman arrived. JoAnn (Crawford) Wood (BSN 1962) took over as acting director of continuing education and arranged many new, short, non-credit offerings.

Among the workshops offered in the late 1970s were: "Communicating in a Helpful Way" given by faculty members Patricia Valentine (BSN 1962) and Ada Butler (BSN 1950, MSN 1971); "Test Construction and Exam Writing" for nursing instructors given by faculty members Ray Thompson and Edie Benoit; and "Writing Skills for Nurses" given by Glennis Zilm (BSN 1958). Most other workshops were clinically focussed, in accord with the demand for continuing education needs identified by the Registered Nurses Association of B.C., and these were developed and offered by expert clinical nurses. For example, excellent cardiac care and critical care nursing workshops were developed in the late 1970s by Karen Webber (BSN 1977), who also taught in the UBC Nursing undergraduate program, Pamela Miller (BSN 1975), a part-time instructor who worked on the cardiac care unit at St. Paul's hospital, and, later, Marilyn Porter (MSN 1984), who left a full-time critical care position to join the teaching staff. These cardiac and critical care programs slowly grew from short workshops into a long, in-depth, two-part critical care course. This was offered several times in the early 1980s, and included a part-time Level I evening course offered in the Vancouver area. The course also travelled to other centres in the province. Often a hospital would arrange to purchase this course so that it could prepare staff to work in a newly opening cardiac care unit; these new units would have the latest cardiac monitors and other equipment but suddenly would require nurses with advanced clinical skills. The courses were discontinued at UBC in 1987; governmental funding was reassigned so that colleges could offer them.

The continuing education workshops were highly successful and well-attended, including those that travelled to centres such as Prince George, Fort St. John, Kamloops, and Sechelt. However, they proved time consuming for School of Nursing faculty members and, as well, some philosophical differences arose about the program. Many faculty members believed the School should not be developing "dead-end" specialty courses for diploma-level graduates, but should be offering degree completion courses for graduate nurses.

In her 1979 report to the UBC President, Marilyn Willman announced that, "after a two-year search," the School had been "successful in attracting a director of continuing education in nursing – Mrs. Shirley Brandt, formerly director of continuing education in nursing at the U. of California, San Diego."[21] Shirley Brandt, who was also a clinical expert in infection control and had taken part in several continuing education programs on this subject, held appointments as both director of continuing education for nursing and a faculty member in the School.[22] The faculty caucus in December 1982 voted to continue to finance the continuing education program, and the minutes noted accordingly that 3.1 per cent of the School's budget (slightly more than $83,000) would go to continuing education.[23]

The demands for continuing university education and for ways to deliver it to students outside the Vancouver area were not restricted to nurses alone.[24] In 1981, UBC President Douglas Kenny released a document entitled *Looking Beyond*[25] in which he suggested UBC had a responsibility to take the university "beyond" the campus. This responsibility fit with the increasing interest in use of satellite television, videotaping, and telephone conference teaching. The Department of Biomedical Communications was anxious to become involved in this kind of teaching as was the newly developed campus support department, Audiovisual Services. The new government-funded Knowledge Network, established by the provincial government in 1980 as a non-profit society, had moved onto the campus in 1981. It was looking for courses, particularly credit courses, that could be offered via a proposed "television university."

Shirley Brandt attracted a number of grants for pilot projects that would allow nursing to use some of these newer technologies for reaching students throughout the province. In particular, she obtained grants for a pilot series for nurses using the Knowledge Network. The one drawback for this pilot project was its timeframe. She received notice of the grant for "Nursing Assessment and Management of Acute Cardiovascular Disease" late in the calendar year – but the program was to air beginning in mid-January 1982. The course was to draw on the cardiac nursing workshops that had proved so popular, but even with this background a whole new method for delivery of courses via television had to be learned almost overnight.

Ethel Warbinek was the nursing instructor for the opening program. The teaching skills were new and challenging. In addition to finding time to prepare the course on short notice, she had to locate visual materials suited to television, lecture to a camera rather than a classroom of students, and work within an exacting time period that had to accommodate station breaks for commercials. The two-hour lecture segment was to be delivered live, with an interactive phone-in session for student groups in Kelowna, Kamloops, and Prince Rupert. Furthermore, the budget did not allow for many of the production techniques now taken for granted. Working over the Christmas break, Ethel Warbinek managed to put together a presentation, opening with a lecture by Charles Slonecker, professor of anatomy, and followed by her own segment on physiology of the cardiovascular system.

> The night before I was to go on TV, my husband used a video camera to tape a rehearsal – and that's when I discovered that I was keeping my eyes on my notes rather than looking into the camera. We did not have any teleprompters or the like, so I spent the whole next day – the program went on air at 3 o'clock – memorizing the script. We needed a script, so that the visuals would come in at the right places. I have never been as scared as I was that night; nothing that I ever faced in teaching before or after that time was as traumatic. I thought my heart would jump out of my chest.[26]

Despite all these worries, this live television program was rated a huge success by the Knowledge Network, which wanted to continue the live shows. However, the stress placed upon teachers who were not experienced television professionals was prohibitive and the Division of Continuing Nursing Education decided that remaining programs would be videotaped for presentation. This created its own challenges, including the videotaping of some segments with patients in hospitals. The entire pilot series was successful and several other programs, such as one on neurological nursing, were prepared and aired. However, a tremendous amount of work was required for each series and the School usually could not afford to release faculty from regular campus duties. Furthermore, academic disciplines were wary of recognizing this new kind of teaching through promotion and tenure, which made some faculty leery about devoting time to it rather than to research and scholarly work. Also, once the pilot projects were completed, the Continuing Education Division usually could not find funds to subsidize the programs on a regular basis, especially when pressures were increasing to develop credit courses for television.

EVOLUTION OF THE BSN OUTREACH PROGRAM

In March 1980, the School set up an ad hoc committee to determine the feasibility of designing a "Baccalaureate Outreach Program" whereby nursing courses could be offered to nurses living in outlying areas of the province. The committee reported back to faculty caucus and recommended a degree-completion Outreach program designed for registered nurses who could not come to campus. The Outreach program would use flexible scheduling and innovative teaching strategies, such as independent study, correspondence courses, television, and off-site classes offered by UBC faculty who would travel to other centres. The committee recommended working collaboratively with community colleges, the University of Victoria, the Knowledge Network, and the new Open Learning Institute (OLI), which had been formed in 1978 and offered its first programs in 1979. (In 1987, OLI and the Knowledge Network merged and became known as the Open Learning Agency, or OLA.)

In June 1982, funding was obtained through a special grant from the Universities Council of B.C. for a BSN Outreach Program and Olive Simpson, who had been on the Nursing faculty since 1974, was appointed director. Financing for the Outreach Program was separate from budget for the School. For 1982-1983, the first year of the program, the budget was $167,000. The funding was conditional on the schools of nursing at UBC and University of Victoria working together to develop joint credit courses.

The first course selected for development was Professional Issues in Nursing. Janet Ericksen and Mary Regester from UBC and Mary Richmond from University of Victoria developed the course, which included six one-hour television programs, a course manual containing 12 lessons, and a book of readings. The one-hour television programs were broadcast, one every two weeks, via the Knowledge Network's regular scheduling. If students lived in a part of the province that did not receive the Knowledge Network's signal, tapes could be sent to a community college or hospital for student use.

Helen Elfert of the UBC Nursing faculty reviewed a course called Understanding Research in Nursing offered by the Open Learning Institute and it was subsequently approved for transfer credit toward the nursing program at UBC. This was the first of many courses that were available from the Open Learning Institute. Such transfer courses offered nurses throughout B.C.

Figure 7.3   Some of the faculty teaching in the UBC Outreach Program, circa 1991. L-R: Joanne Ricci, Ethel Warbinek, Janet Ericksen, Sylvia Holmes, Mary Jane Duke, Cheryl Entwistle, Louise Tenn, Lynda Anderson.

greater flexibility in planning for their degrees. In the early 1990s, many post-basic students were taking electives, such as first-year English and statistics courses, through the Open Learning Agency or community colleges, mainly because other UBC faculties and departments have not become as involved as Nursing in outreach programming.

At first, UBC Nursing Outreach offered only a portion of the program leading to the degree; none of the clinical courses was offered. Also, until the late 1980s, students had to take at least one full year on campus because the University had a residence requirement. As well, the University did not allow any challenge credits, which were allowed by some universities to enable students who had not taken a course to obtain credits if they could demon-strate knowledge of the course content. As the Outreach program developed during the 1980s and early 1990s, more nursing courses were made available. In 1989, Cheryl Entwistle was appointed director of the Outreach Program on a part-time basis and more emphasis was placed on developing a post-basic degree-completion program that could be offered entirely through distance education or used by Vancouver area students who wished a more flexible schedule.

The fourth-year clinical courses were the last to be developed because they needed well-prepared clinical facilitators in the students' clinical practice sites. These facilitators supervise clinical practice and work with the UBC

Figure 7.4   Cheryl Entwistle, Director of the Outreach Program
starting in 1989. She is shown teaching CPR to a group of students in the
Wesbrook lab, circa 1979.

faculty tutors to ensure that course objectives are met. The first fourth-year
clinical course to be developed was Nursing 441, "Nursing Care of Older
Adults," which was written by Jo-Ann Perry (MSN 1976) and offered in
1989. Nursing 440, "Nursing Care of Young and Middle-Aged Adults," the
first to use clinical facilitators, became available in 1990 and was written by
Anne Wyness (BSN 1965) and Ethel Warbinek (BSN 1957, MSN 1970). All
Outreach courses parallel those offered on campus.

The development of the Outreach Program has meant greater flexibility
for all nursing students at UBC. On-campus basic students as well as post-
basic students can opt to take one or more of their courses through independent study. As well, because several Outreach courses are offered during
summers, students may take them at that time and reduce the course load
during the academic year. In 1993, approximately one-half the students in
some courses chose the independent study route. Another major change is
that the program no longer is used only by those outside the Lower Mainland
area, but is open to any student, including those living in Vancouver. Such a
program allows students to work on their degrees on a part-time basis over a
longer period than the traditional four years; this is particularly appealing to

Figure 7.5   Acute Care Unit, circa 1980, when the School
moved to the third floor.

registered nurses who juggle nursing careers, family responsibilities, and educational responsibilities. By 1991, registered nurses could complete the entire BSN degree through independent study. In November 1991, the first 10 such students graduated.

THE MOVE AND THE LEARNING CENTRE

During the 1979-1980 academic year, the School moved to the third floor of the new Acute Care Building of the Health Sciences Centre Hospital. Completion of a modern acute care hospital on campus was the realization of plans that dated back to 1912, three years before the University opened its doors. A hospital, which would also have teaching space for medical and nursing students, was part of the original design for the UBC campus and was planned for the exact site now occupied by the 240-bed Walter Koerner Acute Care Unit.

Nursing faculty supported the belief that proximity of the School to the hospital would allow closer liaison between education and practice. They believed the School could influence the quality of nursing care that was offered. Because there would be easier access to faculty expertise and research, nursing care would reflect these influences and be of a higher standard than in non-university hospitals. The faculty wanted a collaborative relationship between the nursing department and the School in which there was a "shared responsibility ... to ensure the provision of effective nursing care and effective learning experiences."[27] The faculty had strong hopes that this town-gown relationship would provide a model of excellence for student learning, and to a certain extent this happened. The new director of the Walter Koerner Acute Care Unit, which opened in May 1980, was Shirley Mermet (BSN 1975) and many of the staff were UBC graduates so the environment was a positive one and the UBC Health Sciences Centre became renowned for its nursing care.

The acute care unit initially was planned as a community hospital, but had developed into a research-oriented centre with the latest in technological advances in certain specialties. For example, the modern diagnostic equipment included a Positron Emission Tomograph (PET) for taking three-dimensional pictures of the brain using radioisotopes produced at UBC's TRIUMF nuclear cyclotron facility.[28] A well-equipped emergency department was part of the unit and provided care for the growing University community. Student Health Services moved at the same time from the Wesbrook Building into new quarters on the main floor of the hospital.

After many years in temporary sites in various parts of the campus, the move once again located all nursing faculty members in one building. The top floor of the hospital was devoted to educational facilities, with Nursing occupying the larger part but sharing the floor with the School of Rehabilitation Medicine. Enough room was planned for up to 600 undergraduate students and 150 graduate students. In addition to 80 individual offices for faculty members and a large reception area and work space for support staff, the School had eight seminar rooms as well as a modern, 20-bed nursing laboratory that resembled hospital facilities, a faculty lounge (shared with Rehabilitation Medicine), student lounges (graduate and undergraduate), and a new home for the Learning Resource Centre.

Many nursing faculty members had long envisioned a separate building for the School of Nursing. However, the University administration wanted the hospital to be closely allied with teaching and therefore included academic space in the planning for the Health Sciences Centre. Although many Nursing faculty were disappointed, faculty caucus minutes noted that "refusal ... to accept some 20,000 square feet of space would negatively affect ... hopes for a building."[29] The plans originally called for a skywalk to connect the teaching floor of the hospital to the Woodward Instructional Resources Centre (IRC), but this idea was abandoned because of costs. IRC was adjacent to the new hospital, and its lecture theatres continued to be used for nursing's large classes.

The move into the new building went smoothly except for some ruffled feelings over office allocation. About one-half of the new faculty offices had windows, most of them with excellent views, and the other half were in

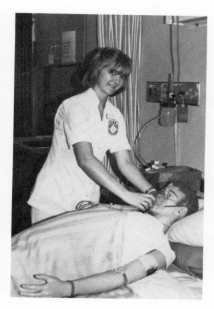

Figure 7.6

Student practising oxygen therapy in the nursing lab of the newly opened Learning Resource Centre, circa 1981.

interior hallways that had no windows. Feelings ran high over who should have the windowed offices. Some maintained that they should go to those who had higher academic credentials, such as doctoral preparation, while others believed those who had seniority should have first choice. In the end, the longest-employed tenured faculty members selected their offices first. The remaining faculty had offices assigned.

The offices of the Director, her secretary, and the administrative assistant remained on the third floor of IRC, along with offices of the other deans and directors of the health sciences programs. The philosophy remained that interactions between students and faculty of all health sciences would be enhanced by this interdisciplinary mingling, although by now several deans and directors had found it more efficient and effective to be closer to their own faculty members. As well, it became more costly to maintain the intrafaculty interactions when the director's office was in another building, and in 1985 Marilyn Willman decided to move out of IRC and into offices in the School.

The move to the new building brought many improvements in the ways that nursing skills were taught. The expanded Learning Resource Centre became the main practice laboratory. Closed circuit television was introduced so that students could watch procedures demonstrated close-up on camera and replay these as they practised. Eileen Campbell was the first coordinator of the Learning Resources Centre and initially assisted faculty members to supervise the skills practice. Later a small team of Resource Centre instructors

Figure 7.7   Joanne Ricci (BSN 1975, MSN 1977) teaching first year
students in the nursing lab.

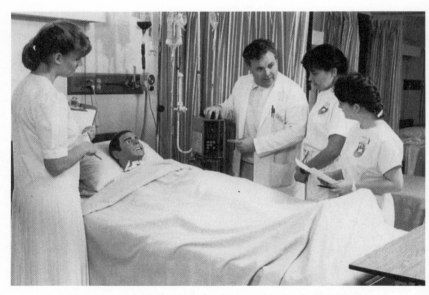

Figure 7.8   Doug Yochim, faculty member in the UBC/VGH
collaborative program, teaching a group of students advanced intravenous
therapy in the learning labs.

Figure 7.9   Student working on a computer in the Learning Resource Centre, circa late 1980s. UBC was one of the first schools of nursing in Canada to introduce computer learning.

organized all teaching and supervision in the laboratories. Rosemary Knechtel then took over as coordinator for a short time.

In 1982, Cheryl Entwistle became coordinator, and under her supervision the Learning Resource Centre has become one of the most advanced such facilities in Canada, attracting frequent visitors from around the world. Several other centres in university and college nursing schools in Canada have been modelled on the one at UBC. The Learning Resource Centre concept at UBC combines more than just a nursing laboratory and reading room; it is a focal point for clinical skills teaching and for independent study and learning. Among the first such centres in Canada to introduce a bank of computers for nursing students, it has audiovisual facilities where the most recent interactive learning materials can be borrowed and used on site. In 1994, plans were underway to have the computers connect with the University's libraries.

Although use of the Woodward Library is encouraged as a major student resource, a reasonably large collection of current books, slides, video- and audiotapes, pamphlets, and journals is available in the Learning Resource Centre. Students also have access to nursing equipment in the laboratory where they can drop in at scheduled practice hours for either supervised or unsupervised practice.

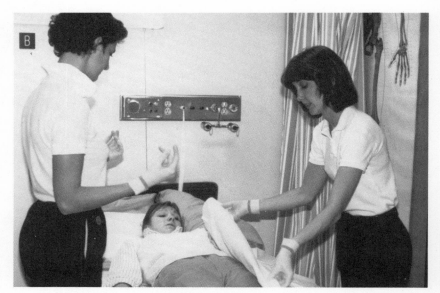

Figure 7.10   Students practising nursing skills during the open practice
hours in the nursing lab circa 1990.

ANNIVERSARIES OF THE SCHOOL

In 1979, the School celebrated the 60th anniversary of its founding. Beth
McCann chaired a committee of faculty and alumni to plan celebratory
events. The first event of the year was an afternoon reception at the Graduate
Student Centre on February 24, followed by a special international seminar,
"Toward the Year 2000," on February 26 and 27. Guest speakers included
four internationally renowned nurses from the International Council of
Nurses and the World Health Organization.

In May, a special banquet was held at the faculty club attended by Chancellor J.V. Clyne and Mrs. Clyne and other university luminaries as well as 150
nursing alumni and faculty. The following evening, Alice Baumgart (BSN
1958), dean of nursing at Queen's University, was the 10th Marion Woodward
Lecturer and spoke on "Sixty Years of University Nursing Education: Political
Values and Sexual Politics." This was the culmination of a full day of events
involving an open house at the School and tours, lectures, and other activities
planned for visiting alumni. A special slide-tape presentation on the UBC
School of Nursing had been prepared by Ada Butler for the University's Open
House that spring, and this was shown as part of the display.

As well, this anniversary marked the launching of what was to become the
notorious spoon sale. Five hundred silver teaspoons with the School's graduation crest were ordered from Birks at a cost of about $1,850. The first 100 of

Figure 7.11

The "infamous" School of Nursing silver teaspoon, which was introduced when the School celebrated its 60th Anniversary in 1979.

these spoons were also engraved in the bowl with "1919-1979" and were to be a fund-raising project for the Nursing Division of the UBC Alumni. Unfortunately, sale of these spoons, which were to provide a profit of $2 per spoon, never caught on, and they became a long-term liability. The spoons were used for presentations to guest speakers and retiring faculty and at special alumni events for the next 15 years. More successful was the introduction of a Diamond Jubilee Director's Fund, which raised money from the alumni to be used to support faculty projects.

The 70th anniversary in 1989 featured a dinner for about 100 held on May 11, 1989, at Cecil Green House, a beautiful 1912 mansion donated to the University by Cecil Green, a UBC alumnus. Nursing alumni of the 1920s and 1930s were honoured guests. Dorothy (Byers) Logan (BSN 1950) received the Nursing Division's Award of Distinction; she had recently retired as director of nursing education at the Vancouver General Hospital. Sue Rothwell, a former UBC faculty member who was president of the Registered Nurses Association of B.C., was speaker at the dinner. During the weeks preceding the dinner, a Phone-a-thon by alumni and students raised $4,710 in pledges from nursing alumni for the Golden Jubilee Scholarship Fund. This fund, which had been started at the 50th anniversary in 1969, provides scholarships for graduate students.

Guest speaker for the Marion Woodward Lecture in the 70th anniversary year was Margretta Styles, professor and Livingston chair in nursing, University of California, San Francisco. She spoke on "The Challenge of Quality Nursing Education." The Woodward Lectures had been changed to the fall by this time and the lecture was held in October preceded by a pot-luck dinner hosted by the Nursing Alumni Division.

FACULTY OF THE 1980s and 1990s

The first five years of Marilyn Willman's term as director had some critical moments. Some faculty members were openly dissatisfied with her style of leadership. She first spoke out at a faculty meeting in November 1978 about the lack of trust among faculty and lack of respect for each other and for her.[30] Some faculty wanted more active support of Canadian professional organizations, including the Canadian Association of University Schools of Nursing and the Canadian Nurses Association; previous directors had been extremely involved in the national associations. Although she had continued her involvement in many of the American associations, she initially was not active in the Registered Nurses Association of B.C., for example, except as required by her position as director of the School. She made her views in this regard clear in an interview in 1981 with Beth McCann:

> I do not believe that the full responsibility for representing the School and for taking the message of the School should fall on the director. There is no way that one person can do that. So ... I am very supportive of the idea that faculty begin to get much more involved – and I think some of that is happening.[31]

As well, some faculty members criticized the use of faculty caucus as the decision making body, where the voices of the large number of new, inexperienced, junior faculty members could outweigh the opinions of more senior and experienced faculty. Furthermore, she got into trouble with faculty fairly soon over some administrative directives regarding faculty vacation time. One in particular related to Christmas breaks. She passed along a memo from the office of the Dean of Applied Science which noted that faculty were expected to be on campus on all except the statutory holiday days.[32] Some faculty insisted they had spent much time in evenings and on weekends on School business and felt that they need not be in their offices during this period. Although this was a minor point, and was University rather than School policy, some faculty blamed her for infringements on their professional accountability.

Criticism of her administration continued. Some faculty members strongly believed that the director should be more involved in campus and professional nursing politics and affairs. In 1982, Marilyn Willman requested an evaluation. She had been one of the last directors to be appointed under the old rules of the University, where deans and directors were appointed without term. The University had since changed the policy to appointment for five-year terms. So, even though she was not obliged to seek a review at the end of her first five years, she requested that a review be carried out.

Although the University had no policies or procedures for such a review, Axel Meisen, then associate dean of Applied Science, chaired a committee that interviewed and received submissions from faculty members who wished to speak out. The committee included Beth McCann and Helen Elfert representing the School, and Mary Murphy, vice-president of the Vancouver General Hospital, and Bernard Riedel, dean of the Faculty of Pharmaceutical Sciences and coordinator of UBC Health Sciences. The committee received several submissions and prepared a confidential report that was given to her. She made the report available to faculty on request. The report praised her administrative abilities, including the fact that she had managed to bring the budget under control and had accomplished a major curriculum revision and restructuring of the faculty organization within a short period. As well, it noted that she had brought a period of stability to the School. It raised a few areas of concern, including comments about her lack of involvement in University affairs and nursing organizations. The evaluation on the whole was a positive one. She then made a conscious effort to address the concerns that had been raised by faculty.

During her first five-year period, the School, its programs, and its faculty had noticeably improved. The Registered Nurses Association of B.C. had approved the new curriculum, first of all for two-year periods while the curriculum was in transition and then for a five-year period; this was the first full five-year approval since the late 1960s. The School was beginning to attract more faculty with doctorates, and Marilyn Willman, with the support of the dean of Applied Science and the academic vice-president, encouraged faculty to apply for sabbatical leave to pursue doctoral study.

The School at the time of her arrival had about 500 undergraduate students, a number that remained relatively constant throughout her 17 years although the number of students in the graduate program grew. On her arrival, the number of tenure-track faculty positions was about 70. Then, in 1981, all faculty at UBC received an 18 per cent salary increase, and this put new pressures on the School's budget, especially when the government tightened financial allocations to the University in 1982. Marilyn Willman recalled that the School was initially asked to cut its overall budget by 33 per cent. She found this completely unacceptable, but after discussions among the heads and directors in Applied Science, and with the dean, she agreed to a cut in the School's budget amounting to 25 per cent over the next three years. She elected to do this by not filling tenure positions as they became vacant and employing more faculty in sessional and short-term positions. This also meant continuing a practice started in the Uprichard years of employing clinical faculty holding baccalaureate rather than graduate degrees. "That's the explanation for the fact that we now have some 34 tenure-track positions when we had 70," she said in a 1992 interview.[33]

In 1994, with sessional faculty and the large number of faculty employed by the Vancouver General Hospital as part of a collaborative program between the UBC and VGH schools of nursing, the actual number involved in teaching was 109. This included 35 tenure-track faculty at UBC, 30 VGH faculty, 32 sessional faculty (clinical assistants and lecturers), and three nursing staff in the Learning Resource Centre. Of the clinical assistants and lecturers, 18 (56 per cent) were part-time. This rising number of part-time appointments, a trend in all Canadian university schools of nursing,[34] has sparked some criticism among nurse educators because responsibility for clinical teaching usually falls to part-time faculty. Full-time tenured faculty then often are not seen as clinical role models and this tends to make clinical instruction seem less important.

Among the well-known senior faculty during the Willman years were Beth McCann, Elizabeth (Betty) Cawston, Helen Shore, Sheila Stanton, Helen Elfert, Kirsten Weber Hyde, and Olive Simpson, all of whom retired during this period. Other senior faculty who remained included Sylvia Holmes, Ray Thompson, Janet Gormick, Ethel Warbinek (BSN 1957, MSN 1970), Anne Wyness (BSN 1965), Ann Hilton (BSN 1968), Elaine Carty, Clarissa Rogers Green, Helen Niskala, Alison Rice (BSN 1967), Linda Leonard (BSN 1966, MSN 1975), and Joan Anderson (MSN 1973). A long-time sessional faculty member was Florence (Flo) Mann.

Sylvia Holmes took over the difficult role of coordinator of clinical experiences, formerly held by Beth McCann. She took on the position in the late 1970s and held it throughout the Willman years as well as serving as undergraduate academic advisor, particularly for post-basic students.

Other well-known faculty who came to the School during the early Willman years and remained for long periods included Carol Jillings (MSN 1977), Janet Ericksen, Mary Regester, Connie Canam (MSN 1980), Donelda Ellis (MSN 1978), Joanne Ricci (BSN 1975, MSN 1977), Sally Thorne (BSN 1979, MSN 1981), Carole Robinson (MSN 1981), Judith Mogan, Judy Lynam (MSN 1979), Louise Tenn, Virginia (Ginny) Hayes, Roberta Hewat (MSN 1980), Marilyn Dewis, and Gloria Joachim (MSN 1976). Those who joined later include Wendy Hall (MSN 1984) and Angela Henderson (BSN 1981, MSN 1983).

Several of these faculty members were encouraged, and in some cases assisted, to pursue doctoral studies, including Joan Anderson, who was one of the first, Ann Hilton, Sally Thorne, Carol Jillings, and Ginny Hayes. Several others were still completing doctoral studies, including Roberta Hewat, Jo-Ann Perry (MSN 1976) and Carole Robinson. In recent years, the School has appointed only faculty with doctoral preparation and some of these included

Betty Davies, Sonia Acorn, Anna Marie Hughes, Joan Bottorff, Joy Johnson (BSN 1981), and Barbara Paterson. Joan Bottorff and Joy Johnson were the first and second nurses to graduate from a Canadian doctoral program in nursing (at the University of Alberta) in 1992 and 1993 respectively. Doctorally prepared faculty at UBC are increasingly involved in nursing research and generally have major teaching responsibilities in the graduate program.

Some faculty who left during the Willman years took senior positions in hospitals and created close linkages between the School and the health agencies. Mary Cruise became director of nursing at the Purdy Extended Care Pavilion of the Health Sciences Centre Hospital, followed in the position by Rose Murakami (BSN 1962). Sue Rothwell became director of nursing, Cancer Control Agency of B.C. All three held joint appointments with the School through a program established under Marilyn Willman's leadership. The School now has 26 adjunct professors and 25 clinical associates, many of whom have active teaching roles. The document describing School beliefs and policies regarding joint (adjunct) appointments frequently is requested by other nursing programs in Canada.

The death in a traffic accident of Sheena Davidson, a popular faculty member who had graduated from the MSN program in 1978, occurred in December 1980. A research fund in her honour, the Sheena Davidson Nursing Research Fund, was established to provide grants for faculty or graduate students doing research in maternal/child care areas. The first award went in 1985 to Roberta Hewat (BSN 1962, MSN 1980) and Donelda Ellis (MSN 1978) for a study on a comparison of the effectiveness of two modes of breast hygiene on the pathogen content of expressed breast milk. As well, a student bursary in Sheena Davidson's honour was set up by the Friends of the University and augmented by funds from the Nursing Undergraduate Society.

Also during this period, a significant financial contribution from Katherine MacMillan, a VGH graduate, became the base for the Katherine MacMillan Director's Research Fund.

UBC/VGH COLLABORATIVE PROGRAM

The move to college-based diploma schools in B.C. had left the VGH three-year program as the only hospital school in the province. However, in early 1988, the Vancouver General Hospital's school of nursing began to have difficulty filling its classes with qualified applicants. At about that time, Marilyn Willman and Inge Schamborzki, chief nursing officer at VGH, began to talk about the possibility of a partnership or collaboration between VGH and UBC for the education of nursing students. The main goal was to try to increase the number of baccalaureate graduates in the province and at VGH. As well, both recognized a need for a link with a strong clinical setting as a learning environment for nursing students at both the undergraduate and graduate levels.

Inge Schamborzki came to a faculty caucus meeting to discuss the idea and there was support, in principle, for development of a collaborative program. A seven-member education advisory committee, called the Project 2000 Committee, was formed; it was chaired by Rosalie Starzomski, who had a joint appointment as clinical nurse specialist at VGH and clinical assistant professor in the School, and had three members from UBC and three from VGH. Colleen Stainton (BSN 1961), a professor and assistant dean of the Faculty of Nursing at the University of Calgary, was hired by VGH as a project director to spend two or three days a month in Vancouver working with both UBC and VGH teaching staffs to help create a climate for change.

Marilyn Willman and Inge Schamborzki determined, for several reasons, that it would be wise to implement the joint program as soon as possible. A recommendation to that effect was approved in October 1988 by David Strangway, UBC president, and James Flett, VGH president. Although many details still needed to be worked out, it was decided that VGH would not admit a class in February of 1989 and, starting with the September 1989 class, nursing students would be registered at UBC in a UBC/VGH program. The four-year generic curriculum of UBC would be followed and students would graduate with a BSN degree from UBC.

Marilyn Willman said that both she and Inge Schamborzki thought the move was a wonderful and timely idea, but some faculty were distressed by the decision.

> I have said to many people that I miscalculated, because I thought our faculty would think it was a wonderful an idea. And they didn't – partly because there was a committee and the committee felt that it had been pre-empted. Here it had been busily working and planning and suddenly they were told 'we are going to do it' so they were not pleased.[35]

The program was organized so that existing VGH teaching staff would continue to be employees of VGH and members of the B.C. Nurses Union; they would be appointed and paid by VGH. Basically, they would be VGH employees who taught in the joint program. UBC faculty are paid by UBC and are members of the UBC faculty association. Financial arrangements are rather detailed. Programs are funded by the respective institutions and the University returns to VGH an amount from the additional student fees generated by the program. The VGH director is Gail Bishop (MSN 1981) and she is responsible to the UBC director for the teaching carried out by the 30 VGH faculty members.

The generic program now is known as the UBC/VGH Nursing Program. As a result of the joint program, the enrolment in the generic program doubled. Since 1986, the UBC School had been limited to 80 first year admissions. Starting in 1989, the quota for first year was raised to 160 students, although this number was not reached until 1993. All students are required to meet UBC criteria for entrance and for progression in the program.

One point of contention that bothered some UBC faculty was that they had to meet University criteria both for appointment and for involvement in research and scholarly work, while VGH faculty had to meet less stringent criteria established by the School for adjunct appointments. VGH faculty members attend faculty caucus, although for the first four years of the program they did not have voting privileges. Since the fall of 1993, they hold voting membership in caucus, but vote only on matters pertaining to the UBC/VGH program; they have no vote on matters relating to the post-basic program or to the graduate programs.

1987 CURRICULUM REVISIONS

Revisions to the undergraduate curriculum were implemented in September 1987. The psychiatric nursing course that had been in the second year of the program was moved to fourth year and became a course in nursing of adults and families with mental health concerns; this change reflected the increasing move to mental health care in the community rather than just in hospitals. The third year maternal/child and pediatric courses were lengthened to reflect the greater emphasis on care in the community. Another change was the greater number of options and opportunities for fourth-year students to focus on a specific clinical area. Although this did not represent a move to clinical specialization per se, it allowed students to pursue an area of interest, such as maternal/child, pediatric, adult, mental health, or gerontological nursing.

As well, an extended practicum in professional nursing was introduced in fourth year; this three-week, 120-hour practice period allowed the student to work with a nurse preceptor in a clinical agency, such as a hospital, home care service, or community health unit. The practicum was another contentious issue for UBC faculty. The idea for one had long been proposed by some faculty and students and the concept was strongly supported by the Registered Nurses Association of B.C. A majority of faculty had rejected the idea when the curriculum was revised in 1978, but it was accepted after heated debate in 1987.

Program revisions were also made in the master's curriculum. The Master of Science in Nursing (MSN) program, begun in 1968 with six students, had grown steadily. When Marilyn Willman arrived at UBC in 1977, the average graduating class was about 15 students, a level that remained until the mid-1980s. Faculty wanted to make the program more flexible and relevant. Courses were restructured for students in the teaching stream so that there were opportunities to do practice teaching in clinical nursing. A longer and more applicable practicum also was introduced in the adminstration stream. As well, the clinical specialization stream was strengthened, in accord with the changing emphasis on specialization in nursing. Students could select an area for specialization and work closely with regular and adjunct faculty members who had expertise in that area.

As well, the number of units required for a master's degree was reduced to be more consistent with those in other graduate programs at UBC and in other nursing programs in Canada. In accord with changes in graduate education at UBC, the School allowed more flexibility for students who wished to enrol in the master's program on a part-time basis. The time limit for the program is five years; most students opt to take the program on a part-time basis.

These changes, coupled with increasing awareness of the need for greater numbers of better prepared nurses, meant progressively larger enrolments in the master's program beginning in the late 1980s. In 1993, 34 new students were admitted into the program, bringing the total enrolment to 156 in 1993-1994.

INTRODUCTION OF THE DOCTORAL PROGRAM

Although nursing leaders in Canada had long stressed the need for a doctoral program in nursing in Canada, even as late as the mid-1980s no such program existed. In 1983, Marilyn Willman established a committee to look into the concept of a doctoral nursing program at UBC. About a year later, the faculty caucus approved a recommendation that the School establish such a program "within the next five years."[36]

The School had much politicking to do on campus because university colleagues questioned the need for a PhD program in nursing. "After all," they protested, "there isn't much nurses can study, is there?" Professors and deans in long-established disciplines still looked askance at explanations about growth of the nursing discipline. However, UBC nursing faculty members persevered and submitted a program to the UBC Senate.

Marilyn Willman said later that the committee had originally developed quite an elaborate program, heavily course-oriented and structured, but the Senate curriculum committee had rejected it and recommended fewer organized courses and more emphasis on research under the mentorship of a faculty member.

> I think our planning was influenced a great deal in that a number of people on the committee had doctorates from American universities, [which] are big on course work – almost endless course work. So we had that influence on one side and on the other side the British influence where they have almost no course work at all.[37]

Axel Meisen, dean of Applied Science, also believed that a doctoral program should have a relatively small number of courses, as did Peter Suedfeld, dean of Graduate Studies. The School made changes along these lines and the final proposal for a Doctor of Philosophy (PhD) in Nursing was approved by Senate. The program, when it began admitting students in September 1991, was the second doctoral nursing program in Canada; the University of Alberta had launched its program in January 1991 with four students.[38]

The UBC program is research-intensive and applicants must have a master's degree in nursing and identify their research area before being admitted to the program. This requirement is to ensure that qualified faculty members are available to help the student develop a research project. The program consists of three major components: core courses, support courses, and a doctoral thesis. Students must sit a comprehensive examination upon completion of course work, usually at the end of the first year of study. The purpose of the program is to prepare nurse researchers capable of advancing nursing knowledge through scholarly research, disseminating research findings, and applying findings to nursing and health care.

The first two students – Patricia (Paddy) Rodney (MSN 1988) and Rosalie Starzomski – entered the program in September 1991. Three students – Lynne Maxwell (BSN 1986, MSN 1990), Janice McCormick, and Joanne Roussy – were admitted to the program in September 1992. Three more – Ruth Grant-Kalischuk, Frances Legault, and Colleen Varcoe (BSN 1975) – were admitted in September 1993. Most of the students obtained scholarships or other kinds financial assistance. For example, Rosalie Starzomski, a clinical nurse specialist working in the area of renal disease, obtained fellowships from the Kidney Foundation of Canada. Two received awards from the Canadian Nurses Foundation. Two received Margaret Campbell Scholarships, which were generated in honour of long-time faculty member Margaret Campbell (BASc(N) 1948), who had helped develop the doctoral program. One received the Reid-Wyness Graduate Scholarship in Nursing, donated by Alison Reid Wyness (BASc(N) 1934), who had taught at the Vancouver General Hospital during the Mabel Gray years and whose daughter Anne Wyness (BSN 1965) began teaching at UBC during the Uprichard years.

GROWTH OF NURSING RESEARCH AT UBC

In the report to the UBC President for the year from September 1977 to August 1978 (her first report as director), Marilyn Willman noted that research efforts had become increasingly visible, although funding support for nursing research "was not readily available and nurses must spend a great deal of time seeking out funding sources."[39] In the 1980-1981 year, the amount and kind of research activity in the School increased sharply. That year there were 25 projects; nine were studies of student learning or behaviours related to nursing education and the remainder were clinically oriented.[40] Three studies were funded by the B.C. Health Care Research Foundation, and 10 by the Social Sciences and Humanities Research Council; faculty also received funding through other sources.

Joan Anderson, who finished her doctorate in 1981 and came back to the faculty, was one of the major people to help get research established. As Marilyn Willman noted:

> We began just about at that point to emphasize that people appointed to the faculty needed to think in terms of research and publication if they wanted tenure. Prior to that we had a real problem [with the senior appointments committee for the University] ... because [nursing faculty] did not meet the criteria. For a while the dean was able to talk them through, [but] it became apparent that was not going to work any more. So we really had to work very hard at making research possible, developing some things that would facilitate faculty research, and I think that we made fairly major breakthroughs during that period.[41]

In 1982, UBC and University of Victoria jointly planned a National Nursing Research Conference, which was held on the Victoria campus April 28-30, 1982. This was the eighth such conference; the School had organized the first, held in Ottawa in 1971. The theme for the 1982 conference was "Nursing Research – A Base for Practice: Service and Education," and the chief organizers were Ann Hilton (BSN 1968) of UBC and Mary Richmond from the University of Victoria. More than 200 nurses from across Canada and the United States attended to hear more than 25 presentations. A book of the proceedings of the conference was published by the UBC School of Nursing.[42]

In 1984, the School started an annual UBC Nursing Research Day to which nurses interested in research were invited to hear presentations by UBC faculty and graduate students. This was a forerunner to larger research conferences hosted by the School in the 1990s. An international research conference, Making a Difference: Meeting the Challenge, was planned for May 1994 to celebrate the 75th anniversary of the School. Joan Bottorff, who joined the faculty in 1992, was chair of the planning committee.

A major development in the evolution of research in the School was the opening on February 23, 1989 of the Research Unit. It provided an administrative framework to facilitate development of nursing research and also compiled resource information about funding opportunities. A full-time supervisor of research administration was appointed to seek possible funding sources, assist with grant applications and budgets, and administer the grant funds. In 1989, the School began publishing periodic reports on research activities and on awards and current research projects being carried out by faculty members.

Development of the Research Unit was helpful in promoting research in nursing at UBC and in attracting funding.[43] For example, research funding for faculty in 1986-1987 was $70,016; it rose in 1990-1991 to $341,186. However, funding dropped in 1992-1993 to $124,649; the drop was related to major cuts in research funding linked to growing deficits and the economic recession.

Research activities of faculty fall mainly within four broad areas: family health care, especially the health care of women and children; management of chronic illness and disability; cross-cultural health care; and aging. School faculty are actively engaged in collaborative research efforts at several affiliated hospitals and agencies. A brochure on the School's research resources for 1992-1993[44] identified 22 faculty involved in more than 115 major projects.

STUDENT HIGHLIGHTS

Growth in numbers of students in both undergraduate and graduate programs in this period led to some loss of a strong student identity. Class sizes of 160 students for first year meant individuals had difficulty in getting to know classmates. Further, only a few classes involved all students. Gone were the small classes and residence life of early years, when students lived and worked together and life-long friendships were formed. Nevertheless, the Nursing Undergraduate Society (NUS) continued to maintain an active presence in the School and on the campus.

The Nursing Undergraduate Society grew out of the Science Girls' Club of the 1920s. The various executives continued to organize events and maintain traditions established by previous generations of nursing students at UBC. In 1993, for example, NUS organized presentations in which individuals from the nursing community, most of them UBC graduates, met with students to discuss the role of baccalaureate nurses as well as career opportunities and options.

The location of the School, in the hospital and on the southeastern edge of the campus, sometimes made interaction with students from other faculties difficult, but nursing students continued to participate in such events as the interfaculty "mixers" with Engineering and with other health science students. The tradition of the annual Teacup game continued, but in 1993 was played, for the first time, against students in the School of Rehabilitation Sciences rather than students in the School of Home Economics, now named Family and Nutritional Sciences.

Students also continued to organize Nursing Week every year, and to set up a booth in the Student Union Building (SUB). There, they demonstrated various nursing activities, such as checking blood pressures and doing health teaching and promotion. As well, students often invited special guest speakers and the final event of the week was a Nursing Dance. During Homecoming Week, NUS remained active in team events arranged for all faculties on

Figure 7.12   Students taking part in the 1986 Teacup game, which started
in the 1950s and has continued to be a tradition in the 1990s.

campus, such as the traditional Arts 20 Relay to commemorate the Great
Trek of 1922.

Links between Engineering and Nursing, so long a tradition at UBC,
periodically broke down during this era. A crisis occurred in 1979 when
Engineering students published a newspaper in which they caricatured
women and children in denigrating and disgusting ways. Women on campus
objected strenuously both to this publication and to the traditional Lady
Godiva ride, and the Nursing Undergraduate Society was among the most
outspoken protesters against the pornographic portrayals. Star Mahara, NUS
president, was then made the sole object of a lewd publication by the
Engineering Undergraduate Society, which included her phone number.

Figure 7.13   Students, Class of 1986, taking part in the traditional Nursing Week.

Figure 7.14   The 1985 NUS relay team that took part in the
Arts 20 relay held during Homecoming week each fall to
commemorate the Great Trek of October 29, 1922.

This caused her extreme distress and led to threats against her. She sought legal redress against the Engineering Undergraduate Society, the Alma Mater Society, and the University itself. Other groups on campus took the matter to the B.C. Human Rights Branch. Star Mahara was supported in her protests by the Nursing Undergraduate Society, the School, and Nursing faculty as well as campus women's groups. However, the Lady Godiva ride continued until the late 1980s, despite protests from University administration.[45]

Affiliation between the Nursing and Engineering societies remained strained, largely because small groups of radical engineering students continued to support activities demeaning women and promoting violent acts. However, as Gail Jeffreys, NUS president for 1991-1992, reported:

> In my year, they [Engineering students] made a tremendous effort.... They had blood donor clinics, they supported us for the Tea Cup, they apologized for what had happened with previous Engineers. The rapport was better, certainly by the end of my term. They showed up at all our dances and our fund-raisers.[46]

Although the number of male students enrolled in the School has increased, the percentages have remained stable in recent years and males continue to make up less than three percent of graduates (comparable to the number of males in nursing generally). Because most students are females, the School is affected by the feminist movement and gender politics on campus, although most students do not take a particularly active role. However, more courses included content dealing with gender issues. Faculty members such as Joan Anderson and Alison Rice have been affiliated with the new Centre for Research in Women's Studies and Gender Relations, which opened in 1991 under Director Veronica Strong-Boag. However, the long-time position of dean of women, established in 1922, was discontinued in 1978 and replaced with a Women Students' Office administered by a director. This was perceived by some as a significant loss of support for women on campus.

Undergraduate students from this period who were interviewed generally recalled their experiences in a positive light. Kris Cholyk (later Gustavson) (BSN 1986), NUS president 1985-1986, was an active student while at UBC and she recalled some of her campus activities in a 1993 interview. She was one of the students involved in the prank of painting a bright blue (washable) N on the Engineering cairn. Her first clinical experience was in extended care; from it she learned she could make a difference in people's lives, something that was important to her. She also recalled her experience in a zoology course in first year.

> That was a tough, tough course, because the amount of content to be covered was just phenomenal. I still remember Mary Jackson [the professor] throwing

Figure 7.15   NUS students (circa 1985) painting the Engineer's cairn during Engineering week.

Figure 7.16   First year students during their experience in Extended Care in the Purdy Pavilion at UBC in the early 1980s.

on and off overheads as quick as you could blink, saying 'You know this is all
testable material.' You are sitting there thinking I can't do this. There was a
significant attrition from first to second year; we started out with about 120 in
first year and ended up with about 80 in second year. Zoology was the killer.[47]

Kris Gustavson held a variety of positions after graduation, and in 1990 was
appointed director of the pediatric unit at Mount St. Joseph Hospital in Vancouver. Her sister, Natalie Cholyk (BSN 1977), also got her degree from UBC.

Kris Gustavson stressed that she found the nursing program excellent. She
believed baccalaureate preparation is essential for those who want a nursing
career and that she would not have had the opportunities she had if she did
not have a degree. She recognized that a master's degree was preferred for
administrative positions such as the one she held, and she planned to pursue
graduate studies in nursing.

Nancy Chin (later Burget) (BSN 1978) recalled using videotape equipment to tape an interview with one of her families and that she had "an
ordeal" in setting it up in the kitchen of the family home. Another recollec-
tion concerned a debate among her classmates over the appropriateness of
demonstrating backrubs to raise money for charity during Nursing Week; the
class decided this would be sexist and elected to take blood pressure record-
ings instead.[48]

Catherine Tustin (later DeGusseme) (BSN 1979) recalled the increased
emphasis on prevention and related it to release of the Lalonde report on
lifestyles and their effect on health. She also remembered the 1978 "crisis" at
the Vancouver General Hospital and the firing of four clinical directors. She
thought this "sparked a unified reaction from a large body of nurses growing
ever more political" and that it "probably helped to fuel a more effective
labour relations division of the RNABC."[49]

Morrie Steele (BSN 1980), who had been active in the Registered Nurses
Association of B.C. before he became a post-basic student, criticized the
School's failure to acknowledge the expertise of registered nurse students and
the contributions they had made to nursing.

Doris Wong (BSN 1981) was elected as a student member to the Senate
in 1980-1981. An NUS report to faculty caucus stated that this election
was an indication of the increasing visibility of nurses in student and
university affairs.

Brenda Eng (BSN 1984) joined the staff of the B.C. Children's Hospital
following graduation and was particularly involved with development of
Canuck Place, a hospice for children with progressive life-threatening illnesses and their families. This project, in which Nursing faculty member
Betty Davies also was active, involved mobilizing the support of the Vancouver Canucks hockey team and their fans to raise funds to purchase and
renovate a large heritage mansion near the hospital.

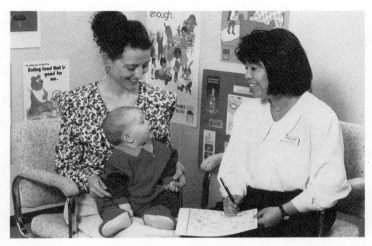

Figure 7.17   Student administering a DDST – Denver Developmental
Screening Test – to a young child, circa late 1980s.

One of the MSN students of this period has a connection with the origins
of the School; Dawn Faris (MSN 1979) is the daughter-in-law of Marion
Fisher Faris (BASc(N) 1923), one of the first three graduates of the UBC
Nursing program.

While most students from the Willman period are just beginning their
progress up the career ladder, many are likely to become nursing leaders
during the next decade. Those in the graduate programs are also likely to
make major contributions to nursing by the turn of the century. Some MSN
graduates of this era are already beginning to make names for themselves.
Several have joined the UBC faculty and have already been mentioned.
Among those active in administration are Dianne Doyle (MSN 1981), Sally
MacLean (MSN 1981), Lynette Best (MSN 1982), Carol Mitchell (MSN
1982), Jenise Brouse (MSN 1985), Wendy Winslow (MSN 1985), Ruth Lamb
(MSN 1985), Theresa Orlando (MSN 1988), Laurel Brunke (MSN 1989),
and Elaine Baxter (MSN 1989). Among those active in nursing education,
other than at UBC, are Thelma Brown (MSN 1979), Mary Kruger (MSN
1980), Jill Peregrym (MSN 1983), Pauline Dunn (MSN 1984), Penny Dunn
(MSN 1985), Mary Thompson (MSN 1988), Susan Duncan (MSN 1989),
Linda Pickthall (MSN 1990), and Linda Gomez (MSN 1990).

CLOSING OF THE WILLMAN PERIOD

The 17 years during which Marilyn Willman was director included some
turbulent times but also encompassed a period of steady growth and
development for the School. New and excellent physical facilities brought

Figure 7.18   Three students of the Class of 1991 taken at Graduation.

all personnel together and made communication, planning, and collaboration among faculty easier and more effective. The joint UBC/VGH baccalaureate program was the first of its kind in Canada and became one of
the largest and most significant undergraduate programs in Canada. The
post-basic program and BSN Outreach evolved and became more flexible
to better meet the needs of the province's registered nurses. The growth of
the master's program has been steady and the program attracts graduate
students of high calibre. Establishment of the Research Unit and opening
of the doctoral program are major achievements and in themselves can be
considered an important legacy of the Marilyn Willman years. Difficult
economic times plagued the School throughout her tenure, but she persevered and left stronger and more viable programs.

Another major achievement of this period is the seven-year accreditation
of the School by the Canadian Association of University Schools of Nursing
(CAUSN). An accreditation program for baccalaureate programs in nursing
had long been proposed in Canada and in 1972 it was determined that
CAUSN would be the appropriate body to develop and administer accreditation standards. However, the CAUSN program took considerable time to
develop and did not become fully established until 1985. Through this
voluntary program a CAUSN committee determines whether participating
university-level programs meet established standards and offers public
assurance of the high quality of the programs. Accreditation standards are
generally considered exacting and considerably higher than the minimum

standards for program approval by provincial nurses' associations. The UBC School elected to submit to the process in 1992 and, after an extensive external review by a CAUSN committee, was awarded a seven-year accreditation, the maximum term allowed before another review.

In addition, Marilyn Willman herself considered one of the important legacies from her period was establishment of the UBC Nursing Honour Society. The Society brings together, from both community and academia, nursing leaders who have demonstrated high standards and commitment to quality health care and to nursing; it provides recognition for these leaders and a network in which they exchange ideas and promote endeavours supporting excellence in nursing. Several senior nursing administrators in the Vancouver area as well as several UBC faculty, including Marilyn Willman, were members of Sigma Theta Tau, a nursing honour society with chapters organized at many universities in the United States. They wanted a western Canadian chapter of this group that would help bring together nursing leaders from both the community and the university, and from administration, research, and education. A committee was formed at UBC, chaired by Nursing faculty member Anna Marie Hughes, and the UBC Nursing Honour Society was formed as a first step to joining the international organization. The Society held its first induction ceremony and meeting in the spring of 1991. In 1994, the Society will be chartered as a chapter of Sigma Theta Tau, the ceremony coinciding with the 75th anniversary of the UBC Nursing program.

An indication of the increasing visibility of the School within the community and the University was the award in 1992 of an honorary doctorate to a graduate of the UBC Nursing program. This was the first time a UBC Nursing graduate had been so honoured by the alma mater. The recipient was Lyle Creelman (BASc(N) 1936), who was recognized as a distinguished nursing leader at the international level through her work with the World Health Organization and United Nations committees. In 1994, UBC will recognize another nursing leader with an honorary doctorate to Helen K. Mussallem, a distinguished B.C. nurse who was executive director of the Canadian Nurses Association for many years and who is internationally known and honoured.

As the School's 75th anniversary approached, Marilyn Willman was nearing retirement age. She informed faculty of her impending retirement at a faculty caucus meeting in September 1991 and noted that her retirement date would be December 31, 1993. A search for a new director then began.

In the discussions about a search for a new director, the question of faculty status for the School once again was raised. Faculty caucus approved a proposal be sent to Senate recommending that the School be granted faculty status. The motion was brought before Senate on November 18, 1992, by Elaine Carty, a Nursing faculty member and a member of Senate, and was supported by Axel

Meisen, dean of the Faculty of Applied Science, and by Daniel Birch, UBC's academic vice-president. In the background to the motion, Elaine Carty stressed that the growth of the graduate program, including opening of the doctoral program, justified the move to faculty status. As well, faculty status would provide the opportunity to have a nurse as a leader for the discipline. As in previous attempts, several members of Senate expressed reluctance to create another faculty and said such a move would create a precedent for the many other schools on campus. UBC's structure was not based on a large number of decentralized faculties, but was a more traditional hierarchical one. The suggestion was raised, once again, that perhaps the School of Nursing should be included with a number of other health sciences disciplines under one faculty. Robert Will, former dean of Arts, suggested that organization of the whole structure of the University should be examined before any decision was made on the School of Nursing's request. The matter therefore was referred to the Senate Academic Policy Committee, which would report back on recommendations for the best model for UBC.[50] At the beginning of 1994, no further action had been taken.

For several years throughout her term as director, Marilyn Willman taught courses in administration in the master's program and was a well-respected teacher. She chaired 17 thesis and 8 major essay committees in the School and served as a committee member for 16 students. Students praised her abilities to encourage them throughout the writing of the theses and noted that she was able to get them to meet deadlines. She served on numerous University committees and was a member of Senate for six years and of the Senior Appointments Committee for three years, the first nurse on this committee. She was an active member of the Nursing Education Council of B.C., serving as vice-chair and member-at-large of the executive.

In response to criticisms about her lack of involvement in professional organizations early in her term, she soon became more involved in nursing associations. She was an active member of the Nurse Administrators Association of B.C. and chair of its Lower Mainland region for two years. She served as a member of several major committees of the Registered Nurses Association of B.C. She also served on committees for many health agencies and organizations in Vancouver and throughout the province. She was frequently asked by agencies such as St. Paul's, Shaughnessy, and Vancouver General hospitals to be on search committees for senior nursing administrators. She also was a member of several search committees for heads of other UBC departments and faculties.

Marilyn Willman had wonderful editorial skills and was an excellent editor. Throughout her term at UBC she continued as an editorial consultant and reviewer for three well-known American nursing journals, including *Nursing Leadership*, *Nursing Papers*, and *Nursing Outlook*. She also maintained an active involvement with some of the senior professional associations in the United States and, in 1993, the American Academy of Nursing honoured her, for her many contributions, as one of 36 outstanding American nurses.

Sheila Stanton, who was acting director when Marilyn Willman arrived, noted in an interview in 1993 that Marilyn Willman brought a sense of stability and a sense of order to the School. She respected Marilyn Willman's judgment and said that, although Marilyn Willman rarely offered thanks or praise for faculty work or special assignments, this was based on a belief that faculty were intelligent and should get their rewards from doing a good job without necessarily having to be told about it. "That's the type of administrator she was – and from that point of view I don't think she was appreciated."[51]

Jeannette Bouchard, executive director of the Canadian Association of University Schools of Nursing in Ottawa, had great praise for Marilyn Willman's contributions to CAUSN during her latter years on the CAUSN's council. As a director who had been on CAUSN council for many years, she frequently was able to provide the long term view. Jeannette Bouchard noted that her "quiet influence" had not always been recognized but that, during the 1990s especially, Marilyn Willman had made several significant contributions at the national level, including a much respected revision of CAUSN's *Position Statement: Graduate Education in Nursing.*[52] Because UBC had opened the second doctoral program in nursing, Marilyn Willman was in an ideal position to describe the needs of graduate nursing education in Canada. She prepared a letter for the Medical Research Council detailing the financial resources that needed to be in place for nursing research at UBC that was circulated by CAUSN to all its deans and director.[53]

Axel Meisen, who became dean of Applied Science in 1985 and worked closely with Marilyn Willman until her retirement, respected her enormously. At the retirement reception in her honour in November 1993, he noted that she had achieved the mandate set for her when she was appointed and especially praised her ability to manage the budgets and to come up with practical and reasonable solutions to problems.

She had not wanted an official reception, but agreed to an informal gathering at the Faculty Club. Although the guest list, at her request, was limited, the event was well attended, mainly by faculty and staff but also by representatives from the Nursing Alumni Division, University administration, and the nursing community. She was presented with a beautiful, handcrafted gold brooch because of her interest in fine jewellery. As well, she received the now traditional silver spoon as an informal ending to the afternoon.

Margaret Street, professor emerita since 1972 who remained an active observer of the history of the School, praised Marilyn Willman in an interview for the University Archives in 1990: "Under her leadership the School has made notable progress and is very strong today."[54]

Figure 7.19   Marilyn Willman, just prior to her retirement in December, 1993, just as the School was getting ready to celebrate its 75th anniversary.

Whenever a dean or director leaves a senior position at UBC, an external review panel is brought in to assess the program. The panel that reviewed the UBC nursing program at the end of 1992, in preparation for the search for a new director, stated that it was "extremely impressed" with the School. In the panel's report, Chair Judith Ritchie of Dalhousie University concluded: "The School of Nursing is a very strong academic unit that has strong leadership, committed faculty, bright and involved students, very good teaching programmes, and impressive levels of scholarly and research productivity."[55]

This strength is a appropriate legacy as the Nursing program begins its 75th year and looks to its future. The contributions of most of the students and faculty of Marilyn Willman's period are just beginning, but will no doubt reflect the same quality as those earlier alumni who helped shape UBC's history.

CHAPTER EIGHT

Looking to the Future

In the years from 1919 to 1994, Nursing at the University of British Columbia has grown and developed in response to many changes, both internal and external. The program has been influenced particularly by the six strong women who were its leaders during those 75 years and who were the chief sculptors of the program. Nevertheless, nursing education at UBC also was moulded by the hundreds of dedicated faculty members who contributed their best to the programs throughout the years. More than 3,550 baccalaureate graduates, 660 diploma graduates, and 291 master's graduates also left their marks on Nursing at UBC and many of them went on to distinguish themselves in nursing provincially, nationally, and internationally. Thanks to the efforts of those who have been part of Nursing at UBC, the School today has a proud heritage and leaves a strong legacy.

As the School enters its fourth quarter century, it will have a new director. Katharyn Antle May assumes the position on July 1, 1994.[1] In the tradition of her predecessors, she comes well prepared. Her previous position was as professor and associate dean for research and director of the nursing doctoral program at Vanderbilt University in Nashville, Tennessee. A Bachelor of Science in Nursing graduate of Duke University in North Carolina in 1973, she also holds a Master of Science (Nursing) (1976) and a Doctor of Nursing Science (1978) from the University of California in San Francisco. A well-known researcher in maternal and child care, she is co-author of a textbook on comprehensive maternity nursing. This text received many awards, including the *American Journal of Nursing* book-of-the-year awards in 1986 and 1990 and the 1990 "best book" designation by the Association of Jesuit Colleges and Universities. The third edition of the text, *Maternal and Neonatal Nursing* (Philadelphia, Lippincott), was published in late 1993. Her recent research projects at Vanderbilt led to some major funding, including a $367,000 grant in 1990 to study "the impact of home-managed preterm labor on families."

She takes over a strong program handed down by the former director. Whenever a dean or director leaves a senior position at UBC, an external review panel is brought in to assess the program. The panel that reviewed the UBC nursing program at the end of 1992, in preparation for the search for the new director, stated that it was "extremely impressed" with the School. In the panel's report, Chair Judith Ritchie of Dalhousie University concluded: "The School of Nursing is a very strong academic unit that has strong leadership, committed faculty, bright and involved students, very good teaching programmes, and impressive levels of scholarly and research productivity."[2] The report also made recommendations that will need to be considered as the new director and faculty develop goals for the School for the remaining years of the 1990s. Among these were calls for revisions to the curriculum, which had been in place since 1987, for increased levels of interdisciplinary exchanges in teaching and research, and for an examination of the administrative structure.

The Board of Accreditation for the Canadian Association of University Schools of Nursing (CAUSN) also identified three similar areas that it believes the UBC program needs to address in the final years of the century.[3] The first concerns relationships between the University and the Vancouver General Hospital about the basic program and, in particular, the two-tier system that has developed because faculty from the Vancouver General Hospital do not meet academic standards required by universities. The second concerns a lack of consensus among faculty over the School's basic philosophy, its approaches to teaching, and its evaluation mechanisms. The third concerns a need to revise the curriculum once again in light of major societal trends.

Political, educational, cultural, scientific, technological, and economic trends will, as always, have an effect on the School as the new era begins. Perhaps the most important trend of the mid-1990s concerns the economic restraints being placed on health and education. Under new government policies of restraint and of emphasis on "closer to home" care, hospital beds are being closed. This will, once again, place emphasis on care in the community, one reason that the UBC Nursing program was started in 1919. Unfortunately, community health care budgets have not been increased, so UBC nursing students being prepared for the new world of the 21st century will need to learn how to do more with less.

Another effect of the economic restraint is that health care agencies are merging into larger and larger corporate entities. For example, the Vancouver General Hospital absorbed the campus hospitals late in 1993 and had a name change in early 1994 to become the Vancouver Hospital and Health Sciences Centre. Although the real focus of these large agencies, particularly the hospitals, is *nursing* care, the role of nurses in senior executive positions is being eroded and downplayed. Thus education for better and more effective nursing administration must become a priority for the next decade. As well, those being prepared for the coming years need to be more aware of their political roles in shaping the health care systems of the future so that nursing's role is better understood and valued.

Education has changed markedly during the 75 years, with increased emphasis on postsecondary education. Nursing education has changed as well. Similar challenges to those that led to introduction of Canada's first university nursing degree in 1919 have dictated that the baccalaureate should be the basis for entry to practice for all nurses by the year 2000. By the fall of 1994, four universities in B.C. will have nursing programs. The University of Victoria's long-time degree-completion program for registered nurses has expanded to include a collaborative program with six B.C. colleges; some of these colleges, such as the University College of the Cariboo in Kamloops, already have degree options to follow their diploma programs, either on their own or through collaboration with the University of Victoria. Trinity Western University, a privately funded university in Langley, admitted the first 35 students into its four-year nursing degree program in September 1993. The new University of Northern British Columbia in Prince George will admit the first students to its nursing program in September 1994.

One of the great challenges for science and technology in the mid-1990s is the search for a response to HIV/AIDS and the new drug-resistant bacteria and viruses. The UBC School of Nursing was the first in Canada to establish an undergraduate course directly concerned with nursing care of those with HIV/AIDS, and UBC must continue with such innovative responses. Nursing research at UBC finally is gaining recognition and taking its place in examining new frontiers, both in theoretical and in applied research. Other challenges for Nursing include discovering the best ways to respond to genetic engineering, ethical issues regarding the right to live and the right to die, multiple organ transplantation, and care for those with chronic conditions such as cancer, multiple sclerosis, and cystic fibrosis.

Canada's demographics are changing yet again. The cultural face is becoming more diversified, with changing immigration patterns. An aging population and growth of mega-cities are just two trends that will continue into the next century. The changing ratio will see fewer young people entering the educational stream and this will have its effect on enrolments and recruitment into nursing in the late 1990s.

As the preceding chapters have shown, UBC Nursing has, in the past, often led in innovative responses to the challenges of the times. Graduates of the 1930s faced economic times that were even more restrictive than those of the mid-1990s. Rapid advances in science and technology – automobiles, radios, television, space travel, computers – occurred in previous generations and were taken in stride by those who have gone before.

One thing has remained constant – the value of a university-based nursing education program. UBC Nursing graduates have the knowledge and skills to adapt in a changing world. If the history of nursing education at UBC is any indication, graduates of the present generation and of coming generations will respond in the same way as those of earlier times – with courage and creativity. This is the real legacy.

Notes

PREFACE

1   Cantor and Schneider, 1967, p. 20.

CHAPTER I: A CLIMATE FOR CHANGE

1   Johns, 1920, p. 3.
2   Kloppenborg et al., 1977, p. 49.
3   Ormsby, 1958, p. 338.
4   Barfoot, 1991, p. 363.
5   Con et al., 1982, p. 83.
6   Morton, 1973, p. 267.
7   Ormsby, 1958, p. 350.
8   Con et al., 1982, p. 85.
9   Barfoot, 1991, p. 363.
10   Ormsby, 1958, p. 350.
11   Morton, 1973, p. 226.
12   Ormsby, 1958, pp. 369-370.
13   Baer, 1990, pp. 2-4.
14   Pearson, 1985, p. 1. The 1891 date was accepted by the Royal Jubilee Hospital as the "official" opening. Pearson's book makes it clear that the board had established a school and enrolled two students in August 1890. An active educational program for these students did not start, however, until the arrival, in 1891, of Grace Mouat, by which time other students were also enrolled.
15   Meilicke and Larsen, 1992, pp. 530-533.
16   Kelly, 1973, p. 3.
17   Davis, 1976, pp. 276-278.
18   Kelly, 1973, p. 6.
19   Kelly, 1973, p. 15.

20 Kelly, 1973, p. 19.
21 Ross, 1971, p. 23.
22 Stewart, 1972, pp. 3-4.
23 Hives, 1990, p. 12.
24 Johnson, 1971, p. 135.
25 Hives, 1990, p. 12.
26 Hives, 1990, p. 12-13.
27 Gibson, 1973.
28 Stewart, 1990, p. 93.
29 Connelly, 1985, pp. 1958-1959.
30 Gibbon, 1947, p. 1.
31 French, 1988, p. 223.
32 Gibbon, 1947, p. 119.
33 Stewart, 1990, p. 21.
34 Stewart, 1990, pp. 21-22.
35 Dock and Stewart, 1931, p. 242.
36 Mussallem, 1992, p. 498.
37 O'Brien, 1987.
38 Kerr, 1944.
39 Registered Nurses Act. S.B.C. 1918, c. 65.
40 Registered Nurses Act, S.B.C. 1918, c. 65, s.21.
41 Canadian Nurses Association, 1968, p. 72.
42 Kerr, 1944.
43 Kerr, 1944, p. 4.
44 Johns, 1920.
45 Johns, 1920, p. 7.
46 Dock and Stewart, 1931, p. 175.
47 Stewart, 1947, pp. 160-161.
48 Dock and Stewart, 1931, p. 175.
49 Dock and Stewart, 1931, 176.
50 Paffard, 1913, p. 298.
51 Paffard, 1913, p. 301.
52 Street, 1973, pp. 98-99.
53 Wesbrook, 1918, p. 1. Also quoted in Street, 1973, p. 99.
54 Whyte, 1988, p. 18.
55 Green, 1984, pp. 5-6.
56 Green, 1984, p. 7.
57 Green, 1984, p. 5.
58 Stewart, 1979, pp. 7-10.
59 Report of the [CNA] special committee on education, 1914, p. 571.
60 Stewart, 1990, p. 32-33.
61 McDonnell, 1992, pp. 292-294.
62 B.C. Hospitals Association, 1919, pp. 46-47.

63   Green, 1984, pp. 8-9.
64   Senate Minutes, Feb. 12, 1991, pp. 80-81.
65   Senate Minutes, Mar. 5, 1919, pp. 85-86.
66   Board of Governors Minutes, May 26, 1919.
67   Street, 1973, pp. 119-121.

CHAPTER 2: THE ETHEL JOHNS YEARS, 1925-1941

1   Street, 1973, p. 115.
2   The full story of her life is available in the truly excellent book *Watch-Fires on the Mountains: The Life and Writings of Ethel Johns*, by UBC Associate Professor Emerita Margaret M. Street (Toronto: University of Toronto Press, 1973). As well, Margaret Street organized and catalogued the Ethel Johns' papers for UBC Library's Special Collections; these include notes for an autobiography that was never completed. Most of the information on Ethel Johns' early life is drawn from Street.
3   For more information on Cora Hind: Haig, 1966; Saunders, 1958.
4   Street, 1973, pp. 16-17.
5   Ethel Johns Papers (notes for an autobiography), UBC Special Collections.
6   Johns and Fines, 1988, pp. 11-27.
7   Johns and Fines, 1988, pp. 28.
8   Street, 1973, p. 35.
9   Street, 1973, p. 41.
10   Street, 1973, p. 42.
11   Street, 1973, p. 75.
12   Ethel Johns Papers (notes for an autobiography), UBC Special Collections. Also cited in Street, 1973, p. 81.
13   Street, 1973, p. 86.
14   Kelly, 1973, p. 30.
15   Gibbon and Mathewson, 1947, pp. 360-361.
16   Street, 1873, pp. 98-99.
17   Government of Manitoba. (1919, February). *Second Interim Report of the Public Welfare Commission of Manitoba*, Winnipeg: Provincial Library of Manitoba. Cited in Street, 1973, pp. 102-104.
18   Street, 1973, p. 105.
19   Davis, 1973, p. 9.
20   Ormsby, 1958, pp. 409-410.
21   Saturday, June 21, 1919. Story, 1967, p. 832.
22   Street, 1973, pp. 107-111.
23   Johns, 1945. Cited in Street, 1973, p. 108.
24   Masters, 1950, p. 128. The quotation is not in Masters' book, although he acknowledges other contributions from Johns. The quotation is cited in Street, 1973, pp. 108, 294, but apparently comes from a copy of the memo to Masters.

25 Street, 1973, pp. 110-111. In these pages, Margaret Street writes wonderful detail of this particular period of Ethel Johns' career.
26 Street, 1973, pp. 120-121.
27 MacEachern, M.T. Letter to President L.S. Klinck, September 23, 1919. Quoted in Street, 1973, p. 121.
28 Senate Minutes, Wed. October 29, 1919, pp. 121-135.
29 King, 1970, pp. 67-73.
30 McDonnell, 1972, p. 293.
31 Senate Minutes, Wednesday, Oct. 29, 1919, p. 121.
32 Senate Minutes, Oct. 29, 1919, p. 124.
33 Beatrice Wood Interview Tape, Feb. 22, 1981.
34 Senate Minutes Wed. Oct. 29, 1919, p. 124.
35 Marion Fisher Farris Interview Tape, January 1981.
36 Esther Naden Gardom Interview Tape, Nov. 24, 1987.
37 Beatrice Wood Interview Tape, Mar. 21, 1991.
38 Beatrice Wood Tape, Feb. 22, 1981.
39 Gibbon and Mathewson, 1947, p. 342. The five universities were Toronto, McGill, Alberta, Dalhousie, and UBC.
40 Senate Minutes, Tuesday, April 20, 1920, pp. 145-146.
41 From a single sheet resume in the CNA Library Files, taken from the Mathewson files at the Library School for Graduate Nurses, McGill University. Information on Mary Ard. MacKenzie is culled from a variety of sources, but relatively little information is available about her life and work.
42 UBC Calendar, 7th session, 1921-1922, p. 185.
43 UBC Calendar, 7th session, 1921-1922, p. 185.
44 Green, 1984, p. 12.
45 Davis, 1976, p. 342.
46 Ormsby, 1958, pp. 405-427.
47 Nicol, 1978, p. 144.
48 Green, 1984 , p. 14.
49 Pearson, 1985, pp. 47-50. See also Pearson for information on the various individual nurses.
50 Pearson, 1985, p. 48.
51 Green, 1984, p. 20; Gibbon, 1947, p. 55.
52 Pearson, 1985, pp. 49-50.
53 Smith, 1990b, p. 38.
54 Smith, 1990b, p. 38. The eight districts were: Sayward, Melville, Cowichan, and Colwood, all on Vancouver Island; Waldo in the East Kootenay Valley; Shusway Lake (including Magna Bay and Celista, and Eagle Bay, Blind Bay, Sorrento, and Notch Hill); East Arrow Park on the Arrow Lakes; and Creston.
55 Smith, 1990b, p. 38.
56 Smith, 1990a, pp. 39-40.
57 Cross, 1991, p. B15.

58 Cross, 1991.
59 Ida May Snelgrove Elliot Interview Tape, Mar. 10, 1981.
60 Balf, 1989, p. 69.
61 Green, 1984, p. 32.
62 Gibbon and Mathewson, 1947, pp. 432-436.
63 Aiken, 1921.
64 Marion Fisher Faris Interview Tape, Jan. 28, 1981.
65 Esther Naden Gardom Interview Tape, Nov. 24, 1987.
66 Esther Paulson Interview Tape by Natalie Bland, July 12, 1988. (Esther Paulson was a friend of Margaret Thatcher, and was also the nurse who followed up the adoption process in 1930.); see also Paulson, 1989, p. 5.
67 Green, 1984, pp.24-25.
68 UBC Catalogue, Eighth Session, 1922-23, pp. 196-197.
69 Mallory, 1961, p. 4.
70 Letter from Ethel Johns to Muriel Uprichard, Sept. 16. 1965, Ethel Johns Papers, UBC Special Collections. Also quoted in Street, 1973, p. 161.
71 UBC Calendar, Eleventh Session 1925-1926, pp. 12, 197-200.
72 Johns, 1919, p.2.
73 Johns, 1919, pp. 9-10.
74 McLeod, 1919, p. 2103.
75 Cavers, 1949, p. 29.
76 Cavers, 1949, pp. 30-31.
77 Cavers, 1949, p. 29.
78 Esther Naden Gardom Interview Tape, Nov. 24, 1987.
79 Esther Naden Gardom Interview Tape, Nov. 24, 1987.
80 Johns, 1948, p. 721.
81 Johnson, quoted in Cavers, 1949, p. 37.
82 Florence Innes Interview Tape, Mar. 11, 1981.
83 Beatrice Johnson Wood, Mar. 20, 1991.
84 Beatrice Johnson Wood quoted in Cavers, 1949, p. 36.
85 Hives, 1990, pp. 14-15.
86 Florence Innes Interview Tape, March 11, 1981.
87 Marion Fisher Faris Interview Tape, Jan. 28, 1981; also see Street, 1973, p. 145.
88 Mrs. Charles Vater, 1970, quoted in Street, 1973, pp. 157-158, 297.
89 See Street, 1973, pp. 129-137.
90 Street, 1973, p. 130.
91 Board of Governors Minutes, Dec. 20, 1922.
92 Minutes of UBC Board of Governers, 1921-1924; Street, 1973, pp. 140-142.
93 Proceedings of Twenty-eighth Annual Convention of the N.L.N.E. June 26-July 1, 1922, quoted in Street, 1973, p. 144.
94 Street, 1973, p. 297.
95 Davis, 1973, p. 236.
96 Carswell, 1980, p. 44.

97   Pearson, 1985, p. 54.
98   CNA, 1968, p. 85.
99   Ethel Johns Papers, UBC Special Collections, File II-3. Notes for Autobiogra-
     phy: Vancouver Unit.
100 Ethel Johns Papers, UBC Special Collections, File II-3. Notes for Autobiogra-
     phy: Vancouver Unit.
101 Minutes of the Board of Governers, 1924.
102 Street, 1973, p. 161.

CHAPTER 3: THE MABEL GRAY YEARS, 1925-1941

1   Information on Mabel Gray's early life is drawn from a number of sources,
     including: the Mabel Gray papers in the UBC Special Collections; vertical
     files on Mabel Gray from the Canadian Nurses Association; *The Canadian
     Nurse*, 1941, 37 (11), 755-756; Johns and Fines, 1988; and Street, 1973.
2   Hugg, J.B. (1898). Letter of reference. Mabel Gray Papers.
3   Johns and Fines, 1988, pp. 49-50.
4   Johns and Fines, 1988, p. 52.
5   Information on Mabel Gray's tenure at the University of Saskatchewan and the
     courses at the University of Saskatchewan is from University of Saskatchewan
     Archives: Presidential Papers, Series 1, B.90 "Registered Nurses."
6   Robinson, 1967, pp. 53-54.
7   Letter to Dean G.H. Ling, University of Saskatchewan, from Ethel Johns,
     August 18, 1922. University of Saskatchewan Archives: Presidential Papers,
     Series 1, B.90 "Registered Nurses."
8   "Miss Gray retires," 1941, p. 755.
9   University of Saskatchewan Archives: MG61, J.E. Murray Papers, A.IV.48,
     "Nursing Housekeepers."
10   Gray, 1932, pp. 4-5.
11   Ormsby, 1958, p. 441.
12   UBC, 1936, p. 20.
13   Information related to the growth of the University comes from: UBC, 1936
     (21st anniversary report) and from the UBC Calendars of the time.
14   UBC Calendar, 1930-1931, p. 41.
15   UBC Calendar, 1930-1931, pp. 40-41.
16   "Compulsory registration ...," 1934, p. 530.
17   *The Canadian Nurse*, 1931, p. 484.
18   McIntosh, 1930, pp. 289-294.
19   RNABC Archives, Box 27, File 4/27.
20   O'Brien, 1987, p. 11.
21   RNABC Archives, Box 27, File 4/27.
22   Johns, 1920, p. 1.
23   Weir, 1932, p. 279.
24   Weir, 1932, p. 183.

25 "The conference on nursing ...," 1927, p. 364.
26 Weir, 1932, p. 6.
27 Weir, 1932, p. 6.
28 Weir, 1932, p. 391.
29 Weir, 1932, p. 393.
30 Struthers, 1985, pp. 770-771.
31 Davis, 1976, pp. 30-31.
32 Cavers, 1949, pp. 43-44; Kelly, 1973, pp. 77-77.
33 Creese, 1992, pp. 365-367.
34 Ormsby, 1958, p. 445.
35 Creese, 1992, p. 378.
36 Creese, 1992, p. 379.
37 "Courage and optimism ...," 1932, p. 8.
38 Gunn, 1933, p. 144.
39 RNABC, 1987, p. 15.
40 Cotsworth, 1930, p. 312.
41 RNABC, 1987, pp. 13-14.
42 Geary, 1933, p. 358.
43 Various RNABC and BCNU documents, esp. RNABC, 1987, pp. 14-15.
44 Mallory, 1961, p. 15a.
45 Johns, 1939, p. 201-202.
46 Written communication from Esther Paulson, Feb. 3, 1993, available in UBC
    SoN Archival Collection.
47 "75 years of caring ...," 1987, p. 15.
48 Helen Saunders. 1981, April. Alumnae Questionnaires 1933-40. UBC SoN AC.
49 MacLennan, 1934, pp. 307-309.
50 MacLennan, 1934, p. 308.
51 Whitehead, 1933, pp. 361-362.
52 Fairley, 1933, p. 303-304.
53 Stewart, 1990, pp. 51-58.
54 McCullough, 1932, pp. 171-178.
55 Myers, 1986.
56 Pearson, 1985, p. 64.
57 Kelly, 1973, p. 100.
58 Geraldine E. Homfray Langton Interview, 1988.
59 Forbes, 1933, p. 29.
60 Catholic Hospital Association of B.C., c1990, p. 18.
61 Kelly, 1973, pp. 83-86.
62 Louise Lore Yuen, 1981 April. Alumnae Questionnaires 1933-40. UBC SoN AC.
63 Louise Lore Yuen, 1981 April. Alumnae Questionnaires 1933-40. UBC SoN AC.
64 Duffield, 1941, p. 337-338.
65 Mallory, 1961, p. 5; Gray, 1933, p. 3; UBC Calendars for relevant years.
66 UBC Calendars, 1935-1936 ff.

67 Alumnae Interview (unnamed), 1981.

68 UBC Calendar 1938-1939, p. 183.

69 UBC Calendar 1938-1939, p. 183.

70 Gray, 1932, p. 4.

71 Alumnae Interview, 1981.

72 Dorothy Tate Slaughter Interview, 1988.

73 Alumnae Interview, 1981.

74 Cavers, 1949, p. 40.

75 Kelly, 1973, pp. 102-104.

76 Alumnae Interview, 1981.

77 Alison Reid Wyness Interview, 1993.

78 Alumnae Interview, 1981.

79 Alumnae Interview, 1981.

80 Alumnae Questionnaires 1933-40. UBC SoN AC.

81 Esther Paulson Interview, 1993.

82 Esther Paulson Interview, 1993.

83 Quoted in Stewart, 1979, p. 105.

84 Kelly, 1973, p. 98.

85 Robinson, 1967, pp. 140-142.

86 Cavers, 1949, p. 42; Kelly, 1973, p. 101.

87 Alumnae Interview, 1981.

88 Alison Reid Wyness Interview, 1993.

89 Papers from the CNA Archival Files on Margaret Kerr, especially a press release signed by Dorothy Percy, CNA President.

90 Margaret Kerr (Obituary) ..., 1976, p. 10; and other materials from the Vertical files of the CNA.

91 Creelman, 1947, p. 532.

92 Green, 1984, p. 98.

93 Shore, 1991, p. 2.

94 Mary Henderson Interview, 1988.

95 Information on Monica Green is obtained from a variety of sources, including: Green, 1984; personal correspondence; and files in the UBC SoN AC.

96 Alumnae Interview, 1981.

97 Alison Reid Wyness Interview, 1993.

98 Nursing profiles, 1948, p. 122.

99 Hill and Kirkwood, 1991, p. 10.

100 Stewart, 1979, pp. 119-123.

101 *The Canadian Nurse*, 1948, 44 (8), 650.

102 Green, 1984, p. 18.

103 Green, 1984, pp. 52-64.

104 Green, 1984, pp. 61-62, 110-111.

105 Alice Beattie, 1981, April. Alumnae Questionnaire 1933-40. UBC SoN AC.

106 Phillips, 1985, pp. 85-88.

107 Nursing profiles. (1948). *The Canadian Nurse,* 44 (1), 51.
108 Nursing profiles. (1949). *The Canadian Nurse,* 45 (11), 836.
109 Nursing profiles. 1949. *The Canadian Nurse,* 45 (1), 51.
110 Cavers, 1949, pp. 68-69.
111 Alison Reid Wyness Interview, 1993.
112 Geraldine Homfray Langton Interview, 1988.
113 Miss Gray retires, 1941, pp. 755-756; see also the Mabel Gray Papers, compiled by Margaret M. Street, in the UBC Special Collections.
114 Letter from Elizabeth Copeland Merrick to Beth McCann, April 20, 1981. Included with Alumnae Questionnaires 1933-1940, UBC SoN AC
115 Geraldine Homfray Langton Interview, 1988.
116 Miss Gray retires, 1941, pp. 755-756; the original typescript for this article is also available in the CNA files on Mabel Gray; see also the Mabel Gray papers, UBC Special Collections.

CHAPTER 4: THE EVELYN MALLORY YEARS, 1941-1967

1 The early family history was obtained in an interview with Evelyn Mallory's niece, Mrs. Georgie M. Irvine of Vernon, May 27, 1993.
2 A large portion of the information on Evelyn Mallory's personal life and career comes from tapes, transcripts, and notes prepared by Beth McCann following interviews with Evelyn Mallory, November 27, 1980, and January 25-26, 1981 in Vernon, B.C. These are part of the UBC SoN AC, File: Evelyn Mallory Papers. These may later be refiled as part of the UBC Special Collection as the Evelyn Mallory papers. All quotations in this section come from these tapes/transcripts. At the time this book was prepared, Evelyn Mallory was too ill to be interviewed.
3 Gillett, 1981, pp. 354, 357.
4 Kelly, 1973, p. 108.
5 Evelyn Mallory Transcript, Nov. 27, 1980, p. 3.
6 Data related to attitudes to the Japanese is drawn from a number of sources, but chiefly from Barman, 1991.
7 Barman, 1991, p. 266.
8 Barman, 1991, p. 266.
9 Williams, 1941, pp. 339-342.
10 Barman, 1991, p. 269.
11 The information in the following paragraphs, including quotations, comes from the Trenna Hunter Interview, 1987.
12 Trenna Hunter Interview, 1987.
13 Trenna Hunter Interview, 1987.
14 Kelly, 1973, pp. 128-129.
15 Hood, 1956, pp. 583-585.
16 Barman, 1991, p. 262.

17 Myers, 1986, p. 120.
18 Kirstine Adam Griffith Interview, 1993.
19 President's Report, 1945, p. 1.
20 President's Report, 1943, p. 15.
21 President's Report, 1943, pp. 75, 78.
22 Kerr, 1942, pp. 661-663.
23 Report of the Dean of Women, President's Report, 1944, p. 47.
24 President's Report, 1943, p. 14-15.
25 Kirkwood and Bouchard, 1992; Ellis, 1942, pp. 845-846.
26 Langton and Chodat, 1943, p. 742.
27 Alumnae Questionnaires 1947-54. UBC SoN AC.
28 Kelly, 1973, p. 116; Palliser, 1944, p. 843-844.
29 Palliser, 1944, pp. 843-844.
30 Kelly, 1973, pp. 117-188.
31 Gibbon and Mathewson, 1947, p. 460.
32 Gibbon and Mathewson, 1947, pp. 456-458.
33 Fairley, 1942, p. 613.
34 Fairley, 1942, p. 613.
35 Munroe, 1946, p.737; Mallory, 1942, pp. 715-717.
36 Mallory, 1942, pp. 715-717.
37 Letter from Margaret Kerr to Mrs. C. Normansell Burn, September 17, 1942. UBC SoN AC: File: Correspondence.
38 Alumnae Questionnaires 1941-46. UBC SoN AC.
39 Alumnae Questionnaires 1941-46. UBC SoN AC; Stewart, 1979, pp. 289-292.
40 MacLean, 1949, pp. 95-99.
41 Alumnae Questionnaires 1941-46. UBC SoN AC.
42 Alumnae Questionnaires 1941-46. UBC SoN AC.
43 Kirstine Adam Griffith Interview, 1993.
44 Evelyn Mallory Transcript, Nov. 27, 1980, p. 3.
45 Evelyn Mallory's Annual Report for 1948-49, p. 8. SoN HoN AC, File: Annual Reports Submitted to the President, 1945-1953.
46 Lorna Horwood Interview, 1981.
47 Scoones, 1945, pp. 984-985.
48 Both quotes from Alumnae Questionnaires 1947-54. UBC SoN AC.
49 President's Report 1948-1949, 1950, pp. 18-19.
50 Logan, 1958, p. 186.
51 Logan, 1958, p. 192.
52 Letter from N.A.M. MacKenzie to Mrs. A.G. Shugg, June 3, 1949. UBC SoN AC, File: School Correspondence; Mallory, 1958.
53 Beth McCann Tape (recording notes of interview with Dr. C.E. Dolman), December 1980, UBC SoN AC. [Transcript available].
54 Transcripts of notes by Beth McCann of an interview with Lorna Horwood, UBC SoN AC, File: Transcripts.

55 Mallory, 1961, p. 10.
56 See also Kerr, 1978, who shows the breakdown of financial assistance to other Canadian university schools of nursing.
57 Letter from Evelyn Mallory to Dr. C.E. Dolman, July 7, 1949. Available UBC SoN AC as part of the Evelyn Mallory papers.
58 From the philosophies of the School expressed in the Calendars of the 1950s.
59 Mallory quoted in Wright, 1948, p. 846.
60 Mallory, 1952, Annual Report to the President 1951-52.
61 Kelly, 1973, pp. 124-128.
62 Mallory's annual report for 1951-52 to the President of UBC. UBC SoN AC: Mallory papers.
63 Barman, 1991, pp. 279-280.
64 Green, 1984, p. 99.
65 Alumnae Questionnaires 1947-54. UBC SoN AC.
66 Beth Walton Fitzpatrick Interview, 1993.
67 Beth Walton Fitzpatrick Interview, 1993.
68 Beth Walton Fitzpatrick Interview, 1993.
69 Letter from Alice Baumgart to Elizabeth Robertson, June 16, 1993.
70 Elizabeth Robertson. Personal letter to Glennis Zilm, October 1956.
71 Ann-Shirley Goodell Interview, 1993. Information and quotations in this and the following paragraphs are from this interview.
72 Ann-Shirley Gordon Goodell Interview, 1993.
73 A complete *Workbook for Field Experiences* outlining the Port Alberni small hospital experience, dated April 1958, was preserved by Beth McCann and is available in the UBC SoN AC.
74 Alumnae Questionnaires 1947-54. UBC SoN AC.
75 Ann-Shirley Gordon Goodell Interview, 1993.
76 Kloppenborg et al., 1977, p. 147.
77 Ann-Shirley Gordon Goodell Interview, 1993.
78 Information on Pauline Capelle was obtained from a variety of sources. Rose Murakami, who knew her well, provided many details of her early life and career.
79 Capelle, 1944, pp. 487-489.
80 Kirkwood and Bouchard, 1992.
81 Morrison, 1964.
82 Anne Wyness Interview, 1993.
83 Horwood, 1981. Transcript UBC SoN AC.
84 Evelyn Mallory's Annual Report to the President for 1963-1964, UBC SoN AC, File: Annual Reports Submitted to the President.
85 Beth Walton Fitzpatrick Interview, 1993. All quotes in this paragraph are from this interview.
86 Information on Margaret Street is drawn from a number of sources, but in mainly from the Biographical Files of the RNABC History of Nursing Professional Practice Group. Vancouver: RNABC.

87   Mallory, 1958.

88   An exceedingly interesting document outlining the proposed changes – *Proposed Program for the Second and Third Years of the Basic Professional Curriculum* (March 1957), prepared by the UBC nursing faculty for the Subcommittee of the Joint VGH-UBC Committee – is available in the UBC SoN AC.

89   Mallory, 1961, p. 13.

90   Mallory, 1958, p. 8.

91   Correspondence and contracts. UBC SoN AC. File: St. Paul's Initial Contacts.

92   Letter from Evelyn Mallory to Sister Florence Mary, March 12, 1958. UBC SoN AC. File: St. Paul's Initial Contacts.

93   M. Anne Wyness, personal communication, June 24, 1993.

94   Mallory, 1961, p. 36.

95   Logan, 1958, p. 85.

96   Mussallem, 1960.

97   Mussallem, 1964b.

98   Mallory, 1961, p. 35.

99   Green, 1984, p. 130.

100   Mallory Report to the President for academic year 1965-1966, 1966.

101   Alumnae Questionnaires, 1961-66 (Delcie Hill (BSN 1964)). UBC SoN AC.

102   Alumnae Questionnaires, 1961-66. UBC SoN AC.

103   Alumnae Questionnaires, 1961-66. UBC SoN AC.

104   Alumnae Questionnaires, 1961-66. UBC SoN AC.

105   Alumnae Questionnaires, 1961-66. UBC SoN AC.

106   Miller, 1991, p. 13.

107   Green, 1984, p. 124.

108   Trout, 1987, p.5

109   Alumnae Questionnaires, 1961-66. UBC SoN AC.

110   Comments in this section are from Alumnae Questionnaires, 1947-1954, 1955-1961, and 1961-1966.

111   Report of the President, 1966-1967, p. 10.

112   Personal communication from Margaret Street to Ethel Warbinek, July 17, 1993.

CHAPTER 5: THE BETH MCCANN YEARS, 1967-1971

1   Sister Anna McCann said 1916, but School of Nursing records indicate 1917, including Beth McCann's Curriculum Vitae.

2   Information on Beth McCann's life comes from many sources, including an interview with her sister Anna McCann, an interview at the time of Beth McCann's retirement, her curriculum vitae in the School of Nursing AC files, and from various friends and acquaintances on the UBC SoN faculty.

3   Kirkwood and Bouchard, 1992, p. 15.

4   Kirkwood and Bouchard, 1992, p. 26.

5   Basil Dunell Interview, 1993.

6   Basil Dunell Interview, 1993.

7   Basil Dunell Interview, 1993.

8   Elizabeth Cawston Interview, 1993.

9   Anna McCann Interview, 1993.

10 The President's Report, 1967-1968, pp.7-8; Alma Mater Society Brief "The Future of Education at the University: Fair Weather or Foul," 1968.

11 President's Reports, 1968-69, 1969-70, 1970-71.

12 UBC School of Nursing Programmes, August 1969.

13 Elizabeth K. McCann's Report to the President for 1967-1968, p. 3. SoN HoN AC; File: Annual Report submitted to the President 1968.

14 The President's Report 1971-1972, p. 28.

15 The President's Report 1971-1972, p. 34.

16 Elizabeth K. McCann Report to the President 1967-1968.

17 Some documents in the UBC SoN AC Filing Cabinet 3, MSN Program refer to *four* other programs (Western Ontario, McGill, Montreal, and Ottawa) as preceding the UBC MSN.
    However, although a program was approved at Ottawa in 1961, it was never implemented. See University of Ottawa School of Nursing, 1973, p. 111, and Stinson, 1992, pp. 426-435.

18 *Manual MSN Program* [First Manual], June 1968 (Section on Forms); this and other documents on the MSN program were used in preparation of this section and are available in the UBC SoN AC, File: Cabinet 3, MSN Program.

19 *First National Conference ...*, 1971.

20 *Slipstick*, 19, p. 38.

21 Letter from Elizabeth K. McCann to Helen K. Mussallem, September 22, 1969. UBC SoN AC, File: Marion Woodward Lectureship.

22 Helen Gemeroy Interview, 1981.

23 Helen Gemeroy Interview, 1981.

24 Mallory, 1965.

25 President's Report, 1969-1970.

26 McCann, 1969.

27 President's Report, 1969-1970.

28 *Report of The President's Temporary Committee, Administrative Structure for the Health Sciences Centre, The University of British Columbia*, October 1969, p. 19. [Available UBC SoN AC]

29 School of Nursing, *Supporting statement in relation to faculty status for School of Nursing*, November 18, 1969. UBC SoN AC, File: Historical Material Faculty Status for School of Nursing.

30 Interview with Ann Taylor, May 18, 1993.

31 Alumnae Questionnaires, 1966-1971. UBC SoN AC.

32 Transcript of a Coffee Party with 1969 graduates, interviewed by Beth McCann, May 6, 1981. UBC SoN AC: Book of Interviews.

33 Well-known senior faculty members retire. (1982). *UBC Nursing Today*, 3(6), 1-2. [Available UBC School of Nursing Archives]

34 Anna McCann Interview, July 13, 1993.

CHAPTER 6: THE MURIEL UPRICHARD YEARS, 1971-1977

1 Information on the background of Muriel Uprichard was compiled from a number of sources, including her curriculum vitae, various newspaper articles, clippings on reports of her appointments. This information is available in the Uprichard File, UBC SoN AC.

2 Bateson, 1977 [Clippings from UBC SoN AC: File: Uprichard]

3 Hamley and Uprichard, 1948.

4 Muriel Uprichard Curriculum Vitae on application to the UBC School of Nursing, 1971. UBC SoN AC, File: Uprichard, Muriel.

5 Canadian Nurses Association, 1968, p. 90; Larsen and Meilicke, 1992, p. 536.

6 Muriel Uprichard Curriculum Vitae on application to the UBC School of Nursing, 1971. UBC SoN AC, File: Uprichard, Muriel.

7 Janet Gormick Interview, 1993.

8 Muriel Uprichard Curriculum Vitae. UBC SoN AC: File, Uprichard. The UBC Woodward Library could find no evidence that this had been published.

9 Janet Gormick Interview, 1993.

10 Letter, plus supporting documents, to Muriel Uprichard from Mary Richmond MacBean, May 2, 1972. UBC SoN AC, File: VGH-UBC Proposal. The information in these two paragraphs, including quotes, comes from this letter and documents.

11 *UBC Senate Summary*, December 13, 1972, p. 3.

12 *UBC Senate Summary*, December 13, 1972, pp. 3-4.

13 Memo from the Senate New Programmes Committee to Senate, November 30, 1972, p. 1.

14 Green, 1983, pp. 151-152.

15 Letter to David V. Bates, Faculty of Medicine, from Muriel Uprichard, September 26, 1972, and his reply, October 10, 1972. UBC SoN AC, File: Curriculum 1971-1977.

16 *Report submitted to the Registered Nurses' Association of British Columbia*, July 1974, pp. 1-2.

17 Letter to President W.H. Gage from RNABC Executive Director F.A. Kennedy, September 30, 1974. UBC SoN AC, File: Curriculum 1971-1977.

18 Letter to President D.T. Kenny from RNABC Executive Director F.A. Kennedy, September 16, 1975. UBC SoN AC, File: Curriculum 1971-1977. All information in this paragraph comes from this letter.

19 Willman, 1977, pp. 3, 6.

20 Report of the RNABC Committee on Approval of Schools of Nursing, U.B.C. Nursing Program, August 1975. Submitted to President D.T. Kenny by

RNABC Executive Director F.A. Kennedy, September 16, 1975. UBC SoN AC, File: Curriculum 1971-1977.

21 UBC School of Nursing Programs, August 1969. UBC SoN AC.

22 *Nursing Papers/Perspectives en nursing,* Summer 1976, pp. 1-43.

23 Proposed Master's Program, Nursing. [Unpublished document outlining the changes for submission to the Senate.] April 1973. UBC SoN AC, File: MSN program, Uprichard years.

24 Sheila Creeggan Stanton Interview, 1993.

25 Campbell, 1973, p. 79.

26 Sheila Creeggan Stanton Interview, 1993.

27 Unpublished report by Muriel Uprichard to J.V. Christensen, Chair, B.C. Medical Centre, Nov. 5, 1973. UBC SoN AC, File: Articles on the New Nursing Program.

28 "AV aids ...," 1974, p. 49.

29 Sheila Stanton [Acting Director], *Report for the President,* October 19, 1976. UBC SoN AC, File: Annual Reports 1973-1976.

30 Letter from Barbara J. Lee, Program Director, W.K. Kellogg Foundation, to President Walter H. Gage, November 13, 1973. UBC SoN AC, File: Curriculum 1971-1977.

31 Bateson, 1973a, p. 52.

32 Minutes, Full Staff Meeting, September 6, 1973, p. 2.

33 Letter from W.J. Lyle, Deputy Minister of Hospital Insurance, to Muriel Uprichard, May 1, 1974. UBC SoN AC File – Margaret Campbell papers, "Budget."

34 Uprichard, 1975, p. 8.

35 Transcript of a coffee party with Mary Fewster and Deborah Taylor, interviewed by Beth McCann, May 7, 1981. UBC SoN AC: Book of Interviews.

36 Personal Communication Sylvia Holmes, November 15, 1993.

37 UBC 75th Anniversary Award of Merit, 1990.

38 Helen Shore Interview, 1993.

39 Memo to All Faculty from Muriel Uprichard, May 12, 1975. UBC SoN AC File UBC SoN Memos 1973-1975.

40 "B.C. govt. announces ...," 1974, p. 9.

41 Barman, 1991, pp. 312-325.

42 Green, 1984, pp. 144-146.

43 Ratsoy, 1974, pp. 42-44.

44 Lalonde, 1974b, pp. 19-20.

45 "CNA statement ...," 1974, p. 12.

46 Canadian Nurses Association, 1981, pp. 17-26.

47 Letter from E. Margaret Fulton, dean of women and chair of the Ad Hoc Committee on International Women's Year, to Douglas T. Kenny, president of UBC, Dec. 15, 1975. UBC SoN AC, File: International Women's Year.

48 Stewart, 1990, pp. 127-128.

49   School of Nursing *Newsletter*, March 21, 1974. UBC SoN AC, File Newsletters.
50   Transcript of a coffee party with graduates of 1972-1976, interviewed by Beth McCann, May 7, 1981. UBC SoN AC: Book of Interviews.
51   Alumnae Questionnaires 1972-1976. UBC SoN AC.
52   Alumnae Questionnaires 1972-1976. UBC SON AC.
53   *University of British Columbia School of Nursing Report*, submitted to the Registered Nurses Association of British Columbia for Initial Approval of a New Baccalaureate Programme in Nursing, May 1973, p. 15.
54   Transcript of a coffee party with graduates from 1972-1976, interviewed by Beth McCann, May 7, 1981. UBC SoN AC: Book of Interviews.
55   Transcript of a coffee party with Mary Fewster and Deborah Taylor, interviewed by Beth McCann, May 7, 1981. UBC SoN AC: Book of Interviews.
56   Minutes, Special Faculty Meeting, February 9, 1976, p. 2.
57   Minutes of the Full Faculty Meeting, February 18, 1977, p. 3.
58   Uprichard, 1976, p. 3.
59   Memo to All Faculty from Sheila M. Stanton, Acting Director, Nov. 30, 1976. UBC SoN AC. File: Uprichard.
60   Sheila Stanton Interview, 1993; Sheila Stanton Biographical Form for the History of Nursing Group, Feb. 17, 1993.
61   Minutes, Faculty meeting, June 24, 1977.
62   Bateson, 1977. Clipping, UBC SoN AC, File: Uprichard.
63   Judith MacDonald, personal communication with Ethel Warbinek, Nov. 26, 1993.
64   Muriel Uprichard Interview, 1979.
65   Muriel Uprichard Interview, 1979.

CHAPTER 7: THE MARILYN WILLMAN YEARS, 1977-1993

1   Marilyn Willman Interview, 1992.
2   Marilyn Willman Interview, 1981.
3   Marilyn Willman Interview, 1992.
4   Marilyn Willman Interview, 1992.
5   Marilyn Willman Interview, 1992.
6   Marilyn Willman Interview, 1981.
7   Marilyn Willman Interview, 1992.
8   Minutes of Full Faculty Meeting, Friday, July 15, 1977, p. 3.
9   Minutes of Full Faculty Meeting, Friday, July 15, 1977, p. 2.
10   Minutes of Full Faculty Meeting, Friday, July 15, 1977, p. 3.
11   *Faculty Organization and Committee Structure of the School of Nursing: Faculty Caucus By-Laws*, December 16, 1977. UBC SoN AC, File: School of Nursing.
12   *Report of the Ad Hoc Committee on Roles and Responsibilities of UBC Faculty and Community Health Field Guides*, June 1983. UBC SoN AC, File: Community Health Field Guides.

13 Bajnok, 1992, p. 411.
14 Ethel Warbinek, personal communication, December 3, 1993.
15 University of B.C., 1979, p. 28.
16 Kermacks, 1979.
17 Baumgart, 1992, p. 38.
18 Lovell, 1981, p. 11. This book is a sociological study of the year-long crisis.
19 Hibberd, 1992, p. 586.
20 Alcock, 1992, p. 3.
21 *The President's Report* 1978-79. UBC SoN AC File: President's Reports 1977-1984.
22 *The President's Report* 1978-79. UBC SoN AC File: President's Reports 1977-1984.
23 Faculty caucus minutes, Dec, 9, 1982, p. 3.
24 Entwistle, 1985. This thesis contains much valuable information on the development of the continuing education program at UBC.
25 Kenny, 1981.
26 Ethel Warbinek personal communication, December 20, 1993.
27 Report to Faculty Caucus of a Nursing Advisory Committee – Acute Care Unit, November 22, 1979.
28 *The President's Report* 1979-1980, p. 25.
29 Minutes of Faculty Caucus, Dec. 6, 1979, p. 7.
30 Minutes of the Faculty Caucus, Nov. 17, 1978, pp. 13-14.
31 Marilyn Willman Interview, 1981.
32 Minutes of Faculty Caucus Meeting, Nov. 17, 1978.
33 Marilyn Willman Interview, 1992.
34 Westera, 1992, pp. 47-59.
35 Marilyn Willman interview, 1992.
36 Faculty caucus minutes, November 8, 1984, p. 2.
37 Marilyn Willman Interview, 1992.
38 Godkin and Bottorff, 1991, pp. 31-34.
39 *Report to the President* 1977-1978, UBC SoN AC, File: Marilyn Willman's Reports to the President 1978-1984.
40 *Report to the President* 1980-1981, UBC SoN AC, File: Reports to the President, 1977-1993.
41 Marilyn Willman Interview, 1992.
42 Zilm, Hilton, and Richmond, 1982.
43 Communications from SoN Research Unit, January 1994.
44 *Resources for Nursing Research Guide* 1992-1993 [Pageproof Draft], 1993. UBC SoN AC.
45 Gould, 1991, pp. 34.
46 Gail Jeffreys Interview, 1993.
47 Kris Gustavson Interview, 1993.
48 Alumni Questionnaires 1977-1981.

284 Notes to pp. 256-264

49 Alumni Questionnaires 1977-1981.
50 Senate Minutes, Nov. 18, 1992.
51 Sheila Stanton Interview, 1993.
52 Willman, 1992.
53 Jeannette Bouchard, personal communication, Feb. 16, 1994.
54 From notes, written by Margaret Street, for her interview as part of an Oral History Project, Professor Emeriti Division, carried out by UBC Alumni Association, Oct. 25, 1990.
55 Ritchie, 1992, p. 1.

CHAPTER 8: LOOKING TO THE FUTURE

1 Information on Katharyn Antle May comes from her curriculum vitae submitted to the School in 1993. UBC SoN AC.
2 Ritchie, 1992, p. 1.
3 Letter from Susan E. French, chair of Board of Accreditation, Canadian Association of University Schools of Nursing, to Marilyn Willman, April 13, 1992. UBC SoN AC.

Bibliography

The bibliography contains the full information for the references cited in the endnotes of the various chapters as well as selected other important materials and sources consulted. The bibliography is organized under the following headings:

Primary Sources:

(1) Interviews, including taped interviews available in the UBC School of Nursing Archival Collection and the RNABC Library
(2) Questionnaires, initiated by Beth McCann, available UBC School of Nursing Archival Collection, File Alumnae Questionnaires
(3) Documents from Museum and Archives, including the UBC Library and Woodward Biomedical Special Collections; the School of Nursing Archival Collection, Newspapers, and Interviews

Secondary Sources:

(1) Books
(2) Articles (Journal and Newspaper)

The style used in the endnotes and bibliography is based on that recommended in the *Publication Manual of the American Psychological Association* (3rd ed.) (Washington, DC: American Psychological Association, 1983). The style used for archival documents is based on that recommended for use in Canadian archives. The style has been adapted slightly to provide additional information (such as the full first names of authors where these are known).

Please note that surnames beginning with Mac and Mc or M' (the abbreviated forms of Mac) are filed at the beginning of the M section, with these prefixes all being filed as if they were Mac and based on the capital letter following.

Libraries and Archives consulted during the research for this book included the following (with their abbreviations):

UBC School of Nursing Archival Collection (UBC SoN AC), possibly to be housed, eventually, in the UBC Special Collections and Archives. This collection includes seven large filing cabinets, containing files, most of which were collected by Elizabeth (Beth) McCann in preparation for a history of the School. These files were arranged alphabetically and listed by Natalie Bland and by Anne Keski-Salmi under the direction of Ethel Warbinek. Additional material was obtained for the collection by Glennis Zilm and Ethel Warbinek starting in 1989.

UBC Special Collections and Archives

UBC Library, including the Woodward Biomedical Library and the Charles Woodward Memorial Reading Room Archives and Files

Registered Nurses Association of B.C. (RNABC) Library and Archives. The library holds the RNABC Oral History Tape Collection, which has many taped interviews with UBC graduates

Canadian Nurses Association Library and Archives

British Columbia Provincial Archives

University of Saskatchewan Archives

Saskatchewan Registered Nurses Association Library and Archives

Newspapers, including *The Vancouver Sun* and *The Vancouver Province*

PRIMARY SOURCES

Interviews

Alumnae Interview [unnamed], Class of 1940. (1981). Interview of group by Beth McCann, March 19, 1981. Vancouver: UBC SoN AC. [Transcript available]

Elizabeth Cawston. (1993). Interviewed by Ethel Warbinek, September 17, 1993. Vancouver: UBC SoN AC. [Transcript available]

Beverly Witter DuGas. (1993). Interviewed by Ethel Warbinek, July 8, 1993. Vancouver: UBC SoN AC. [Transcript available]

Basil Dunell. (1993). Interview (with Anna McCann) by Ethel Warbinek and Glennis Zilm, July 13, 1993. Vancouver: UBC SoN AC. [Transcript available]

Mary Jane Duke. (1993). Interview by Ethel Warbinek, October 1, 1993. Vancouver: UBC SoN AC. [Transcript available]

Ida May Snelgrove Elliot. (1981). Interview by Beth McCann, March 10, 1981. Vancouver: UBC SoN AC. [Transcript available]

Marion Fisher Faris. (1981). Interview by Beth McCann, January 28, 1981. Vancouver: UBC SoN AC. [Transcript available]

Beth Walton Fitzpatrick. (1993). Interview by Ethel Warbinek, March 31, 1993. Vancouver: UBC SoN AC. [Transcript available]

Esther Naden Gardom. (1987). Interview by Mary Richmond, November 24, 1987. Vancouver: RNABC Oral History Collection. [Transcript by Ethel Warbinek available UBC SoN AC]

Helen Gemeroy. (1981). Transcript (partial) of interview by Elizabeth McCann, March 18, 1981. Vancouver: UBC SoN AC, File: Book of interviews.

Ann-Shirley (Gordon) Goodell. (1993). Interview by Ethel Warbinek, April 28, 1993. Vancouver: UBC SoN AC. [Transcript available]

Janet Gormick. (1993). Interview by Ethel Warbinek, September 29, 1993. Vancouver: UBC SoN AC [Transcript available].

Kirstine Adam Griffith. (1993). Interview by Ethel Warbinek, March 3, 1993. Vancouver: UBC SoN AC. [Transcript available]

Kris Gustavson. (1993). Interview by Ethel Warbinek, November 19, 1993. Vancouver: UBC SoN AC. [Transcript available]

Sylvia Holmes. (1993). Interview by Ethel Warbinek, November 25, 1993. Vancouver: UBC SoN AC. [Notes only available.]

Lorna Horwood. (1981). Transcipt of interview by Elizabeth McCann, March 20, 1981. Vancouver: UBC SoN AC.

Trenna Hunter. (1987). Interview by Sheila Zerr, March 1987. Vancouver: RNABC Oral History Collection. [Transcript by Ethel Warbinek available UBC SoN AC]

Florence Innes. (1981) Interview by Beth McCann, March 11, 1981. Vancouver: UBC SoN AC. [Transcript available]

Georgie Irvine. (1993). Notes from interview by Glennis Zilm, May 27, 1993. Vancouver: UBC SoN AC.

Gail Jeffreys. (1993). Interview by Ethel Warbinek, March 12, 1993. Vancouver: UBC SoN AC. [Transcipt available]

Geraldine E. Homfray Langton. (1988). Interview by Eva Williamson, August 1988. Vancouver: RNABC Oral History Collection. [Transcript by Ethel Warbinek available UBC SoN AC]

Anna McCann. (1993). Interview (with Basil Dunell) by Ethel Warbinek and Glennis Zilm, July 13, 1993. Vancouver: UBC SoN AC. [Transcript available]

Rose Murakami. (1993). Interview by Ethel Warbinek, August 18, 1993. Vancouver: UBC SoN AC. [Transcript available]

Esther Paulson. (1988). Interview by Natalie Bland, July 12, 1988. Vancouver: UBC SoN AC.

Esther Paulson. (1993). Interview by Ethel Warbinek, February 3, 1993. Vancouver: UBC SoN AC [Transcript available].

Helen Shore. (1993). Interview by Ethel Warbinek, October 29, 1993. Vancouver: SoN AC [Transcript available].

Dorothy Tate Slaughter. (1988). Interview by Nora Whyte, April 20, 1988. Vancouver: RNABC Oral History Collection. [Transcript by Ethel Warbinek available UBC SoN AC]

Sheila Creeggan Stanton. (1993). Interview by Ethel Warbinek, February 18, 1993. Vancouver: UBC SoN AC. [Transcript available.]

Ann Taylor. (1993). Transcript of interview by Ethel Warbinek, May 18, 1993. Vancouver: UBC SoN AC, File: Biographical Files.

Fern Trout. (1987). Interview by Audrey Stegan, December 22, 1987. Vancouver: RNABC Oral History Collection. [Transcript by Ethel Warbinek available UBC SoN AC]

Muriel Uprichard. (1979). Taped Inverview at McGill with a group of students in the MSc(N) program, January 24, 1979. [Transcript by Ethel Warbinek available UBC SoN AC]

Marilyn Willman. (1981). Interviewed by Beth McCann, June 24, 1981. Vancouver: UBC SoN AC, File: Book of taped interviews. [Transcript available UBC SoN AC]

Marilyn Willman. (1992). Interview by Glennis Zilm, taped by Sheila Zerr, January 22, 1992. Vancouver: RNABC Oral History Collection. [Transcript by Glennis Zilm available UBC SoN AC]

Beatrice Fordham Johnson Wood. (1981). Interview by Beth McCann, February 22, 1981. Vancouver: UBC SoN AC. [Transcript available]

Beatrice Fordham Johnson Wood. (1991). Interview by Sheila Zerr, March 20, 1991. Vancouver: RNABC Oral History Collection. [Transcript by Ethel Warbinek available UBC SoN AC]

Alison Reid Wyness. (1993). Interview by Ethel Warbinek, April 30, 1993. Vancouver: UBC SoN AC. [Transcript available]

Anne Wyness. (1993). Interview by Ethel Warbinek, June 30, 1993. Vancouver: UBC SoN AC. [Transcript available]

Questionnaires

Questionnaires to Graduates. (1920-1980). UBC SoN AC. Questionnaires were sent by Elizabeth (Beth) McCann in the early 1980s to all graduates of the UBC Nursing program for which the Alumni Division had addresses. Those that were returned are filed, usually by decade within the term of a director of the program, in the UBC SoN AC, File: Questionnaires 1920 ff.

Documents

Annual reports. (1960-). [Only a few copies of *Annual Reports* from the early Directors of the Nursing Department or School have been found.] Available UBC SoN Archival Collection: Files Annual Reports.

Gray, Mabel. (n.d.) *Papers.* Available UBC Special Collections.

Gray, Mabel F. (1932). Department of Nursing and Health: The University of British Columbia (Reprint). *Methods and problems of medical education,* 21st series. New York: The Rockefeller Foundation, 1932. Available Mabel Gray files, UBC SoN HoN Archival Collection.

Johns, Ethel. (n.d.) *Papers.* Available UBC Special Collections.

Johns, Ethel. (1919). *Address to mass meeting.* Manuscript of speech given at the Vancouver General Hospital on her appointment as director of nursing. Original in UBC Woodward Biomedical Library.

Johns, Ethel. (1922, June 30). *Administration of schools of nursing.* Paper presented at the National League of Nursing 28th Annual Education Convention. (Photocopy

of this, from the proceedings of the Convention, is in the Beatrice Fordham
Johnson Wood papers, UBC SoN HoN Archival Collection.)

Kenny, Douglas. (1981). *Looking beyond* [President's report]. Vancouver: University
of B.C.

Kerr, Margaret. (1944). *Brief history of the Registered Nurses' Association of British
Columbia.* Unpublished manuscript. Available RNABC Library, Vancouver.

McCann, Elizabeth K. (1969). *Interim submission to the co-ordinating committee
concerning role and relationships of the School of Nursing in the Health Sciences
Centre.* March 12, 1969. Unpublished typescript. Available UBC SoN AC.

Mallory, Evelyn. (1958, May). *Background information regarding developments which
led to the formation of a joint (UBC-VGH) committee ... May 1958.* Unpublished
typescript. Available UBC SoN AC.

Mallory, Evelyn. (1960, Oct.). *General progress report – September 1960.* Unpublished
typescript. Available UBC SoN AC.

Mallory, Evelyn. (1961, Dec.). *Report of the School of Nursing – including specific data
for the year 1960-61.* Unpublished typescript. Available UBC SoN AC.

Mallory, Evelyn. (1965). *Brief recommending the establishment of a Faculty of Nursing.*
Unpublished typescript. Available UBC SoN AC.

Ritchie, Judith (Chair). (1992). *Report of the Review Panel for the School of Nursing,
University of British Columbia.* Unpublished report. UBC SoN AC.

Shore, Helen. (1991). *Tribute to Lyle Creelman.* Unpublished manuscript of speech to
UBC School of Nursing Alumnae 1991 annual dinner, May 2, 1991. Copy in UBC
SoN AC.

UBC School of Nursing Programmes, August 1969. Unpublished manuscript. UBC SoN
AC.

University of British Columbia . (1915-1993). *UBC Calendars.* Available UBC
Library.

University of British Columbia. Board of Governors. (1919–). *Minutes.* Available
UBC Special Collections.

University of British Columbia. Senate. (1919–). *Minutes.* Available UBC Special
Collections.

University of British Columbia School of Nursing (1988–). *Research Activities*
[Reports]. Available UBC SoN AC.

Uprichard, Muriel. (1973). *Why a model? – and indeed why a nursing model?*
Unpublished notes for presentation, February 18, 1975. UBC SoN AC, File:
Uprichard.

Uprichard, Muriel. (1975). *Annual report, Kellogg Foundation Grant, University of
British Columbia School of Nursing: Progress report – September 1974 to September
1975.* Unpublished document. UBC SoN AC, File: Curriculum 1971-1977.

Uprichard, Muriel. (1976). *Annual report, Kellogg Foundation Grant, University of
British Columbia School of Nursing: Progress report – September 1975 to September
1976.* Unpublished document. UBC SoN AC, File: Curriculum 1971-1977.

Wesbrook, F.F. (1918, May 15). *Letter* (to Dr. Helen MacMurchy). UBC Archives.

Willman, Marilyn. (1977). *Final report, Kellogg Foundation Grant, University of British Columbia School of Nursing September 1973 – September 1977.* Unpublished document. UBC SoN AC, File: Curriculum 1971-1977.

Willman, Marilyn. (1992). *Position Statement: Graduate Education in Nursing* (Canadian Association of University Schools of Nursing) (Rev.). Ottawa: Canadian Association of University Schools of Nursing.

SECONDARY SOURCES

Books (including chapters of books)

A history of the Royal Columbian Hospital School of Nursing: Commemorating its Diamond Jubilee 1901-1976. (c 1976). [New Westminster, n.p.].

Aiken, C.A. (1921). *Clinical studies for nurses.* Philadelphia: W.B. Saunders.

Baer, Ellen D. (1990). *Editor's notes for "Nursing in America: A history of social reform" – a video documentary* (NLN Pub. #41-2342). New York: National League for Nursing.

Bajnok, Irmajean. (1992). Entry-level educational preparation for nursing. In A.J. Baumgart and Jenniece Larsen (Eds.), *Canadian nursing faces the future* (2nd ed.) (pp. 408-419). St. Louis: Mosby Year Book.

Balf, Mary. (1989). *Kamloops: A history of the district up to 1914* (3rd ed.). Kamloops: Kamloops Museum Association.

Barman, Jean. (1991). *The west beyond the west: A history of British Columbia.* Toronto: University of Toronto Press.

Baumgart, Alice J. (1992). Evolution of the Canadian health care system. In A.J. Baumgart and Jenniece Larsen (Eds.), *Canadian nursing faces the future* (2nd ed.) (pp. 23-43). St. Louis: Mosby Year Book.

Baumgart, Alice J., and Larsen, Jenniece. (1992). *Canadian nursing faces the future* (2nd ed.). St. Louis: Mosby Year Book.

British Columbia Hospital Association. (1919). *Report of proceedings of the second annual convention of the hospitals of British Columbia.* Vancouver: Author.

Berton, Pierre. (1983). *The Klondike quest: A photographic essay 1897-1899.* Toronto: McClelland and Stewart.

Brown, Craig (Ed.). (1987). *The illustrated history of Canada.* Toronto: Lester and Orpen Dennys.

Canada. (1983). *Preserving universal Medicare: A Government of Canada position paper* (Cat. No. H21-92/1983). Ottawa: Minister of Supply and Services Canada.

Canadian Nurses Association. (1968). *The leaf and the lamp.* Ottawa: Author.

Canadian Nurses Association. (1981). *The seventh decade 1969-1980.* Ottawa: Author.

Carpenter, Helen M. (1982). *A divine discontent: Edith Kathleen Russell, reforming educator* (History Monograph 1). Toronto: University of Toronto Faculty of Nursing.

Carswell, Sally. (1980). *The story of Lions Gate Hospital: The realization of a pioneer settlement's dream 1908-1980.* West Vancouver: Author.

Catholic Health Association of B.C. (c1990). *Living the mission 1940-1990: Anniversary booklet.* Vancouver: Author.

Cavers, Anne S. (c 1949). *Our school of nursing 1899 to 1949.* Vancouver: Vancouver General Hospital School of Nursing.

Con, Harry, Con, R.J., Johnson, G., Wickberg, E., and Willmott, W.E. (1982). *From China to Canada: A history of the Chinese communities in Canada.* Toronto: McClelland and Stewart/Multicultural Directorate, Department of the Secretary of State, Government of Canada.

Connelly, M.P. (1985). Women in the labour force. In *The Canadian encyclopedia* (Vol. III). Edmonton: Hurtig.

Creese, Gillian. (1992). The politics of dependence: Women, work and unemployment in the Vancouver labour movement before World War II. In Gillian Creese and Veronica Strong-Boag (Eds.), *British Columbia reconsidered: Essays on women* (pp. 364-390). Vancouver: Press Gang Publishers.

Davis, Chuck (Ed.). (1976). *The Vancouver book.* Vancouver: J.J. Douglas.

Dock, Lavinia L., and [in collaboration with] Stewart, Isabel Maitland. (1920). *A short history of nursing: From the earliest times to the present day.* New York: Putnam's Sons.

Dock, Lavinia L., and Stewart, Isabel Maitland. (1931). *A short history of nursing from the earliest times to the present day* (3rd ed.). New York: C.P. Putnam's Sons.

Donahue, M. Patricia. (1985). *Nursing: The finest art: An illustrated history.* St. Louis, MO: C.V. Mosby.

Emory, Florence H.M. (1953). *Public health nursing in Canada: Principles and practice.* Toronto: Macmillan.

Entwistle, Cheryl. (1985). *Distance learning in nursing education ... a challenge for change.* Unpublished master's thesis, Faculty of Graduate Studies (Adult Education), University of B.C., Vancouver.

Engineering Undergraduate Society. (1950–). *Slipstick* (annual yearbooks). Vancouver: Author.

Epp, Jake. (1986). *Achieving health for all: A framework for health promotion.* Ottawa: Health and Welfare Canada.

Field, P.A., Stinson, S.M., and Thibaudeau, M-F. (1992). Graduate education in nursing in Canada. In A.J. Baumgart and J. Larsen (Eds.), *Canadian Nursing Faces the Future* (2nd ed.) (pp. 421-445). St. Louis: Mosby Year Book.

First National Conference on Research in Nursing Practice. (1971). [Vancouver: University of British Columbia School of Nursing.]

Foulkes, Richard. (1973). *Health security for British Columbians.* Victoria: Government Printing Office.

French, Doris. (1988). *Ishbel and the empire: A biography of Lady Aberdeen.* Toronto: Dundurn Press.

Gibbon, J.M. (1947). *The Victorian Order of Nurses for Canada 50th anniversary 1897-1947.* Montreal: Southam Press.

Gibbon, J.M., and Mathewson, M.S. (1947). *Three centuries of Canadian nursing.* Toronto: Macmillan.

Gibson, William C. (1973). *Wesbrook and his University.* Vancouver: The Library of The University of British Columbia.

Gillett, Margaret. (1981). *We walked very warily: A history of women at McGill.* Montreal: Eden Press Women's Publications, pp. 354, 357.

Goldstone, Irene L. (1972). *The origins and development of collective bargaining by nurses in British Columbia 1912-1976.* Unpublished master's thesis, Department of Health Care and Epidemiology, University of B.C., Vancouver.

Gould, Jan. (1975). *Women of British Columbia.* Saanichton, BC: Hancock House Publishers.

Green, Monica M. (1984). *Through the years with public health nursing: A history of public health nursing in the provincial government jurisdiction British Columbia.* Ottawa: Canadian Public Health Association.

Greenhous, Brereton. (1987). *Guarding the goldfields: The story of the Yukon Field Force* (Canadian War Museum Historical Publication No. 24). Toronto: Dundurn Press.

Haig, Kennethe. (1966). E. Cora Hind 1861-1942. In Mary Quayle Innis (Ed.), *The clear spirit: Twenty Canadian women and their times* (pp. 120-141). Toronto: University of Toronto.

Hamley, H.R., and Uprichard, M. (1948). *A study of the Florence Nightingale International Foundation.* London: International Council of Nurses.

Hibberd, Judith M. (1992). Strikes by nurses. In A.J. Baumgart and J. Larsen (Eds.), *Canadian nursing faces the future* (2nd ed.) (pp. 575-595). St. Louis: Mosby Year Book.

Hill, E. Jean M., and Kirkwood, Rondalyn. (1991). *Breaking down the walls: Nursing science at Queen's University.* Kingston, ON: School of Nursing, Queen's University.

Jensen, Phyllis Marie. (1985). Nursing. In *The Canadian encyclopedia* (Vol. II). Edmonton: Hurtig.

Johns, Ethel, and Fines, Beatrice. (1988). *The Winnipeg General Hospital and Health Sciences Centre School of Nursing 1887-1987.* Winnipeg: Alumnae Association Winnipeg General Hospital and Health Science Centre School of Nursing. [Note: Section I – 1887-1953 was written by Ethel Johns and was produced in facsimile in the 1988 edition].

Johnson, F. Henry. (1964). *A history of public education in British Columbia.* Vancouver: University of British Columbia. Cited in Stewart, 1990.

Johnson, F. Henry. (1971). *John Jessop: Goldseeker and educator: Founder of the British Columbia school system.* Vancouver: Mitchell Press.

Kelly, Nora. (1973). *Quest for a profession: The history of the Vancouver General Hospital School of Nursing.* Vancouver: Vancouver General Hospital School of Nursing Alumnae Association.

Kermacks, Claire. (1979). *Nursing education study report* (Discussion paper 04/79). Victoria: Ministry of Education, Science and Technology.

King, M. Kathleen. (1970). The development of university nursing education. In Mary Quayle Innes (Ed.), *Nursing education in a changing society* (pp. 67-85). Toronto: University of Toronto Press.

Kirkwood, Rondalyn, and Bouchard, Jeannette. (1992). *"Take counsel with one another": A beginning history of the Canadian Association of University Schools of Nursing 1942-1992*. Ottawa: Canadian Association of University Schools of Nursing.

Kloppenborg, Anne, Niwinski, Alice, Johnson, Eve, and Greuetter, Robert. (Eds.) (1977). *Vancouver's first century: A city album 1860-1960*. Vancouver: J.J. Douglas.

Lalonde, Marc. (1974a). *A new perspective on the health of Canadians*. Ottawa: National Health and Welfare.

Logan, Harry T. (1958). *Tuum Est: A history of the University of British Columbia*. Vancouver: University of British Columbia.

Longstaff, M.F. (1941). *Esquimalt Naval Base: A history of its work and its defences*. Victoria: Author.

Lovell, Verna. (1981). *I care that VGH nurses care!: A case study and sociological analysis of nursing's influence on the health care system*. Vancouver: In Touch Publications.

Masters, Donald C. (1950). *The Winnipeg General Strike*. Toronto: University of Toronto Press.

Meilicke, Dorothy, and Larsen, Jenniece. (1992). Leadership and the leaders of the Canadian Nurses Association. In A.J. Baumgart and J. Larsen, *Canadian nursing faces the future* (2nd ed.). St. Louis: Mosby Year Book.

Morton, James. (1974). *In the sea of sterile mountains: The Chinese in British Columbia*. Vancouver: J.J. Douglas.

Murphy, Herbert H. (1958). *Royal Jubilee Hospital, Victoria, B.C., 1858-1958*. Victoria: Hebden.

Mussallem, Helen K. (1960). *Spotlight on nursing education: The report of the pilot project for the evaluation of schools of nursing in Canada*. Ottawa: Canadian Nurses' Association.

Mussallem, Helen K. (1964a). *A path to quality: A plan for the development of nursing education programs within the general education system of Canada*. Ottawa: Canadian Nurses' Association.

Mussallem, Helen K. (1964b). *Nursing education in Canada* [Study for the Royal Commission on Health Services]. Ottawa: Queen's Printer.

Myers, Jay. 1986. *The Fitzhenry and Whiteside book of Canadian facts and dates*. Markham, ON: Fitzhenry & Whiteside.

Nicholson, G.W.L. (1975). *Canada's nursing sisters*. Toronto: Samuel Stevens/ Hakkert.

Nicol, Eric. (1978). *Vancouver*. Toronto: Doubleday Canada.

Nutting, M. Adelaide, and Dock, Lavinia L. (1935). *A history of nursing* (Vols. 1-4). New York: Putnam's Sons.

Ormsby, Margaret A. (1958). *British Columbia: A history.* Vancouver: Macmillian of Canada.

Pearson, Anne. (1985). *The Royal Jubilee Hospital School of Nursing 1891-1982.* Victoria: Alumnae Association of the Royal Jubilee School of Nursing.

Prentice, Alison, Bourne, Paula, Brandt, Gail C., Light, Beth, Mitchinson, Wendy, and Black, Naomi. (1988). *Canadian women: A history.* Toronto: Harcourt Brace Jovanovich.

Registered Nurses Act. Statutes of British Columbia 1918. Chapter 65.

Registered Nurses Association of B.C. (1987). *RNABC 1912-1987: 75 years of caring.* (Special publication distributed with *RNABC News,* 19 (6).) Vancouver: Author.

Reminiscing: St. Joseph's Hospital School of Nursing commemorative yearbook 1900-1981. (1981). Victoria: Victoria General Hospital.

Robinson, Marguerite E. (1967). *The first fifty years* [History of the Saskatchewan Registered Nurses' Association]. [Regina: Saskatchewan Registered Nurses' Association.]

Ross, A.M. (1971). The romance of Vancouver's schools (from *The British Columbia Magazine,* VII (6), 443-453). In James M. Sandison (Ed.), *Schools of old Vancouver* (Occasional Paper #2). Vancouver: Vancouver Historcial Society.

Sandison, James M. (Ed.). *Schools of old Vancouver* (Occasional Paper #2). Vancouver: Vancouver Historical Society.

Saunders, Bryne Hope. (1958). *Canadian portraits: Carr, Hind, Gullen, Murphy: Famous women.* Toronto: Clarke, Irwin & Co.

Stewart, Charles M. (1972). *The story of Union College.* Vancouver: Union College of British Columbia.

Stewart, Irene. (1979). *These were our yesterdays: A history of District Nursing in Alberta.* Calgary: Author.

Stewart, Isabel Maitland. (1947). *The education of nurses.* New York: The Macmillan Company.

Stewart, Lee. (1990). *"It's up to you": Women at UBC in the early years.* Vancouver: University of British Columbia Press.

Strangway, David W. (1989). *Second to none: A strategic plan to implement the mission of the University of British Columbia for the decade preceding the 21st century.* Vancouver: University of B.C.

Street, Margaret M. (1973). *Watch-fires on the mountains: The life and writings of Ethel Johns.* Toronto: University of Toronto Press.

Story, Norah (Ed.). 1967. *The Oxford Companion to Canadian history and literature.* Toronto: Oxford University Press.

Struthers, James. (1985). Great depression. In *The Canadian encyclopedia* (Vol. II, pp. 770-771.). Edmonton: Hurtig.

University of British Columbia. (c1936). *Twenty-first anniversary 1915-1936.* [Vancouver: Author.]

University of British Columbia. (1979). *The mission of the University of British Columbia.* Vancouver: Author.

University of Ottawa School of Nursing. (1973). *School of Nursing 1933-1973*. Ottawa: Author.

Uprichard, Muriel (Ed.). (1956). *The Canadian speller*. Toronto: W.J. Gage.

Uprichard, Muriel. (1943). *Three little Indians*. Toronto: Copp Clark.

Weir, George M. (1932). *Survey of nursing education in Canada*. Toronto: University of Toronto Press.

Whyte, Nora. (1988). *Provincial public health nursing in B.C. from 1939-1959: A social history*. Unpublished master's thesis, School of Nursing, University of B.C., Vancouver.

Zilm, Glennis, Hilton, Ann, and Richmond, Mary. (1982). *Nursing research – a base for practice: Service and Education*. Vancouver: University of British Columbia School of Nursing.

Articles (Journal and Newspaper)

Alcock, Denise. (1992). Nursing research (Editorial). *The Canadian Nurse*, 88 (1), 3.

Alsop, Kay. (1971). "Any idiot can count the sheets." *The Province*, March 18, 1971, p. 43. UBC SoN AC, File: Uprichard.

Anderson, Donn. (c1973). Nursing comes to academia. [Unidentified newspaper clipping, likely *The Vancouver Sun*, no date, likely summer 1973, no page.] UBC SoN AC, File: Uprichard.

AV aids. (1974). *The Canadian Nurse*, 70 (1), 49.

Bateson, Helen. (1973a). A grant of recognition. *The Province*, December 6, 1973, p. 52. UBC SoN AC, File: Uprichard.

Bateson, Helen. (1973b). A new prescription for nurses. *The Province*, March 31, 1973, p. 51. UBC SoN AC, File: Uprichard.

Bateson, Helen. (1977). Her lamp lighted a new way. *The Province*, June 29, 1977 [no page number]. UBC SoN AC, File: Uprichard.

Bateson, Helen. (1978). Education key to nursing future. *The Province*, February 9, 1978, p. 16. UBC SoN AC, File: Willman.

B.C. govt. announces start of resource and health centers. (1974). *The Canadian Nurse*, 70 (10), 9.

Campbell, Margaret. (1973). Innovations: University programs. *National conference on nurses for community service* [Proceedings] (pp. 77-80). Ottawa: Department of National Health and Welfare and Canadian Nurses Association.

Capelle, Pauline. (1944). The nurse and venereal disease control. *The Canadian Nurse*, 40 (7), 487-489.

CNA statement on the nurse-midwife. (1974). *The Canadian Nurse*, 70 (4), 12.

Compulsory registration. (1934). *The Canadian Nurse*, 30 (11), 530.

Cotsworth, Olive V. (1930). The ten-hour day for Vancouver nurses. *The Canadian Nurse*, 26 (6), 312.

Courage and optimism (Editorial). (1932). *The Canadian Nurse*, 28 (1), 8.

Creelman, Lyle M. (1947). With UNRRA in Germany. *The Canadian Nurse*, 43 (7), 532-552, 556.

Cross, Susan. (1991). The Red Cross in Kamloops: Almost 80 years of service. *The Kamloops Daily News*, Oct. 19, 1991, p. B15.

Duffield, Margaret. (1941). Nursing care for racial groups. *The Canadian Nurse*, 37 (5), 337-338.

Ellis, Kathleen W. (1942). The Provisional Council of University Schools and Departments of Nursing. *The Canadian Nurse*, 38 (11), 845-846.

Fairley, Grace M. (1933). A new teaching device. *The Canadian Nurse*, 29 (6), 303-304.

Fairley, Grace. (1942). The president's address. *The Canadian Nurse*, 38 (9), 612-613.

Forbes, Jean. (1933). Foods of the foreign born. *The Canadian Nurse*, 29, 9, 485-489.

Geary, Anna L. (1933). British Columbia attains its majority. *The Canadian Nurse*, 29 (7), 358.

Godkin, Dianne, and Bottorff, Joan. (1991). Doctorate in nursing: Idea to reality. *The Canadian Nurse*, 87 (11), 31-34.

Gould, Terry. (1991, May). The engineers of dumb behavior. *Vancouver*, pp. 30, 32, 34, 38, 40, 109, 112.

Gunn, Jean I. (1933). Educational adjustments recommended by the Survey. *The Canadian Nurse*, 29 (3), 139-145.

Hives, Christopher. (1990). From humble beginnings: UBC's origins and first decade. *UBC Alumni Chronicle*, 44 (3), 12-15.

Hood, Evelyn. (1956). Economic security in British Columbia. *American Journal of Nursing*, 56, 583-585.

Johns, Ethel. (1920). The university in relation to nursing education (Reprint). *The Modern Hospital*, 15 (2). [Reprint original in the Ethel Johns papers, UBC Special Collections]

[Johns, Ethel]. E.J. (1939). Introducing Margaret Kerr. *The Canadian Nurse*, 35 (4), 201-202.

Johns, Ethel. (1948, September). The nurse seeks the university. *The Canadian Nurse*, 44 (9), 720-724. (According to a note on a copy of this article, the article was based on the address given at the occasion of the awarding of Miss Johns' Honorary Doctorate at Mount Allison University.)

Johns, Ethel. (1958). The nature of genius. *Just Plain Nursing*, 12 (3), 1-8. (Pamphlet. Montreal: J.B. Lippincott).

Johnson, Beatrice Fordham. (1923). History of nursing. *Pupil Nurses' Annual*, pp. 15-19.

Kerr, Margaret. (1942). Teaching manual for first aid instruction. *The Canadian Nurse*, 38 (9), 661-663.

Lalonde, Marc. (1974b). Guest editorial. *The Canadian Nurse*, 70 (1), 19-20.

Langton, Geraldine, and Chodat, Isabelle. (1943). Planning field experience for a postgraduate course in public health nursing. *The Canadian Nurse*, 39 (11), 739-744.

McCullough, John W.S. (1932). Modern methods and treatment of cancer. *The Canadian Nurse*, 28 (4), 171-178.

McDonnell, C.E. (1992). The evolution of hospital accreditation. *BC Medical Journal*, 34 (5), 292-294.

McIntosh, J.W. (1930). Health insurance. *The Canadian Nurse*, 16 (6), 289-294.

MacLean, John T. (1949). The use of the artificial kidney. *The Canadian Nurse*, 45 (2), 95-99.

MacLennan, Katherine M. (1934). Progress in nursing communicable diseases. *The Canadian Nurse*, 30 (7), 306-309.

McLeod, Maude. (1919). The university and the training school for nurses, Vancouver General Hospital. *The Canadian Nurse*, 15 (11), 2100-2103.

Margaret Kerr (Obituary). (1976). *The Canadian Nurse*, 72 (8), 10.

Mallory, Evelyn. (1942). Ward aides and helpers. *The Canadian Nurse*, 36 (9), 715-717.

Miller, Judy. (1991, July 8). Healing mission. *The [Springfield, IL] State Journal-Register*, 13.

Miss Gray retires. (1941). *The Canadian Nurse*, 37 (11), 755-756.

Morrison, Ruth M. (1964). Public health nursing in the nursing curriculum. *The Canadian Nurse*, 60 (11), 1081-1085.

Munroe, Fanny. (1946). The presidential address. *The Canadian Nurse*, 42 (9), 734-737.

Nursing profiles. (1948). *The Canadian Nurse*, 44 (2), 122.

O'Brien, Vicki. (1987). An instrospective look at the history of the RNABC. *RNABC News*, 10 (1), 10-12.

Paffard, Agnes H. (1913). The history of the Graduate Nurses Association of Ontario. *The Canadian Nurse*, 9, 296-303.

Palliser, Elinor M. (1944). The accelerated course. *The Canadian Nurse*, 40 (11), 843-844.

Paulson, Esther. (1989, Spring). Meg Thatcher – 1892-1987. *Nursing Division Newsletter*, p. 5.

Phillips, Ivan E. (1985). Similkameen's first public health nurse. In Okanagan Historical Society, *Okanagan History: 49th annual report*. [Kelowna: Author.]

Ratsoy, M. Bernadet. (1974). Maternity patients make decisions. *The Canadian Nurse*, 70 (4), 42-44.

Report of the special committee on nurse education. (1914). *The Canadian Nurse*, 10, 570-579.

Scoones, A. Elizabeth. (1945). The student nurse and the VON. *The Canadian Nurse*, 41 (12), 984-985.

Smith, May Buckingham. (1990a). My experience with the Red Cross nurse. *Schuswap Chronicles*, 3, 39-40. (Celista, BC: North Schuswap Historical Society.)

Smith, May Buckingham. (1990b). The history of the Red Cross nurses in B.C. *Schuswap Chronicles*, 3, 38-39. (Celista, BC: North Schuswap Historical Society.)

Sturmanis, Dona. (1990). "Those Canadians from UBC." *UBC Alumni Chronicle*, 44 (3), 16-21.

The conference on nursing. (1927). *The Canadian Nurse*, 13 (7), 364-366.

Toward the year 2000. (1987). *RNABC News*, 19 (2), 21-24.

Uprichard, Muriel. (1974). An experimental nursing curriculum. *The Canadian Nurse*, 70 (5), 30-32.

Westera, Doreen. (1992). A profile of part-time faculty in Canadian university nursing programmes. *The Canadian Journal of Nursing Research*, 24 (4), 47-60.

Whitehead, Ursula. (1933). A sling for a plaster spica. *The Canadian Nurse*, 29 (7), 361-362.

Wigod, Rebecca. (1991). Nursing in the '90s. *The Vancouver Sun*, October 5, 1991, p. B3. UBC SoN AC, File: Willman.

Williams, Eileen. (1941). Public health nursing in a Japanese community in British Columbia. *The Canadian Nurse*, 37 (5), 339-342.

Wright, Alice L. (1948). Annual meeting in British Columbia. *The Canadian Nurse*, 44 (10), 846, 848, 850.

Index

About the Authors

GLENNIS ZILM, RN, BSN, BJ, MA (Cmns), is a 1958 graduate of the UBC School and is a writer, editor, and writing consultant in the health care fields. She has combined her nursing background with journalism for nearly 30 years and was an assistant editor for *The Canadian Nurse* and managing editor for the *B.C. Medical Journal.* Recently, she was developmental editor for two nursing textbooks and she is the editor of the *Newsletter,* History of Nursing Professional Practice Group, Registered Nurses Association of B.C.

ETHEL WARBINEK, RN, BSN, MSN, has both her undergraduate (1957) and graduate (1970) degrees from the UBC School and is Assistant Professor in the School. She is a past president of the UBC Nursing Alumni Division and is now Faculty Advisor to the Division and has served two terms as a Director of the Registered Nurses Association of B.C. She is Vice-President and Chair, Biographical Committee, of the History of Nursing Professional Practice Group of the Registered Nurses Association of B.C.